VISIONARIES

People & Ideas to Change Your Life

VISIONARIES

People & Ideas to Change Your Life

Jay Walljasper, Jon Spayde, and
the Editors of *Utne Reader*

New Society Publishers

Cataloguing in Publication Data: A catalog record for this publication is available from the National Library of Canada.

Cover design by Diane McIntosh. Photo by Darren Robb: Tony Stone Agency.

Printed in Canada by Friesens Inc.

New Society Publishers acknowledges the support of the Government of Canada through the Book Publishing Industry Development Program (BPIDP) for our publishing activities, and the assistance of the Province of British Columbia through the British Columbia Arts Council.

BRITISH COLUMBIA ARTS COUNCIL
Supported by the Province of British Columbia

Paperback ISBN: 0-86571-445-2

Inquiries regarding requests to reprint all or part of *Visionaries: People and Ideas to Change Your Life* should be addressed to New Society Publishers at the address below.

To order directly from the publishers, please add $4.50 shipping to the price of the first copy, and $1.00 for each additional copy (plus GST in Canada). end check or money order to:

New Society Publishers
P.O. Box 189, Gabriola Island, BC V0R 1X0, Canada

Published in cooperation with *Utne Reader* Books, 1624 Harmon Place, Minneapolis, MN 55403 www.utne.com

New Society Publishers' mission is to publish books that contribute in fundamental ways to building an ecologically sustainable and just society, and to do so with the least possible impact on the environment, in a manner that models this vision. We are committed to doing this not just through education, but through action. We are acting on our commitment to the world's remaining ancient forests by phasing out our paper supply from ancient forests worldwide. This book is one step towards ending global deforestation and climate change. It is printed on acid-free paper that is **100% old growth forest-free** (100% post-consumer recycled), processed chlorine free, and printed with vegetable based, low VOC inks. For further information, or to browse our full list of books and purchase securely, visit our website at: www.newsociety.com

NEW SOCIETY PUBLISHERS   www.newsociety.com

Contents

SOCIAL ACTION

SEEING GREEN

CREATIVITY & CULTURE

BODY, PSYCHE & SENSES

ACKNOWLEDGMENTS

FIRST WE WANT to thank the visionaries featured here, who not only shared their time and ideas but who transfused us with a rising sense of hope for a new century. And we want to honor all the thousands of other visionaries from all walks of life all over the world; the limited space of a single book means that we could not include anywhere near all the worthy thinkers and doers of our time.

Special recognition and great thanks go to Elaine Robbins, who wrote the profiles of Roberta Gratz, Frances Moore Lappé, Kenny Ausubel and Nina Simons, Edward Goldsmith, Larry Dossey, Muhammad Yunus, Bill Moyers, Theo Colburn, and George Gerbner; to Joseph Hart, who wrote the profiles of James Hillman, Paul Hawken, Gloria Anzaldua, Bobby McFerrin, bell hooks, Starhawk, and Thomas Berry; and to David Brauer, who wrote the profiles of Tom Hodgkinson and Kalle Lasn.

We are deeply indebted to Margaret Klis, whose hard work showed us the way out of several tough spots, and Craig Cox, whose problem-solving knack and good-naturedness know no bounds. A big thanks to all our *Utne Reader* colleagues, who showered us with specific insights and general support. It's crucial to acknowledge Eric Utne and Nina Utne, who made it all possible by bringing *Utne Reader* into the world.

We are very grateful to Molly Bennett, who masterfully negotiated a series of daunting projects. Also to Terrence Gotz, who helped with research, and Sara Rubinstein, who pitched in on the fact checking.

The efforts of the entire Utne Reader Books team merit big bravos: director Julie Ristau, whose near limitless talents saved our lives, almost literally; managing editor Sharon Parker, whose steady skills brought these words to the page; copy editor Lynn Marasco, who brought out what's best in us, as always; and fact checker Keith Goetzman, who knows almost everything.

—Jay Walljasper & Jon Spayde

FOREWORD

Where there is no vision the people perish

WE NEED visions these days. Not the prognostications of cybergeeks and marketers and statisticians and trend-mongers who try to tell us where we'll end up if we continue in the direction we're going. Useful as these predictions may be, we've got plenty of those kinds of visions. What we need are visions of society the way we want it to be. Creative, seemingly impractical, catalytic visions of human possibility and achievement can inspire and motivate us to change our lives and the world.

This book presents to you some of the most compelling visions from some of the most original minds of our time. These visionaries are a varied lot. Among them are scientists and mystics, activists and business leaders, physicians and poets. You'll find a rabbi, dancer, chef, radio talk show host, jazz singer, and the world's foremost proponent of idleness as a social cause. One has been labeled America's leading dissident while another once worked for George H. Bush at the State Department. A few have written best-sellers while many others are little known outside the communities in which they work. Some ask questions as big as the universe while others offer practical tips on how to improve your everday life. But in every case they offer ideas that can expand your own thinking in exhilarating new ways.

We hope that this book inspires you to become the visionary you were born to be, to articulate and embrace your own vision of who we are and what we could become. Dive into the labyrinth, risk getting lost, and return to your own community with bright ideas that help people see themselves and the world differently. This, according to mythologist Joseph Campbell, has been the role played by visionary heroes throughout all cultures from time immemorial.

If we have any chance of making life gentler, kinder, and more meaningful for everyone on the planet, we as a society must pay attention to the visions of people like you.

—Eric Utne

INTRODUCTION

IN THE PAGES that follow, you'll be introduced to 61 people whose ideas and actions are making a difference in the world—visionaries who can help us imagine this new century in an unexpected and appealing light. You'll meet thinkers who suggest ways to make sense of everday life, activists who stubbornly walk their talk on forgotten city streets, artists who struggle to turn wisps of vision into enduring expression, and healers who restore peace to frightened people, broken communities, and ravaged landscapes.

We first encountered many of these women and men during our years as editors at *Utne Reader* magazine, where we combed through thousands of alternative press publications in search of bright ideas, bold initiatives, and brave deeds. It was our mission to uncover the important and inspiring news the major media overlooked. These people—and others like them—were often right at the center of that news. When the time came to inaugurate Utne Reader Books, we realized that nothing could be more appropriate for a first title than a compilation of these people's insights and examples.

As our plans for the this book took shape, we augmented our original lists by contacting friends and colleagues around the world for their recommendations, holding an *Utne Reader* staff salon to garner more names, and then spending plenty of time in a local coffee shop hashing out the final lineup. We worked intuitively. Our touchstones were simple: aside from a record of solid accomplishment, did a candidate for the list inspire us and give us hope? Were we genuinely excited by his or her message? When our eyes lighted up at every name, we knew we were ready to begin the process of researching, interviewing, and writing.

Coming from monasteries and urban ghettos, working at architecture firms and restaurants, living in Berkeley and Bangladesh, being younger than thirty-five and over eighty, these people share one crucial asset: hope for the future. Hope for finding broader meaning and greater joy in our lives. Hope for the restoration of vast stretches of the planet that lie devastated under the human heel. Hope for the gradual growth of compassion among people, even among political and ethnic enemies. Hope for a social and economic order that uses the welfare of the weakest, not the strongest, as its gauge of success. These are not the "visionaries" usually lauded in the major media, who tell us how the world of tomorrow will be shaped overwhelmingly by globalization, new technology, and market economics. The visionaries in this book take a step back from current trends, to think creatively about what makes a better world for everyone.

They are more than accomplished, articulate toilers in the vineyards of social change and personal growth. Our visionaries, as the word itself suggests, have a unique and illuminating way of seeing. Each one expresses, in accordance with his or her calling, a powerful image of human possibility—whether it's singer-conductor Bobby McFerrin's ideal of the concert hall as town meeting, ecstatic dancer Gabrielle Roth's dream of bodies shaking their way to fulfillment, or community organizer Ernesto Cortes' mission of empowering poor communities.

At this moment, when prophecies of doom and decay are a pop culture staple—and as Canadian novelist John Ralston Saul suggests, the very idea that humans can cooperatively shape their future for the better has been abandoned for blind faith in the great gods of the global market and the Internet—we offer these voices, not of hope only, but of experience and wisdom. Our visionaries are not mere dreamers— they are practical people full of energy and accomplishment. And they show a remarkable willingness to push beyond the boundaries of their professional specialties and personal agendas. Many feel that purely feminist, or racial, or environmental issues no longer exist; nothing can be changed in isolation from what's going on everywhere else. That used to be called holism, and it had a New Age sound to it. Today, as we struggle in a political and economic system that stifles real change by pitting agenda against agenda in rolling gridlock, this idea has lost its utopian tones and rings out as clear truth.

But this book is more than a repository of ideas and resources. It's a collection of stories. The visionaries we've chosen to profile tell tales of their ups and downs, of brainstorms and breakthroughs, of the people and experiences that led them to look at the world in fresh ways. Taken together, these stories herald another clear truth: that determined human individuals, of all sexes and races and incomes and passions, can take a stand, right now, in the light of their deepest values and most energizing dreams. Some of these visionaries are successes, as the culture counts success; many more work hard below the radar of fame and prestige. Mother Teresa once said that what counts is not being successful, but being faithful. This, then, is a self-help book for those who want to be faithful to the never-yet-extinguished dream of a better world.

—Jon Spayde & Jay Walljasper

THE SPIRIT MOVING US

A COMMERCIAL SELF–HELP school advertises a course in spirituality: "Spirituality is magical! It's feeling protected, guided, and in tune with the world around you. It's knowing you have a purpose and the power to make it happen. It's attracting everyone and everything you need right to you! And best of all, it's a blast!"

In this epitome of pop spirituality, you can hear several voices: the nattering, too-perky, egocentric voice of American striving, of course, and a booming echo of the marketing of spirit that's so ubiquitous in the bookstores. But if you're generous, you can hear something deeper as well. A truth about our lives: Many of us hunger for a powerful comfort beyond the fast fading delights of new SUVs and HDTVs. Religious Americans (and there are tens of millions) seek it in church, temple, and mosque. But many secular Americans dwell far enough from this comfort, this sense of connectedness that is the essence of the experience of spirituality, that a self-help course in a pretty rudimentary form of it can present itself as news.

And several truths about spirituality itself are present here too: It is about feeling protected, guided, and in tune with the world. Purpose and power? You are granted them, although neither belongs to you. A blast? Why not? Joy has always been the hallmark of the spiritual path.

And yet, what's left out of this picture is an entire dimension of the spirit: its presence in, and response to, the dark. More than a mere comfort- and power-bringer, spirit is the force that allows us to be, in Robert Frost's phrase, "acquainted with the night." Sometimes the spiritual path itself is a darkness, when pleasure and consolation disappear and we go ahead on pure faith. At other times, spirituality is the ally that allows us to dwell and work inside the personal, political, economic, and social pain of the world without denial, avoidance, anger, or burnout.

Many who have rejected the religions of their childhoods think of spirituality as an alternative to religion: eclectic, personal, experiential, open to surprise and joy in a way that the old shul or the church on the hill never was. There is much truth in this perspective, especially

1

for those of us for whom the experience of organized religion was an exercise in superficiality—a pleasant weekend ritual cleansed of life-changing power—or "bad profundity": the inculcation of guilt.

But can we be sure that religion and spirituality are really distinct from one another, with religion the bad, failed, and superseded member of the pair? Religion is more than dogma, after all. It's a body of believers united—and if there's one thing the great spiritual writers of all traditions can agree about, it's the dangers of isolated spirituality. The most radical mystics, from the Desert Fathers to Saint Teresa to Thomas Merton, have insisted that community—spiritual direction, congregational worship, the daily exercise of loving-kindness to other real humans—is integral to the spiritual path. *Sangha*—community—is the third "jewel" of the Buddhist path, equal in importance to the Buddha's example and the *dharma* (way of living) he set down.

Not that the religious dimension of life always needs to be expressed in a church or a denomination. The men and women of spirit in this chapter are, I think, shining examplars of the religious impulse even though none of them wear the label of a sect. And all of them engage the multiple darknesses of our time, from ecological devastation to war and economic injustice, with steadfast faith and courage.

Thomas Berry, an ordained Catholic priest from North Carolina who no longer wishes to be called "Father," is nevertheless profoundly catholic ("universal") in that in his many books of ecotheology he takes the entire universe as his community—indeed, as the body of Christ. Care of the planet becomes, then, nothing less than sacramental, and the story of the evolution of the cosmos a sacred story of even greater beauty and significance than the poetic account of creation in the Bible.

Earth-care and feminism are at the core of Starhawk's proudly pagan articles of faith. Her pioneering books on goddess spirituality, witchcraft, and paganism gave birth to a flourishing movement. This prophetess of the sacred earth is also a political worker whose activism around the San Francisco Bay area is linked to her convictions: If "the earth and the elements that sustain our lives are sacred," she says, "then we must work to preserve them."

And here is a key to an important dimension of these visionaries' work. If religion, in the best sense, is the communal face of spirituality, then the religious impulse takes the well-being of the community as a sacred trust. Satish Kumar is a case in point. A peace pilgrim who once walked around the world carrying a message of human solidarity in the face of nuclear weapons, he's now a journalist and an advocate of a simple and thoughtful relationship with the world. As editor of the British magazine *Resurgence*, he presents peaceful, poetic social and political solutions to the world's ills.

For Kumar, a former Jain monk, the sacred expresses itself in a pattern of everyday relationships: how well and deeply we care for one another and the world that has been entrusted to us. Because the gigantism and complexity of modern life damage the planet, pervert justice, and steal energy from the cultivation of the arts and sacraments of relationship, Kumar remains a passionate advocate of the local, the small-scale, the face-to-face.

Thich Nhat Hanh is another formidable spiritual force—a Vietnamese Buddhist monk who prefers to begin the transformation of the world with simple and local acts: acts of awareness, breathing, and mindful smiling, all of which bring pleasure and contentment right away. But Nhat Hanh does not stop there. Upon these foundations he has created "engaged Buddhism," a worldwide movement of disciples, students, friends, and admirers who join him in extending compassionate awareness from the self to others and then to all who suffer from poverty, injustice, and exploitation around the world. Some discover Nhat Hanh's gentle but firm path to justice by visiting his Plum Village community in France and many more by reading his books—more than eighty volumes to date.

Buddhism is also the mainstay of the work Stephen and Ondrea Levine do with the dying. This New Mexico–based couple stand in darkness with people at the end of their lives, using simple techniques based on Buddhist meditation to help them soften their hearts, meet and learn from the pains of their lives. It is all a means of preparing them to let go. In their many books, the Levines have drawn on the lessons the dying have taught them to present a vision of life for those of us not yet on our deathbeds: conscious living, rooted in meditation, curious and courageous in facing the hardnesses of our hearts and softening those places. In short, it is a method of living as if we didn't have time for anything but what really matters.

Is this work political? Profoundly. The Levines, and the other visionaries of spirit in the pages that follow, all testify that what we need, in the dawning days of a new century, is a change of heart. A renaissance of love for the planet, for others, and for the Source of love. In their various ways, they are all promoting it, with faith that this awakening will transform the world. In Rabbi Zalman Schachter-Shalomi's tradition, this transformation is called tikkun-ha-olam, the restoration of the world. Trained in the intricacies of Jewish mysticism by the traditionalist Lubavitcher Hasidim, Reb Zalman, who now teaches at the Naropa Institute in Boulder, has reached out, in knowledge and love, to other faiths, to the worlds of humanistic psychology, feminism, environmentalism, and progressive politics. In the process, he deepened his Judaism instead of diluting it. Speaking to the concerns of the moment, the rabbi has found, like the others in this chapter, an ancient and ever-new prophetic voice.

—Jon Spayde

THOMAS BERRY

"The natural world is subject as well as object. The natural world is the maternal source of our being as earthlings and the life-giving nourishment of our physical, emotional, aesthetic, moral, and religious existence. The natural world is the larger sacred community to which we belong. To be alienated from this community is to become destitute in all that makes us human."

Lou Niznik

T HOMAS BERRY, an eighty-six-year-old Catholic priest and philosophical thinker of immense proportions, stands as an intellectual bridge between spiritual thought and the environmental movement. "He married religion and ecology in a way no one before him ever had," notes environmental activist Andrew Kimbrell. "He deserves the distinction of being called the founder of the religion-and-ecology movement and the grandfather of Creation Spirituality."

Berry is an accomplished scholar of Sanskrit, Dante, Buddhism, Jung, Confucianism, Native American culture, John Dewey, Asian Art, and evolutionary science. Yet in crediting the source that has most influenced his thinking, he looks beyond all the books he has read, beyond all the academic research he has pursued, to an obscure little meadow in the Appalachians.

"I discovered it when I was ten years old," he says. "It was filled with lilies and ran down to a little creek. As the years passed I realized that the little meadow was normative for everything. That a good economics would preserve it; a good science would help us understand it; a good religion would interpret its message."

All the monumental achievements of modern civilization mean little if places like this are spoiled in pursuit of worldly goals. If all our knowledge is truly worth anything, he observes, it should contribute to the preservation of spots like this all over the world. This is the essence of Berry's "Creation Spirituality," which discards old dichotomies like physical and spiritual, humanity and nature, in favor of a holistic approach to earth and civilization.

Berry was born in 1914 into a large Catholic family and grew up rambling the hills of North Carolina. In 1934, at the age of twenty, he entered the Passionist Monastery of Religious Congregation. After he finished his Ph.D. in history from Catholic University of American in 1948, he journeyed to China with the intention of studying language and Chinese philosophy in Bejing—plans that were cut short when Mao's Red Army claimed the city. Instead, Berry returned to the United States to pursue a life of dedicated scholarly and spiritual inquiry that has included three years as an army chaplain and teaching positions at seven universities.

He taught a seminar on the Bhagavad Gita at Columbia University, consulted on education policies for the T'boli people of the Philippines, and founded the Riverdale Center for Religious Research in New York City. His extensive work on integrating the findings of empirical science with the creation origins of many faiths gained him wide recognition. Indeed he is credited with founding a whole new profession: geologian.

In 1978, Berry published a booklet titled *The New Story* that set out his philosophy—a compelling blend of history, environmentalism, and religious teachings. The goal of the profoundly learned book was to illuminate the interconnectedness of life on earth. His aim was "to evoke . . . psychic and spiritual resources to establish a new reciprocity of humans with the earth and of humans to one another," explains Bucknell University theology professor Mary Evelyn Tucker. "As Berry has frequently said, there can be no peace among humans without peace with the planet. . . . The underlying assumption is that with a change of worldview will come an appropriately comprehensive ethics of reverence for all life."

This marriage of human and nonhuman concerns is the essential ingredient of Creation Spirituality, which has been embraced by environmentalists and theologians, and has been vigorously promoted by

Episcopal (and former Catholic) priest Matthew Fox. Creation Spirituality teaches us to worship God's creation—the earth and all its inhabitants—as well as the creator.

Berry has been the movement's champion. In 1988, he revised *The New Story* and republished it as *The Dream of the Earth*. He's meticulously unearthed the links between that meadow in North Carolina, its message for the world, and the deep cultural and philosophical structures of both East and West. With a thorough professional knowledge of European thought, Asian culture, and the religions of India ("where the divine is always immanent in the natural world," Berry points out), he is one of the planet's most erudite and far-seeing advocates of a transformed relationship with nature.

"We have a moral sense of suicide, homicide, and genocide, but no moral sense of biocide or geocide, the killing of the life systems themselves and even the killing of the Earth," he begins a recent paper delivered to the *Harvard Seminar on Environmental Values*. "Clearly there is something strangely wrong with such a position," he continues. Then, drawing on medieval philosophy, St. Thomas' *Summa Theologica*, and contemporary scientists and theologians, Berry advocates an "inner governance of the universe" that encompasses all creatures.

Berry traces our current disassociation between spirituality and nature back to the Great Plague, which struck Europe in 1347–1349, and killed an estimated third of its population. "Since the survivors had no understanding of germs, they could only conclude that the world had grown wicked. God was punishing the world," he writes in a paper delivered before the Harvard Divinity School and the University Committee on Environment. "In this situation the best thing to do was to escape out of the world through spiritual intensity and redemption experience." Beginning, then, with the "Dance of Death," continuing with the myriad forms of spiritual ecstasies that followed, and culminating in mathematician and philosopher Rene Descartes' famous seventeenth century demarcation between the intellect and the world, westerners came to see the "nonhuman world . . . as a mechanism that could be, and even must be, exploited for human benefit."

Berry's philosophy is greatly influenced by Pierre Teilhard de Chardin, the French paleontologist and Catholic priest who theorized in the 1930s that there is a spiritual dynamic in the evolutionary process. But it also looks forward to the transformation of contemporary society. One of Berry's current concerns is changing the worldview in our "establishments—university, government, church, and business." Berry condemns all four for complicity in perpetuating a human-istic—rather than bio-centered—order of thought. "The university, as now functioning," he writes in the Harvard address "prepares students for their role in extending human dominion over the natural world, not for intimate presence to the natural world. Use of this power in a dele-terious manner has devastated the planet."

Relentlessly critical of shortsighted and human-centric policies and philosophies, Berry is also hopeful about the future. His new book, *The Great Work*, offers an intellectual scaffold from which the future might be built. Drawing upon his unusual knowledge of three or four millen-nia of Chinese, Christian, and scientific scholars, he argues that now, more than ever, we are poised to "understand how the human com-munity and the living forms of Earth might now become a life-giving presence to each other." We are living, he continues, in a moment of grace akin to the moment when our sun collapsed and formed the solar system. Berry hails a "developing . . . profound mystique of the natural world" as signaling the end of the industrial age. "The distorted dream of an industrial technological paradise is being replaced by the more viable dream of mutually enhancing human presence within an ever-renewing organic-based Earth community. The dream drives the action. In the larger cultural context the dream becomes the myth that both guides and drives the action."

This isn't hyperbolic; Berry *collapses* religion and science, man and nature. Like many truly original thinkers, his interest lies in overcom-ing seeming oppositions. Dream, myth, spirit, and intellect, after all, are our human contributions to the great story of life on (and of) the earth. Berry—scholar that he is—finds precedent and hope for this immense ecological breakthrough in the Middle Ages, among other times and places. "People in the 11th, 12th, and 13th centuries felt that they were engaged in what they called a Great Work—the establishment of a finer civilization after the chaos of the Dark Ages," says Berry. "There is a Great Work for us to do too, and as we do it, it will not only give us a better world—it will give us a reason to live."

RESOURCES

The Great Work: Our Way into the Future (Bell Tower, 1999)

Religions of India: Hunduism, Yoga, Buddhism (Columbia Univ. Press, 1996)

*The Universe Story: From the Primordial Flaring Forth to the Ecozoic Era
   —A Celebration of the Unfolding of the Cosmos,* with Brian Swimme
   (HarperSanFrancisco, 1992)

Befriending the Earth: A Theology of Reconciliation Between Humans and the Earth, in dialogue with Thomas Clarke, ed. Stephen Dunn and Anne Lonergan (Twenty-Third, 1991)

The Dream of the Earth (Sierra Club, 1988)

SATISH KUMAR

Kate Mount Photography

"There is something more to the world than what you are able to measure, analyze, and quantify. There is a dance between what you know and what you don't know. The place of mystery is an essential ingredient."

THEY SAY A TRIP of a thousand miles begins with a single step, but for Satish Kumar it began with a cup of coffee. He was sitting with a friend at a café near his home in Bangalore, India, looking over the newspaper and noting that philosopher Bertrand Russell had been jailed after a ban-the-bomb protest in London. It was 1962, and people at breakfast tables all around the planet were uneasy as they drank their morning coffee and read about the latest round of nuclear saber-rattling between the United States and the Soviet Union.

But rather than descend into despair and cynicism, Kumar and his friend, Prabhakar Menon, decided to take action. Inspired by the ninety-year-old Russell's deep convictions, the two vowed that morning to take a message of peace to leaders of the world's (then) four nuclear nations. A few weeks later, with no money in their pockets, they set out on their pilgrimage, walking most of the way from Delhi to Moscow to Paris to London to Washington. They were fed and given a place to sleep by the many people they met along the way.

The two sneaked away from their official hosts in Moscow and eluded Soviet police all the way to the Polish border. They engaged in a long discussion about human rights with an East Berlin border guard, were held four days in a filthy Paris jail cell, and deported to England, where they met up with Bertrand Russell, who raised money for their passage to America aboard the luxurious ocean liner *Queen Mary*. Martin Luther King welcomed them to his home in Atlanta, and the owner of a lunch counter in Albany, Georgia—who did not want to serve a brown-skinned man—held a gun to Kumar's head. Kumar and Menon met with representatives of Nikita Krushchev, Harold Wilson, and Lyndon Johnson and gave each of them a packet of tea from a woman they'd met in Armenia, who said that leaders should brew a pot of tea before deciding to fire nuclear weapons.

For Kumar, now sixty-three, this two-and-a-half-year pilgrimage was just one passage in a life's journey devoted to peace, ecology, and spiritual exploration. He has synthesized the ethical philosophies of East and West in a philosophy he calls spiritual consciousness and today stands as one of the world's foremost proponents of the ideas of both Mahatma Gandhi and E. F. Schumacher, the economist who changed how the world thinks about scale in the best-selling book *Small Is Beautiful*.

For twenty-five years Kumar has edited *Resurgence*, an internationally circulated magazine that London's *Guardian* newspaper called "the artistic and spiritual flagship of the Green movement." Kumar's wife, June Mitchell, is managing editor, and they work in a postcard-perfect stone farmhouse surrounded by wildflowers in Devon in southwest England. Kumar also helps direct a college devoted to ecological learning, an alternative school in his local village, and a publishing house. He lectures in Britain, Europe, India, and North America on a panoply of topics, including the principles of spiritual ecology, Gandhian thinking, and misconceptions about progress. He has spoken on spirituality and architecture four times at the Prince of Wales Institute for Architecture. Much of today's architecture is soulless, he said, built without regard to beauty but also designed without the involvement of people who will work or live there. The reason for this is that buildings are too large and constructed too quickly to allow for consideration of the subtle yet crucial spiritual elements. (Prince Charles did not attend, but he told Kumar that he often listens to his lectures on tape.)

Satish Kumar has dedicated his life to tempering the world's devotion to technology, competitiveness, hierarchy, speed, violence, and destruction of nature with awareness of the beauty, mystery, and connectedness of all things.

That sounds quixotic, but Kumar is a man for whom the universe seems to bend a bit, a figure from whom seemingly impossible ideas sound somehow less impossible. A longtime friend, the English writer Richard Boston, says, "His gentleness is accompanied by a will of steel. His schemes are apparently absurd in their Utopianism, but turn out to be quite practical: He is a great deal more hardheaded, shrewder, more canny than he appears at first."

Kumar wins people over with the charming elegance of his manner and the melodious flow of his Indian-accented English. That's how *Resurgence* has been able to publish luminaries like Gary Snyder, Wendell Berry, Vandana Shiva, Thomas Moore, James Hillman, Susan Griffin, Winona LaDuke, Paul Hawken, Jerry Mander, Fritjof Capra, Helena Norberg-Hodge, Ivan Illich, Noam Chomsky, and Prince Charles without paying a single penny.

Some of the same people teach courses at Schumacher College, the academy of spiritual and ecological education that Kumar founded in 1991 in league with the Dartington Trust, a charitable foundation. Named after E. F. Schumacher, the college offers adults "ages twenty to eighty" two to five-week courses on spiritual and ecological subjects. Housed in a fourteenth-century hall on the Dartington Estate in Devon, Schumacher College allows students from around the world to immerse themselves in a subject—to read about it, to meditate on it, and to discuss it in classes, over dinner, while washing dishes, and out in the orchards by moonlight.

"We need to change consciousness," Kumar says, explaining the thread that connects all his projects. "We live under the power of modern consciousness, which means that we are obsessed with progress, and that means that wherever you are is not good enough. The opposite of that is spiritual consciousness. By that I mean you find enchantment in every action you do, rather than in just the results of your action. Modern society is so product-oriented, we always want to achieve something, rather than experience something."

Seeing the universe flowing in cycles rather than progressing along a linear path, Kumar believes that spiritual consciousness eventually will replace, or at least counterbalance, modern consciousness. "Modernity is very powerful," he admits. "It has the media, the corporations. Yet there seems to be a discontentedness in many people, despite all the glamour and achievement and technology and wealth. There is a sense of the loss of meaning. And of course there is pollution, crime, poverty, and ugliness."

The fundamental appeal of Kumar's ideas helps explain his unmatchable skill in enlisting goodwill and financial assistance on behalf of various projects, but so does the practical experience he's acquired throughout a remarkable life.

Against the wishes of his mother, he left home at the age of nine to join an order of itinerant Jain monks, and spent the next eight years wandering the countryside of India, depending on generous villagers for meals and a place to sleep each night. After coming across a book by Gandhi—forbidden reading among monks—he decided to join the land reform campaign led by Vinoba Bhave, Gandhi's successor as leader of India's village movement. He made his way to Vinoba's ashram, where he was taught the important Gandhian craft of spinning cloth, and later helped organize strikes among farmworkers of the untouchable caste. He became an editor at a Gandhian movement newspaper but got sacked for criticizing some prominent Gandhians' plans to build a complex of fancy modern office buildings—a stark rejection of Gandhi's own plea for simple living. Not long afterwards, Kumar embarked on the peace pilgrimage.

After returning to India, Kumar remained involved with the peace movement; he launched a Hindi-language peace magazine and continued to organize peasants seeking land of their own. He also became involved with humanitarian work among refugees fleeing the war in Bangladesh, which led to an invitation to present a photography exhibit in London on the disaster. June Mitchell, an English librarian who had also done relief work in Bangladesh, was invited to speak at the opening of the exhibit, and soon the two of them were living together in London with a baby son, Mukti, making plans to move to India.

But one day when Kumar was walking along a canal near Regents Park, he bumped into John Papworth, an English peace activist who had accompanied him on the United States leg of his peace pilgrimage and who later founded *Resurgence* magazine. Papworth was leaving for Zambia, where he would be an adviser to President Kenneth Kaunda, and he suggested that Kumar take over as editor of the magazine. Although Kumar had no formal schooling, a limited command of written English, and no visible means of support, he took the job, which paid nothing. "I didn't like . . . to refuse something which was coming to me by fate," he recounts in his autobiography, *Path Without Destination.* "I decided to put off thoughts of returning to India. . . . I should have known that life does not operate on the basis of plans, no matter how rational. My nature is to let things happen rather than make them happen."

Unlike many crusaders for worthy causes, Satish and June actually live the simple life they celebrate. He receives no money from *Resurgence,* and she has a small salary; the mortgage on their house and two acres of gardens is held by a trust of *Resurgence* benefactors. Satish lectures for whatever someone is willing to offer above the cost of a plane or train ticket, and Schumacher College pays him a modest salary.

Their house is outfitted with authentic versions of the rustically elegant furniture, rugs, kitchenware, and art that we see in *Martha Stewart Living* magazine and the Pottery Barn catalog. They have no central heat and only a tiny refrigerator—they use an old-fashioned cooling room instead—and much of their food comes straight from the garden. The long table in the middle of the wood-beamed kitchen is the center of their universe, the place where friends and family gather over Satish's delicious Indian dinners and June's spectacular bread and desserts, drinking local cider and inexpensive wine and talking for hours.

"From the office," Satish says proudly, "I can look at black currants, red currants, plums, apples, quinces, and raspberries growing in the courtyard. After a morning of editing, we go to the garden and pick vegetables for lunch. When it's a beautiful sunny day, we'll say let's go outside. No editing today."

No matter how urgent the duties of each day, he always spends two hours in the morning meditating, chanting, and reading, and often takes an afternoon walk with June in the woods or along the nearby seacoast.

"People tell us we are very inefficient and naive," he says, a sly grin crossing his face. "I say, yes, we are inefficient and naive but we are happy. You keep your efficiency and we'll keep our happiness. There is a kind of indivisibility between life and work. If you live this kind of life there is no burnout. Your energy dissipates if you work on just one thing."

Asked if he ever gets discouraged about changing the world, Kumar answers firmly: "Spiritual consciousness holds that the world is sacred. We must celebrate it rather than just try to improve it. Take joy in what's here. Outcome is not the point; we must do what is right."

RESOURCES

Resurgence
  Ford House, Hartland
  Bideford, Devon, EX39 6EE U.K.
  www.resurgence.org

Only Connect: The Best of Resurgence 1990–1999, ed. John Lane and Maya
  Kumar Mitchell (Green Books, 2000)

Path Without Destination: An Autobiography (Eagle Brook/Morrow, 1999)

STEPHEN & ONDREA LEVINE

"Fear of dying is really more like the fear of falling, while our fear of death is our trepidation of the landing. In death we "fall" upward. . . . Dying is the domain of the body. Death is the domain of the heart. Keep dying in its place—the body. Don't let it affect death. Dying is to death as birth is to life. Each is preceded by what seemed the only possible reality, and each is followed by the next remarkable scenario. As one teacher put it, "We fall from grace to grace." Our next moment of grasping, hell, our next instant of letting go, heaven. Dying, like birth, is begun by the body and completed by the heart."

NEWCOMERS TO MEDITATION often think that it's all about being blissed out, blessedly calm. Experienced meditators know that when you're on the cushion, pain is as likely to surface as peace. And then there are Stephen and Ondrea Levine, who have made a career of bringing the treasures of several meditative traditions to those who are facing life's most agonizing situations: bereavement, sexual abuse, chronic pain, and imminent death.

This New Mexico–based husband-and-wife team have spent some twenty years as meditation teachers and counselors in hospitals, prisons, and hospices. They find gentle and truthful ways for people to acknowledge, cope with, and finally move past suffering.

Their partnership with people in dire circumstances has allowed them to see life in new ways, and their work suggests how an enlightened awareness of our mortality can change the way we live right now. "The thing we've seen most on deathbeds is unfinished business," Stephen says. "They married the wrong person, or they didn't put enough energy in the marriage to the right person, or they never were truthful, or they didn't let their heart show. They stayed well protected, and at the end of their lives, they had no contact. They end up saying, 'I'm dying, but what am I dying out of?' "

The Levines' most recent book, *A Year to Live*, in many ways sums up the wisdom they have archived in the meditation manual *A Gradual Awakening*, and other books such as *Who Dies?* and *Healing into Life and Death*. Beginning with the question "If you had only one year to live, what would you do?" the book outlines a year of preparation for mortality. "As we reflect on this life/death riddle," they write, "we may be surprised at how many options it inspires. Rather than our freedom being curtailed by having just a year left, we uncover something quite unsuspected and satisfying: We discover how much more room we have for life and how many more possibilities there are to be fully alive."

The realizations and resources they offer to help people make this discovery are based in Theravada, or Southern, Buddhist practice—although they have learned from other sources of the Indian tradition as well, particularly the *Bhagavad-Gita*. Perhaps the chief resource they offer is "soft-belly meditation," an inner unclenching that allows us to open up to life by letting down our guard against pain. "If there is a single definition of healing," they write, "it is to enter with mercy and awareness those pains, mental and physical, from which we have withdrawn in judgment and dismay." This carefully cultivated openness to pain and fear is transformative, allowing the terminally ill to release into an inner sense of spaciousness, and those not yet in extremity to explore the unlived areas of their lives.

Stephen tells the story of a nurse with many years' experience on the oncology ward who contracted cancer herself. Having seen scores of painful deaths from the disease, she was terrified. "She turned away from her family," Stephen recalls. "She was convinced that she was being punished by Jesus. We tried gently to help her see Jesus' love. We helped her face her pain. And we took care of her in very concrete ways, daily ways, not just prayer by the bedside." Slowly, the former nurse began to reconnect with her family and to embrace her life. She held a "pizza baptism death party" to say farewell to family and friends. "There was a lot of laughter," Stephen recalls. "So often in helping people die, the real issue is to help them be born before their life is over."

The Buddhism the Levines profess isn't encrusted with Sanskrit terms and mental knots. "We've found that a lot of Buddhist practices can be applied very well to dying in this culture, as long as we use words like *focus, soften, kindness,*" says Stephen. When people are on their deathbed, "it isn't the time to give them a course in Theravada Buddhism. In fact, you want to help them get rid of the knowing that blocks a deeper understanding."

Stephen Levine's own Buddhist path was unconventional and improvisational. As a jazz-playing college boy at the University of Miami, he found himself attracted to Zen Buddhism—but in the mid-1950s there were only one or two generally available books on the subject, and no teachers on the horizon. "I started meditating on my own," he says. "Just sitting quietly." And also staying up late playing in black jazz clubs.

Soon Stephen stumbled across his first teacher, in the guise of a Greenwich Village Oriental art-shop owner named Rudi, an eclectic amateur spiritual teacher who was, in Stephen's words, "very far out in some organic, intuitive mystery." Stephen wandered into his shop and "liked him right away. We'd sit on chairs in front of the shop, watching people passing along the street. He'd indicate [people] and ask, 'What's their state of mind?' He trained me to be attentive to body language, body image, energy. He essentially taught me how to read hearts."

Drawn to the Bay Area by the cultural revolution that sprang up there in the mid-1960s, Levine spent a few years as editor of one of the most prominent underground newspapers of the era, the San Francisco *Oracle*. In a typically sixties sideline, Levine and a group of colleagues began publishing meditation books under the imprint Unity Press. (The shoestring operation got financial support from, among others, the Grateful Dead and the Jefferson Airplane.)

In the early 1970s, Levine hooked up with vipassana meditation teachers Jack Kornfield and Joseph Goldstein, who encouraged him to teach meditation in his own right. Tackling extreme cases right away, he began teaching at the infamously tough Soledad Prison. "We meditated, talked about meditation, and talked about life," he says. "There wasn't a single man in my group who didn't have a broken heart. One of them had literally been abandoned by his parents. He came home one night, and his family had moved away. The more pain I saw, the more I wanted to serve; pain either closes your heart or opens it, and

I found that mine was opening." Levine established another meditation group in gentler Santa Cruz. His book *A Gradual Awakening* grew out of talks that Levine gave to the Santa Cruz group.

The newly minted meditation teacher soon crossed paths with three people who would further determine the direction of his life. The first was an old acquaintance from his Haight-Ashbury days, Ram Dass, one of the heavyweights of the spiritual renaissance of the sixties. "We became very close friends," Levine recalls, "and he asked me to teach with him." In Ram Dass, Levine found what he calls a "spiritual friend" rather than a guru. "We became the kind of friends who hold nothing back from each other," he says. "Bit by bit we let go of every-thing that blocked our love for one another. He didn't change my path so much as ripen and deepen it."

Elizabeth Kübler-Ross, the world-renowned author and authority on death and dying, came to one of the Ram Dass/Levine workshops and soon asked Stephen to teach with her. "I had long had a desire to serve others," he says, "but I had no specific direction in mind. Elizabeth gave me that direction, which was working with the dying. And then, at one of the workshops I was doing on conscious dying, I met Ondrea. We looked at each other, and both of us knew we would be together. Later that same afternoon we were actually talking about it, and we've been together ever since."

The Boston-born Ondrea, an intuitive healer who lived in Taos, New Mexico, with her son, and volunteered in hospitals to help the dying, was herself afflicted by many diseases, from grand mal seizures and cancer to narcolepsy. "All these are gone now," she told an inter-viewer in 1999. "I have lived through and with many miracles. Somehow I just seemed to have room to heal. Stephen says it was all part of my 'healer's training.' . . . Maybe he is right."

"Ondrea was born with a lot of gifts," says Stephen. "She can see energy. She can sense traumas in a person's past, so her healing work has always been very natural. Once we had stopped at a gas station on our way from Taos to California. I went to the men's room and came back to see the guy who was pumping our gas talking to Ondrea and weeping. He'd been on cemetery detail on Iwo Jima, taking the half-burned bodies of the Japanese out of caves. He said he didn't know why he started telling her. This happens quite a bit with her, and it can slow things down. She goes out for the mail and comes back two hours later."

For the Levines, who live quietly in rural Chamisal, New Mexico, connected to the world only by a cell phone that can't take incoming calls, the peacefulness of their lifestyle supports caregiving. "I don't think people spend enough time quietly alone," says Stephen. "Alone with their partner, too. There are people out there who are literally giving their whole life to help others. I admire them, but I also think they could give themselves a little break. After all, you are not going to make the world perfect; all you can do is work with what is on your plate. If you start roaming around the whole table, the stuff on your plate is not going to get done. And that's plenty to do. If you are truly open to service, you'll always have plenty to do."

RESOURCES

A Year to Live: How to Live This Year As If It Were Your Last (Bell Tower, 1997)

Embracing the Beloved: Relationship as a Path of Awakening (Doubleday, 1995; Anchor, 1996)

Guided Meditations, Explorations, and Healings (Anchor, 1991)

Meetings at the Edge: Dialogues with the Grieving and the Dying, the Healing and the Healed (Anchor/Doubleday, 1989)

A Gradual Awakening (Anchor, 1989)

Healing into Life and Death (Anchor/Doubleday, 1987)

Who Dies? (Anchor, 1982, 1989)

THICH NHAT HANH

Plum Village

"Many of us worry about the situation of the world . . . We feel that we are on the edge of time. As individuals, we feel helpless, despairing. The situation is so dangerous, injustice is so widespread, the danger is so close. In this kind of situation, if we panic, things will only become worse. We need to remain calm, to see clearly. Meditation is a means to be aware, and to try to help."

O N A TWO-HUNDRED-YEAR-OLD farmstead in southwestern France, lives a small, quiet, infinitely gentle man of seventy-four who has been called a "living Buddha." The Vietnamese Buddhist monk and master Thich Nhat Hanh has also been called, by the American Zen teacher Richard Baker, "a cross between a cloud, a snail, and a piece of heavy machinery—a true religious presence."

Baker's aphorism catches perfectly the paradox of a man who, as one of the world's most famous meditation teachers, emphasizes simple practices—awareness of the breath, mindfulness in daily tasks, happiness, gratitude, and primary acts of love—but who is also one of the great scholars of the Vietnamese Buddhist tradition and one of the most tireless and effective spiritual-social activists since Mohandas Gandhi. In Vietnam he founded a Buddhist publishing house, a university known as the An Quang Buddhist Institute, the School of Youth for Social Service, which aided thousands displaced by the Vietnam war, and a socially engaged order of monks—the Tiep Hien Order, or Order of Interbeing—into which he still initiates disciples.

Author of some eighty books, Nhat Hanh is a poet, novelist, translator, and tireless globe-circler who leads meditation retreats from California to Moscow. He headed the Vietnamese Buddhist delegation to the Paris peace talks that ended the war in Vietnam, and in 1967 was nominated for the Nobel Peace Prize—by Martin Luther King. "His ideas for peace, if applied, would build a monument to ecumenism, to world brotherhood, to humanity," wrote the greatest social reformer of modern America.

And yet he does not overpower his followers and readers with monumental visions, but rather reminds them of quiet truths too easily left behind in the rush of modern life. All of his work, from publishing to international activism, is rooted in the premise that simple happiness, achieved right now with the aid of breathing and a calmed mind, is the deepest and most fundamental "peace work."

"Peace is present right here and now, in ourselves and everything we do and see," he has written. "The question is whether or not we are in touch with it." Walking, smiling, looking into the eyes of friends and children—these are the elements of Buddhist (and universally human) practice that he brings to the foreground. Even doing the dishes—slowly, joyfully, without clocking the time until you're done—can be a spiritual act that brings us contentment. "If while washing dishes we think only of the cup of tea that awaits us, hurrying to get the dishes out of the way," he writes, "the chances are we won't be able to drink our tea either. While drinking the cup of tea, we will be thinking of other things, barely aware of the cup in our hands."

Plum Village, the meditation community in France where Nhat Hanh has based himself since 1982, lacks the buttoned-up solemnity of many Zen centers. Children run about, playing and laughing, chattering in English, French, and Vietnamese. The thirty or so full-time residents (and the international visitors who flock to Plum Village during the one summer month when it is open to the public) pursue everyday tasks like sweeping and kitchen work, or engage in walking meditation, or simply lounge on the grass. Several times daily, they assemble for meditation sessions and dharma talks (informal Buddhist sermons) given by Thay ("teacher"), as Nhat Hanh's friends and followers call him. Compared to the training-camp rigors of many Western retreat centers, this is free and easy. Nhat Hanh likes to call it a "treat," not a "retreat." Plum Village is infused not only with Nhat Hanh's peacefulness, but also with his passion. Thay's followers are "engaged Buddhists," meditators who are likely to be social activists as well, and their mentor's record of social commitment and hard work is always before them.

Born in central Vietnam in 1926, Nhat Hanh knew early on that he wanted to be a monk. "When I was nine," he writes, "I saw on the cover of a magazine an image of the Buddha sitting peacefully on the grass. Right away I knew that I wanted to be peaceful and happy like that." At sixteen, he entered the Tu Hieu Pagoda near Hue as a novice. High-spirited and ambitious (he was the first monk in his monastery to ride a bicycle), he was also idealistic and, along with other young Vietnamese monks in the late 1940s, anxious to do what he could to bring reconciliation and healing to a society that had endured Japanese occupation and was on the brink of a colonial and neocolonial war that would endure for three decades. He moved to Saigon and eventually cofounded the An Quang Buddhist Institute, which would become the most distinguished Buddhist study center in the country.

By 1961, he had achieved sufficient scholarly distinction to teach comparative religion at Princeton and Columbia. But in 1963, colleagues in Vietnam summoned him home. The oppressive American-backed Diem regime was persecuting Buddhists as part of its military campaign against insurgents. The diminutive monk became a whirlwind of compassionate but resolute antiwar activity: He founded the School of Youth for Social Service, which built schools and clinics in the torched and tortured villages; he set up a publishing house and, as editor-in-chief of the official organ of the Unified Buddhist Church of Vietnam, editorialized against the war. Neither communist nor anticommunist, he enraged both the Hanoi and Saigon regimes with his evenhanded desire for peace.

At the same time, as he later told an American audience, he realized that much of Vietnam's agony originated in the hearts and minds of Americans. Their pride, anger, and pain underlay the policies that were prolonging the war. In 1966, he came to the United States at the invitation of the Fellowship of Reconciliation peace group and met with peacemakers and warmakers alike: Thomas Merton, Martin Luther King, Robert McNamara, and many others.

When the war finally came to an end, Thich Nhat Hanh found that the victorious Communist government had no more use for him than its predecessors had, and in 1973 they exiled him for refusing to declare himself pro-Hanoi. Since then he's aided boat people, gathered money and petitions for jailed Vietnamese Buddhist priests and nuns—and brought his wisdom to bear on the many dilemmas that his materially comfortable but spiritually hungry Western students present to him.

When he encourages drivers to think of a stoplight as "a bodhisattva helping us return to the present moment" or offers a devotional verse to say before turning on the television, he shows, as he has all his life, that cultivating the present moment means facing—courageously and compassionately—the world exactly as it is. "Meditation is to be aware of what is going on in our bodies, in our feelings, in our minds, and in the world," he has written. "Children die of hunger. . . .Yet the sunrise is beautiful, and the rose that bloomed this morning along the wall is a miracle. Life is both dreadful and wonderful. To practice meditation is to be in touch with both aspects."

RESOURCES

www.plumvillage.org

Transformation at the Base: Fifty Verses on the Nature of Consciousness (Parallax, 2001)

The Raft is Not the Shore: Conversations Toward a Buddhist-Christian Awareness, with Daniel Berrigan (Orbis, 2001)

Plum Village Chanting and Recitation Book, with the monks and nuns of Plum Village (Parallax, 2000)

The Path of Emancipation: Talks from a Twenty-one-Day Mindfulness Retreat (Parallax, 2000)

Going Home: Buddha and Jesus as Brothers (Riverhead, 1999)

The Blooming of a Lotus: Guided Meditation Exercises for Healing and Transformation (Beacon, 1993)

Present Moment, Wonderful Moment: Mindfulness Verses for Daily Living (Parallax, 1990)

ZALMAN SCHACHTER-SHALOMI

"I do not believe that anyone has the exclusive franchise on the truth. What we Jews have is a good approximation, for Jews, of how to get there. Ultimately, each person creates a way that fits his own situation. While there are differences between Jewish and non-Jewish approaches to mysticism in specific methods, observances, and rituals, there are no differences in the impact of the experiences themselves. When it comes to what I call the 'heart stuff,' all approaches overlap."

Ask Rabbi Zalman Schachter-Shalomi about the path he has taken through seventy-seven years of a complex, active life, and he will stop you and change the verb: "No, the path I was *led* on."

At one level, the phrase expresses the deep piety of a rabbi who seeks God within a great mystical stream, a rabbi trained in the exacting traditions of the Brooklyn-based Lubavitcher Hasidim. It also expresses the courage and broad-mindedness of a religious leader who has opened himself again and again to other classical spiritual traditions from Catholicism to Buddhism, and to psychology, bodywork, feminism, environmentalism, and much else in the great mix of social, personal, and planetary change that came out of the 1960s.

Schachter-Shalomi has become the great sage of a worldwide movement of Jewish renewal by virtue of his keen understanding of where his own tradition can connect with the psycho-eco-spiritual revolutions of our millennial age. As the founder of the P'nai Or (Children of Light) religious fellowship and the rabbinic chair of ALEPH: Alliance for Jewish Renewal, Schachter-Shalomi has inspired and guided a movement for an observant, deeply traditional Judaism that is at the same time warm, experientially based, gender-equal, environmentally aware (thanks to the Schachter-Shalomi-coined concept of "eco-kosher"), nonhierarchical, and grounded in renewed liturgy.

But what "the path I was led on" means to Reb Zalman himself is more personal. It begins with getting out of Europe just before the Holocaust. Born Zalman Schachter in 1924 in Poland, the rabbi-to-be soon moved with his family to Vienna, where he attended both a traditional yeshiva and a socialist-Zionist high school. When the Nazis threatened, the Schachters went to Antwerp; when Belgium came under German attack, the family began an odyssey. Detained in a camp in Vichy France, they escaped to Africa, then to the West Indies, and finally to New York in 1941.

"Having been saved from the Holocaust . . . I felt something was needed from me to give back," he recalled. "I saw what was happening to our tradition, that it was being diminished. That the best and most advanced of our people had been decimated. So I was moved to think about creating a Noah's Ark for our tradition." In other words, he was looking for forces within Judaism that would re-energize it and make it self-confident again. Having been excited by the intense mystical piety of the Lubavitcher movement, Schachter (he would add Shalomi to his name in the 1970s) attended the central Lubavitcher yeshiva in Brooklyn, where he took rabbinic ordination in 1947. Stints of teaching and serving as a congregational rabbi at Lubavitch synagogues in Connecticut and Massachusetts followed.

Already Schachter was showing signs of an iconoclastic temperament. In his congregations, he allowed women to take part more fully in worship and introduced guitars into the liturgy. He also entered a graduate program in the psychology of religion at Boston University, where he enrolled in a class in spiritual disciplines and resources taught by the great African American theologian and social activist Howard Thurman. Uncertain how he would fit into a Catholic-run university and a class taught by a Protestant pastor, the rabbi expressed his anxieties to Thurman.

"He put his coffee mug on his desk and began to look at his hands," Schachter-Shalomi recalls. "Suddenly he spoke. 'Don't you trust the Ruach-ha-Kodesh?'" Not only did Thurman invoke the

Spirit of Holiness in good biblical Hebrew, but he went to his phono-
graph and put on a recording of Max Bruch's setting of the ancient
Kol Nidre prayer, sung on Yom Kippur. "Soon I began saying to myself,
Zalman, relax!"

Thurman's course was another revelation. The students experi-
mented with various kinds of spiritual exercises, which "frequently took
the form of guided meditations," Schachter-Shalomi recalls. "In one
kind of exercise, we were instructed to translate an experience from one
sense to another—we would read a psalm several times, then listen to a
piece by Bach, to 'hear' the meaning of the psalm in the sounds of the
music. . . . In this way our senses were released from their usual narrow
constraints and freed to tune in to the cosmos, to touch God."

When he joined the Near Eastern and Judaic studies department of
the University of Manitoba in Winnipeg in 1956, Schachter was still
looking for ways to restore Jewish traditions, not change or renew
them. The Jewish Essene monastic tradition revealed by the Dead Sea
Scrolls, the vigorous spirituality of the Hasidim, and the treasures of
Kabbalistic mysticism were pre-Holocaust resources that could give
Jews hope and energy after the great European disaster.

But he was also pushing the frontiers of his experience. In 1959,
under the guidance of Timothy Leary, he took LSD; a break with the
Lubavitcher authorities followed. The break may have been inevitable;
while grateful to the Lubavitvher movement for initiating him into the
mystical tradition of Judaism, Schachter was becoming discontented
with the movement's parochialism and insistence that it alone possessed spiritual truth. Through the 1960s, Schachter and a small group
of like-minded colleagues began experimenting with liturgical
changes, meditation, and new modes of prayer.

"In 1968, I had my sabbatical from Manitoba," he said, "and I came
to Brandeis University to do some study for myself. I studied Arabic,
Syriac, Akkadian, Ugaritic—all those ancient Near Eastern languages—
because I was interested in what had happened to our people prior to
the patriarchs. That was when a lot of stuff about the goddess religion
was coming up; there was so much happening around rediscovering the
ways of nature and wicca and so on. I wanted to see what prepatriarchal Judaism was like, what our roots were in these areas."

During his sabbatical, he took part in the founding of a *chavurah*—
a small Jewish study group—in Boston. "We did remarkable things
with liturgy," he says. "Having seen how people sat and meditated on
cushions, we did it too. We used a lot of body movements and dance

in what we were doing, and that was part of the delight. And gradually I was moved from restoration to a whole other idea that had to do
with renewal."

These were among the first stirrings of the Jewish Renewal movement, an effort to re-energize Jewish piety by making it more emotionally satisfying, inclusive, experimental, experiential, and compelling.
For Jews who were alienated from the sometimes tepid rationalism of
the Reform movement and the stern ritualism of the more traditional
denominations, the brilliant neo-Hasidic writings of Martin Buber and
Abraham Joshua Heschel were a call to embrace the living fire of a
slightly different traditionalism—the great tradition of ecstatic union
with God carried by the Hasidic mystics. At the same time it was a call
to link themselves to the world of the moment, its pains, possibilities,
and lessons, its psychospiritual breakthroughs and political changes.

Schachter, with his superb traditional training, omnivorous mind,
and personal warmth, was an immediate natural leader of the movement. Back at Manitoba, he began an intense inquiry into what to keep
and what to alter in a vital Judaism. He corresponded with Catholic
philosopher Thomas Merton and visited the Trappists at the St. Norbert
Abbey outside of Winnipeg, observing the process of *aggiornamiento*
(bringing up-to-date), the modernization of liturgy, language, doctrine,
and the role of lay people that had been mandated by Pope John XXIII
and Vatican II. He talked to Sufi mystics, Indian gurus, and Native medicine keepers. In two books, *The First Step* (1983) and *Fragments of a
Future Scroll: Hasidism for the Aquarian Age* (1975), he laid out his dynamic conceptions of Jewish prayer, meditation, and observance.

When he moved to Temple University in Philadelphia in 1975,
Schachter-Shalomi put his Jewish-renewal activities into high gear.
With the P'nai Or religious fellowship and ALEPH (which subsumed
P'nai Or in 1993) as a base, he has lectured, taught, ordained rabbis, vis-
ited Jewish renewal groups as they sprang up, translated psalms and
prayers into vigorous new English. He even altered his name, adding
Shalomi ("peace") to Schachter ("slaughterer") as an act of peacemak-
ing and balance. Since 1995 he has held the World Wisdom Chair at the
Buddhist-oriented Naropa Institute in Boulder, Colorado, and he
moved to Boulder in 1998.

Schachter-Shalomi's teaching begins with an emphasis on experience over doctrine, the felt yearning for God over abstract ideas about
the Deity. There's also a powerful orientation toward the future in his
idea of faith. "Faith is tossing out into the future an anticipation for

which I don't have proof," he says. "But I feel attracted in a direction and when I follow this direction it is faith that pulls me there." He sees God not as a stern old man living "up there," but as a force both outside and inside us that draws us to Himself (or Herself).

At the same time, his immense erudition in the Hebrew sources of his tradition has allowed him to reveal some powerful spiritual truths hidden in familiar Judeo-Christian words—the fact, for example, that the Hebrew for *commandment* (as in the Ten Commandments) also means "connection, secret communication." The commandments, then, are expressions of God's intimacy with us as well as his expectations of us. "It's like two people who care for each other across the room from each other," he says. "My wife can be over there and I can be over here talking to someone, and a glance, or the way I hold my cup, will communicate that we are not cut off from each other; we are connected."

And, of course, Schachter-Shalomi's psychological training, his experience of several modes of bodywork, and his profound knowledge of other faiths allow him to situate his expanded, welcoming version of Jewish truth in so many different contexts—personal, intellectual, experiential, physical—that learning from him is like taking six courses in six different disciplines, all at once.

Reb Zalman's most recent area of exploration—aging—is of particular poignance for a man of seventy-seven. His 1995 book, *From Age-ing to Sage-ing: A Profound New Vision of Growing Older,* is a spiritual blueprint for a new image of elderhood, not as a period of slow, sad decline culminating in a warehouse called a nursing home, but, as he writes, "a time of unparalleled inner growth having evolutionary significance ... [a] pioneering journey into our unmapped potential." This manifesto calls on elders and those who love them to realize age as a golden time of personal development, in which spiritual tools that have, so far, been associated with the quests of the young and the spiritual crises of midlife—meditation, *zazen,* yoga, shamanic wisdom, the Kabbalah, Sufism—help transform the physical diminishments of old age into powerful spiritual assets: "Spiritual elders use tools from these disciplines to awaken the intuitive capacities of mind associated with inner knowledge, wisdom, and expanded perception. By activating their dormant powers of intuition, they become seers who feed wisdom back into society."

If the plan seems utopian, Schachter-Shalomi can point to his first teachers, the Hasidic masters, who lived to ripe old age with their spiritual fires growing brighter with every passing year. And, for a shining example of a seer who has fed wisdom into society for half a century, we have only to look at Reb Zalman himself.

RESOURCES

ALEPH
  7318 Germantown Avenue, Philadelphia, PA 19119
  www.aleph.org

From Age-ing to Sage-ing: A Profound New Vision of Growing Older, with Ronald S. Miller (Warner, 1995)

Paradigm Shift : From the Jewish Renewal Teachings of Reb Zalman Schachter-Shalomi, ed. Ellen Singer (Jason Aronson, 1993)

Sparks of Light: Counseling in the Hasidic Tradition, with Edward Hoffman (Shambhala, 1983)

The First Step: A Guide for the New Jewish Spirit, with Donald Gropman (Bantam, 1983)

STARHAWK

Deborah Jones

"Spirituality and politics both involve changing consciousness. . . . Yet there are differences. Effective political action, of whatever sort, needs to offer directions and at least propose answers to current problems. But true spirituality must also take us beyond the will, down into the realms of mystery, of letting go, of echoing questions rather than resounding answers."

WHILE IT MIGHT BE going too far to compare pagan priestess Starhawk to Saint Paul or Brigham Young (and she might object to the comparison as strenuously as devout Christians and Mormons would), she has played as instrumental a role in promoting and defining paganism as either man did in his religion. More than a thousand witches' covens and goddess-worship circles across North America have been inspired by her 1979 book, *The Spiral Dance*, according to one estimate. But Starhawk is not a pagan mystic spinning esoteric dogma. Unlike many of her New Age acolytes, she connects spirituality with radical politics, especially feminism, and environmentalism.

Starhawk was born Miriam Simos in St. Paul in 1951. Her parents were Reform Jews, and her grandparents maintained an Orthodox observance. Simos' parents sent her to Conservative Jewish schools: Hebrew High School and later the University of Judaism, both in Los Angeles. During a trip to Israel in 1998, she told the *Jerusalem Post* that she still considers herself a Jew, despite years of advancing the practice of witchcraft and paganism. In her own Jewish education, she "was taught that God was not male or female, but spirit," she explained in an interview with the *Post*. "In that sense, the Goddess tradition is not that different from the Jewish conception of God."

During her first year of college, at UCLA, Simos began an anthropology project on witchcraft. (She later earned a master's degree in psychology). Her research led her to several practicing Celtic witches, and she remembers feeling, "Aha! This is what I have always believed. I just never knew there was a framework for it, or other people [who] believed the same thing." Later, when she wrote *The Spiral Dance*, a practical guide to the beliefs, history, and rituals of contemporary witchcraft, she thought of the book as the introduction to women's spirituality she wishes she'd read in college.

After moving to San Francisco in 1973, she taught witchcraft at the Bay Area Center for Alternative Education and wrote scripts for technical and industrial films. A dream about a hawk that turned into a wise woman inspired her to adopt the name Starhawk in 1975. The success of *The Spiral Dance* allowed her to devote herself fully to spiritual work—she conducts workshops and rituals around the country—and writing more books, including two novels: *The Fifth Sacred Thing* (1993) is a futuristic battle between good and evil set in a Goddess-worshipping San Francisco of the future that is under attack by a fundamentalist army. *Walking to Mercury* (1997), a prequel, explains the roots of the goddess culture of *Fifth Sacred Thing*.

The Reclaiming collective, a spiritual circle that grew out of a course on witchcraft she taught in the early 1980s, offers classes, public rituals, private counseling, and weeklong "witch camps" at which as many as a hundred people gather for daily teaching and ritual.

Insisting that a potent social message is consistent with pagan faith, Starhawk mixes religion with political activism. Paganism, witchcraft, and goddess worship are all part of the same growing movement, she says, and all three spiritual practices raise material concerns about ecology, nature, community, and women's issues. While looking back to the rituals and beliefs of ancient and Native American cultures, this growing religious movement also points the way to new relationships—between humanity and nature, between men and women—that may help us survive the twenty-first century.

Thus, in addition to being a spiritual leader, Starhawk is a radical activist and a self-described anarchist. Her 1987 book, *Truth or Dare: Encounters with Power, Authority, and Mystery*, in many ways a more ambitious work than *The Spiral Dance*, was described in *The New York Times* as "a manual for civil disobedience, an exercise in conceptual art (reminiscent of Yoko Ono), a manifesto for the neo-pagan . . . revival, a feminist version of *Civilization and Its Discontents*, . . . a study in group dynamics" that "aims for nothing less than a complete reshaping of society and psyche."

Starhawk practices what she preaches: She's an outspoken feminist who directed the Westside Women's Center in Los Angeles and has taught classes in feminist theory. She is active in the environmental movement, reasoning that, as she told the *Los Angeles Times* in 1993, if "the earth and the elements that sustain our lives are sacred, then we must work to preserve them." A relentless critic of the American military-industrial complex, she's been arrested more than a dozen times for backing up her beliefs with action.

"I actually would be perfectly happy never to blockade again, never to go to another political meeting in my life. I much prefer doing ritual or working in the garden or hanging out and watching TV to going to meetings," she said in *People of the Earth: The New Pagans Speak Out*. "But it has always seemed to me that when what's sacred to you and what's most important is threatened, you have to take a stand."

In all of her work, Starhawk offers an image of the Goddess that is both more subtle and more radical than the simple replacement of spiritual patriarchy with spiritual matriarchy. "I don't like it when people assume that the Goddess, the great female principle, is just God in skirts," she says. "The Goddess means that the sacred is imminent—it's present right here and now, in nature and in ourselves," she explains. "And by 'sacred' what I mean is not a great something that you bow down to, but what determines your values, what you would take a stand for." The social and political consequences are immediate: "If the forest is sacred, we can't chop it down. If water is sacred, we can't pollute it, even a little bit. If there is sacred authority in the human body, then no external authority can tell people what to do with it—how to love, whether or not to end a pregnancy."

A city kid who came of age in Los Angeles and San Francisco, Starhawk (who is married and has four stepchildren) now lives part of the time in the countryside, where she has taken up subsistence farming—though she continues to travel as a speaker, activist, and writer. She applies the same persistence and calm intelligence she brings to all her activities to her adventures in permaculture, beekeeping, and olive cultivation. "Don't let anyone tell you that moving to the country, getting off the grid, growing your own food, and trying to be self-sufficient is 'simple living,'" she writes in one of her intermittent, informal posts to her Web site. "There's nothing simple about it."

It is fitting that this environmentalist and champion of the earth goddess should turn—between trips to El Salvador to agitate for peace and promoting the twentieth-anniversary reprint of *The Spiral Dance*—to land stewardship. "For me the Goddess is not an abstraction," Starhawk told an interviewer. "She is . . . real. She's alive, in the earth, and in the systems we create in the human community, in all of us. . . . We grow and develop spiritually when we take . . . action [on behalf of] what is sacred to us."

RESOURCES

www.starhawk.org

The Twelve Wild Swans: A Journey to the Realm of Magic, Healing, and Action: Rituals, Exercises, and Magical Training in the Reclaiming Tradition, with Hilary Valentine (HarperSanFrancisco, 2000)

The Spiral Dance: A Rebirth of the Ancient Religion of the Great Goddess (HarperSanFrancisco, 1999; twentieth anniversary edition)

Circle Round: Raising Children in Goddess Traditions, with Diane Baker and Anne Hill (Bantam, 1998)

Dreaming the Dark: Magic, Sex and Politics (Beacon, 1997; fifteenth anniversary edition)

Walking to Mercury (Bantam, 1997)

The Fifth Sacred Thing (Bantam, 1993)

Truth or Dare: Encounters with Power, Authority, and Mystery (Harper & Row, 1987)

A SENSE OF COMMUNITY

MODERN AMERICAN LIFE is positively awash in material abundance and technological splendor. Middle-class people take for granted goods and services that would strike their grandparents as luxurious miracles: Internet communications, instant microwave dinners, richly stocked shopping malls, drugs for every ailment, infinite entertainment options, overseas air travel. It looks like we have finally achieved the centuries-old promise of the Good Life.

Yet doubts persist. Has something important been lost along the way? Most of us don't know our neighbors anymore, except for a hurried hello if we happen to be climbing into our cars at the same moment. We're not really involved in our communities, beyond voting every couple of years and donating to the United Way. And time for family and friends grows maddeningly scarce—we're always stuck in traffic, working late at the office, glued to the television, or caught up in endless rounds of errands. A creeping sense of loneliness hangs in the air, even as the media blare ever more triumphantly about the dazzling inventions and exciting experiences that await us in this new century.

Concerns about the breakdown of community are dismissed as nostalgia, a sentimental yearning for yesterday's church picnics and the corner soda fountain, notes David Morris. But the fast-paced and fragmented lives we now lead have very real consequences: Children grow up in a world of strangers, their perceptions of life colored by feelings that no one besides their parents cares what happens to them. Fear of crime and urban decay hangs over many neighborhoods, and instead of pulling together to fix things, people flee to new subdivisions that sprawl across the countryside. All of us feel increasingly frustrated and powerless as decisions that intimately shape our lives are made thousands of miles away in corporate boardrooms and government agencies.

This shift from the local to the global, from the familiar to the uncertain, from an informal network of personal connections to a structured system of institutional precepts, is often hailed as progress. But progress toward what? This question is raised forcefully by the women and men profiled in this chapter. Is a franchise outlet in a strip mall better than a locally owned neighborhood business? Do outside

35

experts know more about what a community needs than its residents do? What will it take to bring neighborliness back to our busy world? Millions of people are now asking these same questions, and an increasing number of them have begun to seek answers by reaching out to their own communities.

A deeper sense of community can be found by joining a group of like-minded souls in a book club—like those fostered by Virginia Valentine in Denver. Or enlisting neighbors to pressure politicians and business leaders for much-needed community improvements—like the grassroots organizations founded throughout the Southwest by Ernesto Cortes. Writers Jane Jacobs of Toronto and Barbara Brandes Gratz of New York City offer specific suggestions about what qualities promote— and undermine—vitality in our cities and towns. Florida architects Andres Duany and Elizabeth Plater-Zyberk create blueprints for new communities that offer the conviviality and charm of old neighborhoods. David Morris of the Minnesota-based Institute for Local Self-Reliance, and John Papworth, a venerable English social critic, point out that small-scale, locally controlled institutions—from banks to schools to governments—serve us far better than big, distantly managed ones.

Activist Helena Norberg-Hodge draws on her experience with indigenous communities in the Himalayas to remind us of what is being wiped out in the long march of the global economy—in our neighborhoods as well as in the developing world. Michael Lind, a savvy young political commentator from Texas, proposes the idea of America as a single community, and looks at what it will take to hold us together as a nation. Frances Moore Lappé chronicles the reawakening of community consciousness.

While prescriptions for rekindling community vary from locally harvested food to better urban planning, there's full agreement among these visionaries that we can no longer overlook the fact that strong connections between people form the foundation of healthy society— and play a key role in addressing a whole host of critical problems from street crime to failing schools. This rings out as an uplifting message in an era when big technocratic programs to improve society are often seen as ineffective, if not problems in themselves. Focusing our energy on increasing the sense of community across the country offers the added benefit of allowing everyone to take part in the cause. Reaching out to your neighbors, initiating a community garden, joining a movement to protect your local environment or promote affordable housing brings richness to your life as well as tangible results to your community.

—Jay Walljasper

ERNESTO CORTES JR.

"Real politics offers an opportunity to engage people at the core of their values, their vision, their imagination. It begins to offer them some possibilities for change, for transformation of self and of community by beginning to deal with some fundamental issues that affect families."

Frank Curran

A FEW YEARS BACK, *Texas Business* magazine published a list of the most powerful Texans, featuring all the usual suspects: multibillionaire and presidential candidate Ross Perot, notorious corporate raider T. Boone Pickens, U.S. Secretary of Housing and Urban Development Henry Cisneros, vice presidential candidate Lloyd Bentsen. Also listed was Ernesto Cortes—a little-known figure who's never held elective office and has spent most of his career in migrant labor camps, PTA meetings, church basements, ghettos, union halls, and budget motels. At first glance, Cortes seems a preposterous choice for a power broker—especially in a state famed for high-stakes political deal-making and economic empire-building.

Yet upon closer inspection, perhaps it's not preposterous at all. Cortes' whole life has been about gaining power, ever since the day in 1955 at a San Antonio swimming pool when one of his cousins was refused entry because her skin was too dark. "Ernie ran an action right there and then," recalls his wife, Oralia Garza. "He said if she can't go in, none of us are going in." Everyone got to go swimming, notes. Garza, adding that Cortes "has been agitating ever since."

"Power is nothing more than the ability to act in your own behalf," Cortes says. "In Spanish, we call the word *poder*, to have capacity, to be able. Power is such a good thing everyone should have some."

As the Southwest regional director of the Industrial Areas Foundation (IAF), a national network of community groups founded by legendary organizer Saul Alinsky, Cortes has helped spread power a little wider throughout Texas and nearby states. He's founded more than twenty citizen groups from New Orleans to Des Moines to Los Angeles, all of them aimed at increasing the role of average citizens in political and economic decision making.

Power, says Cortes, is important for what it can deliver: water and sewage treatment facilities for 400 communities in the Rio Grande Valley; a $2.8 billion increase in public school funding in Texas; 600 low-income people hired for well-paying positions through a job training program in San Antonio; an initiative that boosts resources and community involvement in thirty-five public school districts in Louisiana, Texas, New Mexico, and Arizona. "I want to teach people how they can take their private pain, their private hopes, their private aspirations, and translate that into public issues that are going to qualitatively improve their lives and those of their children," Cortes says.

There's nothing glamorous about community organizing. You deal with mundane matters like trying to get better storm sewers in poor neighborhoods, arranging car pools so people can get to a city council meeting, worrying if there will be enough hot dogs for the fund-raiser on Saturday. You're often working with people who have built up vast reservoirs of anger and cynicism over a lifetime. And, even in ideal circumstances, change comes slowly. But Cortes has stuck with this work for 30 years, and people are now taking notice. The MacArthur Foundation bestowed on him one of its coveted "genius grants," he was named the Martin Luther King Jr. Visiting Professor of Urban Studies at MIT, and he recently won the $250,000 H. J. Heinz Award. Teresa Heinz, widow of Republican senator John Heinz, whom the grant honors, declared that "Ernesto Cortes embodies the principle of grass-roots organizing and political empowerment."

Outlining the basics of how to empower a community, Cortes says, "You take institutions—the family, the church—and you use them as a source of power, of confidence, of authority. You get people to talk about what's in the interest of their families, what are the threats to their families, what are the threats to their churches and communities.

"Organizing is a fancy word for building relationships," he adds. "If I want to organize you, I try to kindle your imagination, stir the possibilities, and then propose some ways in which you can act on those dreams and those values and your own visions."

The greatest obstacle to empowering communities, Cortes cautions, is "learned helplessness"—the feeling that only someone else can solve your problems—which is widespread in working-class and minority communities. "There's an iron rule in organizing: Never, ever do for people what they can do for themselves," he declares.

Personal transformation is a goal just as important as political change, he emphasizes, because people who have been transformed will continue to stand up for themselves, their families, and their communities. "They get a sense of possibilities for themselves, that their life has meaning and significance," he says. "They see themselves as worthy of respect. It really gives me hope when I see those sorts of changes taking place in people."

Ernesto Cortes might easily have become a true Texas power broker, grabbing a fat share of wealth, fame, privilege, and personal clout. A standout student in San Antonio's Catholic schools, he graduated from Texas A&M University at age nineteen with a double major in English and economics and went on to the prestigious graduate program in economics at the University of Texas. But economics of a different sort grabbed his attention: the rock-bottom wages and deplorable working conditions of farmworkers in the Rio Grande Valley. He initiated a statewide campaign to rally support for a United Farm Workers strike at La Casita farms and has been devoted to political activism ever since. He spent several years in Milwaukee and East Chicago, Indiana, organizing under the tutorship of the Industrial Areas Foundation, and then came home in 1974 to put what he'd learned into practice, founding San Antonio Communities Organized for Public Service (COPS).

In the past quarter-century, COPS has changed the face of San Antonio through what Cortes calls "the art of confrontation and compromise"—sometimes with noisy public actions, other times in quiet negotiations with political and business leaders. The results can be seen all over inner-city San Antonio in new government and private-sector investment. COPS, which is based in Catholic churches on the largely Mexican American West and South sides, has worked with Metro Alliance, another organization Cortes founded, based primarily in Protestant churches, to bring to poor neighborhoods almost a billion dollars in improvements: flood control, health clinics, better schools, better housing, new parks, new libraries, sewers, street repairs, energy conservation, college scholarships, community policing, safe drinking water, job training, and political power. Henry Cisneros, who later became HUD secretary during Bill Clinton's first term, never would have been elected San Antonio's first Mexican American mayor without COPS' successful campaign for single-member city council districts, which do not dilute the strength of Mexican American and African American communities the way previous at-large representation did.

In laying groundwork for similar accomplishments all across Texas and half a dozen other states, Cortes leads an on-the-go life of dizzying proportions: You may need to call him in three time zones just to pin down an interview time. Yet by all accounts he's a devoted family man, squeezing in as much time as possible at home in Austin's South Side barrio with Oralia; their daughters, Ami, a teacher, and Alma, a college student; and son, Jacob, a high school student. At a high-powered political summit at an Austin hotel , the local *American-Statesman* newspaper reported, he snuck off to his room as often as possible—not to rest or hold insider strategy sessions, but to help Jacob with his homework. He mentions family trips to Mexico or Spain as the surest way for him to recharge intellectually.

Fellow Texan Bill Moyers, who interviewed Cortes in his *World of Ideas* PBS series, notes other ways Cortes keeps his mind keen: "He knows his Bible and his *New York Review of Books, The Economist, Dissent*, and *World Press Review*. He carries on a running conversation with John Dewey, Alfred North Whitehead, Dostoyevski, Herman Melville, and Mark Twain. They have been tutors to a man who considers life a continuing course in adult education."

Cortes's intellectual engagement with the great thinkers of American democracy paired with his experiences of working with the everyday people of the American southwest has instilled in him the dream of a new America—one that continues the tradition of "life, liberty, and the pursuit of happiness" but also acknowledges and deepens the bonds between individuals in our society. "I see the schools becoming more connected to parents and the communities they serve," he explains. "I see congregations—Judaism, Islam, Christianity—teaching that religion is not just an internal, mystical experience but a process of building a relational culture among people and becoming a community. I see labor unions not just negotiating contracts but bringing people together. It's about people making connections, making communities, but also about agitating for a new vision, transforming the culture."

SELECTED RESOURCES

Southwest Regional Office of the Industrial Areas Foundation
  1106 Clayton Lane, Suite 120W, Austin, TX 78723

The New Inequality: Creating Solutions for Poor America,
  by Richard B. Freeman (Beacon, 2001), includes an essay by Cortes

Cold Anger: A Story of Faith and Power Politics
  by Mary Beth Rogers (Univ. of North Texas Press, 1990)

A World of Ideas II: Public Opinions from Private Citizens
  by Bill Moyers (Doubleday, 1990)

ROBERTA BRANDES GRATZ

"Preserving the urban fabric, weaving together the treasured old and the needed new, not being afraid to think small—that is what genuine revitalization is all about."

THE LIGHTS ARE SHINING bright again in the American city. From Portland, Maine, to Portland, Oregon, people are rediscovering the charms and comfort of traditional urban neighborhoods. Downtowns are bustling again, not just with new skyscrapers but also lively public markets and squares where people love to gather. And suburban sprawl, once seen as the inevitable product of prosperity, is under challenge by environmentalists, urban activists, and even some elected officials who see it as wasteful, polluting, and unnecessary.

If the American city is the quintessential comeback kid, once on the ropes but now looking strong, then urban observer Roberta Brandes Gratz stands as one of its most important trainers. She's been coaching us for thirty years about what does and doesn't revitalize a city—first as a reporter for the *New York Post* and more recently in magazine articles, books, and lectures. Her 1994 book, *The Living City*, distilled a lifetime's study of what makes cities thrive into a refreshing lesson about "thinking small in a big way." Based on years of carefully observing urban renewal projects and neighborhood activism in New York City and other cities, Gratz concludes that large-scale projects like convention centers, sports arenas, aquariums, casinos, hotels, vertical shopping malls, aren't what bring life back to a town. Renewal comes from the everyday activity of urban residents, shopowners, and neighborhood activists who set out to improve what's there rather than rebuild the city from scratch.

When Gratz started writing about urban issues in the 1960s, cities had already taken quite a few blows. Two post–World War II government programs—the Federal Housing Act and the Federal Highway Act, then the largest public works project in the history of the world—ensured the dominance of sprawling suburban development. Nearly 14 million families fled American neighborhoods for the suburbs, in part because existing homes were usually not eligible for subsidized Veteran's Administration and Federal Housing Administration loans. These policies gave suburbs an enormously unfair advantage over cities, where there was little land left to build new houses. By the 1970s, experts declared many downtowns dead. The Interstate Highway system built freeways through the heart of almost every city, making it easier to move to the suburbs while at the same time leaving many neighborhoods in ruins.

The solutions implemented to fix these problems often just accelerated decline. In the name of "urban renewal," entire neighborhoods were demolished in New York, Chicago, Boston, Detroit, and many towns and cities, replacing rundown but lively neighborhoods with sterile blocks of apartments or office buildings. Our auto-centered transportation policies drove many pedestrians off the sidewalks, killing the street life that is a real city's lifeblood. "In the process of rebuilding America," Gratz says, "we destroyed so much of it, including the greatest transportation network in the world." Before the interstates, "there was not a community of any size in the entire country that did not have a streetcar."

Gratz, like Jane Jacobs a decade earlier, arrived independently at her vision of what makes cities vital, without academic credentials or professional expertise. "It is obvious to anyone who walks the streets, lives in a neighborhood, studies a neighborhood on the street by talking to people, and not from a drawing board or atelier," Gratz says. "The visions that are imposed by highway engineers and urban renewal planners have nothing to do with the improvement of a place."

In *The Living City* and her latest book, *Cities Back from the Edge*, Gratz argues that instead of a quick fix, cities need slow nurturing—"urban husbandry," she calls it. "Urban husbandry respects the existing social fabric, nurtures small business and encourages new ones. Change is gradual, natural, noncataclysmic, and responsible to genuine economic and social needs." And in the process, the seat of decison making usually shifts from city hall and other traditional power centers to the communities themselves.

New York's SoHo is a prime example of how urban husbandry works. It was once a forgotten stretch of dilapidated nineteenth-century manufacturing buildings that the fire department called Hell's Hundred Acres. When transportation officials drafted plans in the late 1950s for a highway that would demolish much of SoHo, Little Italy, and Chinatown, residents of these neighborhoods fought the highway for ten years, until the plans were finally scrapped in 1969. During that time artists had begun moving into the the area, and today it is a world-famous neighborhood of art galleries, loft homes, restaurants, and boutiques in beautifully preserved old buildings. SoHo's success has inspired the creation of similar arts districts in dozens of cities around the country, including the well-known South of Market district (SoMa) in San Francisco and Lower Downtown (LoDo) in Denver. Savannah, Georgia stands as another shining example of how a city can be reborn by paying attention to its architectural and urban heritage. Residents from all walks of life took the lead in restoring the city's splendid historic district, one house at a time.

Perhaps Gratz is such a keen observer of city life because her own life parallels the city's fortunes. Raised in the 1940s in Greenwich Village, where her Jewish immigrant father owned several dry cleaning shops, she moved in the 1950s with her family to suburban Connecticut, where her father opened the first drive-in dry cleaner in the state in one of the earliest malls. Her mother decorated model homes for a tract housing developer.

But Gratz never took to this version of the American Dream. "I had been a happy city kid," she recalls. "I did all kinds of things and had a lot of freedom. I could always go down to the park. Moving was a real culture shock. I was not a happy suburban kid." She grabbed the first chance to move back, enrolling at New York University, and she's never left. After graduating, she got a $55-a-week job as a "copy boy" at the *New York Post*, then worked her way up to reporter and soon gained recognition for her groundbreaking reporting on student protests, the women's movement, abortion, and rape as well as fierce debates over neighborhood development issues. "I used to say that I could not believe how I was paid to get up every day and learn about something new," she says. After more than fifteen years at the *Post*, she left newspaper work when she received a National Endowment for the Arts grant to write the book *The Living City*.

Today she lives just across from Central Park on the Upper West Side with her husband, the owner of a manufacturing company. "I live within twenty minutes of anything," she notes proudly. "I can walk or take the subway to anyplace I want. We can decide at the last minute that we want to go to dinner, or see a movie or a show and we have dozens of choices."

"The big secret that's now becoming evident is that there are a lot of people who really do want to live in a city," she continues. "They want to walk the streets, they want the serendipity of city life. People are jumping ship from the suburbs because there's nothing interesting there. It's a mistake to try and make cities more suburban."

Not everything about city life is rosy, Gratz reminds us. Cities are still spending money on big projects like sports stadiums, casinos, convention centers, and aquariums—which encourage suburbanites to drive in and drive out, but don't bring life back to downtown.

Too often, cities still choose to build new highways to accommodate growth, rather than improve public transportation systems. "It is a familiar dilemma: A modest problem triggers an out-of-scale solution that can be achieved only at an unnecessary economic and physical cost. Local residents, sensitive to aesthetic and ecological issues, oppose the solution and are accused of opposing progress. Local elected officials rationalize the damage rather than reject a large sum of federal money. Proponents argue that the negative impacts are the inevitable price of progress. . . . For several decades now, large and small American communities have been facing this kind of catch-22 development dilemma, too often making the wrong choice. Overscaled, overpriced projects are imposed where smaller, less costly, equally productive, and more aesthetically satisfactory solutions would do."

Gratz is one of the most prominent of a growing chorus of urban critics challenging the merits of this kind of progress. Her writings have inspired neighborhood activists across the country to speak up for a different vision of what their cities could become. She is now taking these ideas into Eastern Europe, where public officials are poised to make the same kind of mistakes that Americans did in the 1950s and 1960s— dismantling mass transit, ripping new freeways through cities, tearing down architecturally rich neighborhoods, and equating progress with newness. She's been commissioned to write a report on the situation for the Rockefeller Brothers Fund and is consulting for civic organizations in Poland, the Czech Republic, Hungary, Germany, and Slovakia.

Spending time in beautiful cities like Prague, Cracow, and Budapest tempts her to think about leaving New York, as does her secret and very un-urban fantasy of buying a vintage Airstream trailer and traveling cross-country. "I don't say that living in a city is the perfect thing for everybody," she says. "but I know that for me, I would always come back to New York."

SELECTED RESOURCES

Cities Back from the Edge: New Life for Downtown, with Norman Mintz (John Wiley, 2000).

The Living City: How America's Cities Are Being Revitalized by Thinking Small in a Big Way (Preservation, 1994).

JANE JACOBS

"At the turn of the century, there was a big wheel in Alaska named Sheldon Jackson, head of education. He came up with the great reindeer-raising project, to help Alaskan natives "rise" from hunters into civilized Christian herders. The whole thing was foolish. It made far more economic sense for native people to go after wild caribou—who care for their own young and protect themselves from disease—rather than take on all these responsibilities and costs themselves. It was a flop—one of those plausible-sounding schemes with absolutely no basis in good sense. A prototype for many foreign, and domestic, aid schemes."

Maclean's Magazine

I N 1961, AT THE height of urban planners' crusade to obliterate all the charming, lovable parts of American cities and replace them with sharp-angled monuments to modernist rationality, an unassuming New York writer defended the urban neighborhoods in a book called *The Death and Life of Great American Cities*. Jane Jacobs celebrated what nearly everyone else called slums and eyesores: the close-knit urban neighborhoods under assault by superhighways and high-rise housing projects. She was savagely attacked for it—not least because she had no formal training as an urban planner, just the knowledge she had accumulated in decades of living in Greenwich Village and as an editor for *Architectural Forum* magazine. But that attention to the nitty-gritty elements of urban living is precisely what makes her thinking so profound. She celebrates the seemingly small things that make a city work well for its residents—the way people on the street deter crime; how a mix of shops and housing makes a neighborhood both convenient and lively. Urban planners tend to overlook these things as they pursue grand visions of architectural splendor without considering what it will be like to live in their masterpieces.

"There is a wistful myth," Jacobs writes in *The Death and Life of Great American Cites,* "that if only we had enough money to spend—the figure is usually put at $100 billion—we could wipe out all our slums in ten years. . . . But look what we have built with the first several billions: Low-income projects that become worse centers of deliquency, vandalism, and general social hopelessness than the slums they were supposed to replace. Middle-income housing projects which are truly marvels of dullness and regimentation, sealed against any buoyancy or vitality of city life. Luxury housing projects that mitigate their inanity, or try to, with a vapid vulgarity."

"One of the great fallacies of planning, urban and otherwise, is that planners project trends onward on a steady line, as though growth or decline will go on at a steady rate," Jacobs adds."One thing you can be sure of is that things won't develop that way; there'll be ups and downs. What planners should plan for is keeping the future open and flexible, with opportunity open for as many people as possible."

The Canadian newsmagazine *MacLean's,* at the time of a 1997 conference exploring Jacobs' work, noted that "the lessons from that one book—that cities are ecosystems that can be smothered by rigid, authoritarian planning, that busy, lively sidewalks help cities thrive as safe, healthy places, that good urban design mixes work, housing, and recreation—have influenced a generation of planners and architects."

Jacobs fell in love with the hubbub of city life upon moving to New York City from her hometown of Scranton, Pennsylvania. "The first time I walked out of the subway and saw Greenwich Village," she remembers, "I knew I had to live there. I liked its human scale, the mix of shops and housing, the little streets and many courtyards. The craft shops. The Italian food stores. It was so full of surprises." This was in the middle of the Depression, and Jacobs had a difficult time finding a job—experience, she says, that offered perspective on what urban life feels like to people scraping by. With no college degree, she started a journalism career at a metals industry trade newspaper; soon she was contributing regularly to *Vogue* and other major publications. During World War II, she met her husband, architect Robert Jacobs. He sparked her interest in architecture, which eventually led to a job as senior editor at *Architectural Forum.* Unlike most couples of the time, they stayed in the city to raise their three children, but the Vietnam war—which Jacobs fiercely opposed and did not want her two sons to fight in—ultimately drove them from New York, and from the United States altogether.

The family moved to Toronto, a city Jacobs feels has done an excellent job in maintaining its urban vitality. In the 1950s, when the United States was plowing billions into urban freeways, Toronto constructed a subway system. Freeways were eventually built on the edges of the city, not through its heart.

Jacobs was partly responsible for saving her adopted home from dissection. Upon arriving in town her family moved into a rented house on Spadina Road that was ground zero for a controversial expressway project. She wrote thundering articles in the local newspaper, accusing city planners of wanting to "Los Angelize" Toronto, and in her kitchen she organized an opposition movement, applying strategic lessons she had learned a decade earlier in a successful campaign to stop a highway from being built through the middle of Greenwich Village's beloved Washington Square Park.

Today, Jacobs still lives in the area known as the Annex, now in a three-story brick house from whose open porch she can monitor activity in the neighborhood. She points out front yard gardens and discusses with a friend on the porch next door the comings and goings of a raccoon family. This middle-class neighborhood in many ways embodies the ideals of urban living celebrated in Jacobs' books. The streets are lined with trees and parked cars, both of which encourage drivers to slow down. The one- and two-family homes are built close together, and alleys run though each block. A busy commercial street with a streetcar line is just around the corner, ensuring that anyone can shop or get around town without a car.

Her house is crowded with books and great stacks of magazines and newspapers, out of which she clips articles for her ongoing research— as well as jigsaw puzzles, a favorite pastime. In a way, her books come together like puzzles, as she doggedly studies the patterns into which elements of information fit. In *The Economy of Cities,* she examined how cities function as economic units, and in *Cities and the Wealth of Nations,* she outlined how cities are the unrecognized secret of national economic prosperity. The latter book influenced University of Chicago economist Robert Lucas' work on human capital—the economic dynamism created from the endless opportunities cities offer for the exchange of ideas—for which he won a 1995 Nobel Prize.

Jacobs relishes her role as an academic outsider because it allows her to look at things—and make connections among them—with fresh eyes. She decided long ago to avoid the trappings of celebrity so she could devote all her energy to her research. She agreed to participate in Ideas That Matter—the 1997 conference that drew economists, sociologists, architects, journalists, artists, ecologists, systems theorists, politicans, generalists, and city lovers to Toronto to discuss her writings—only after being convinced that the event would focus on her work, not on her.

Conference participants spent a lot of time talking about the controversial ideas in her book, *Systems of Survival,* in which she characterizes two distinct human roles: trader and guardian. The traders enrich society with the connections and commerce they make with outside interests, while the guardians, including government and the military, are charged with protecting us from outsiders. The two groups have completely different (and equally valid) systems of values and ethics; complex problems arise when their roles are mixed up, as frequently happens in modern society. "Kick-starting the economy is not a legitimate—or even possible—guardian role," she writes. "Government's role is to create a good climate for new ideas and honest trade."

Medieval knights and Japanese samurai warriors, she points out, were forbidden from trading, or associating with traders. The risk was—and still is—that government officials or military leaders who engage in commerce may betray the interests of the people they serve.

In her mid eighties, Jacobs puts in long days of thinking, writing, and observing the workings of the world through her perceptive gaze. Her latest book, *The Nature of Economies,* looks at how economies function in an intricate, complex, and self-regulating manner almost like ecosystems. She apologetically brought a recent interview to a close by saying, "You'll have to excuse me, but I must get back to work."

SELECTED RESOURCES

The Nature of Economies (Modern Library, 2000)

Ideas That Matter: The Worlds of Jane Jacobs, ed. Max Allen (Ginger Press, 1997), an anthology of unpublished essays, speeches, and letters, along with commentary from Jan Morris, Norman Mailer, and many others

Systems of Survival: A Dialogue on the Moral Foundations of Commerce and Politics (Random House, 1992; Vintage, 1994)

The Death and Life of Great American Cities (Random House, 1961; Modern Library, 1993)

Cities and the Wealth of Nations: Principles of Economic Life (Random House, 1984; Vintage, 1985)

The Economy of Cities (Random House, 1969)

FRANCES MOORE LAPPÉ

"The problems we face are simply too great to be met without our active engagement. Solutions require the ingenuity of those most affected, the creativity that emerges from diverse perspectives, and the commitment that comes only when people know they have a real stake in the outcome. It takes an active citizenry to create public decision making that works— decision making that is accountable and creative enough to address the root causes of today's crises."

WHETHER SHE'S studying world hunger or American democracy, social critic Frances Moore Lappé has spent her career trying to find the solution at the heart of a problem—a process she calls "peeling away layers of the onion." It's a fitting metaphor for the author of *Diet for a Small Planet,* the 1971 combination philosophical treatise and cookbook that revolutionized the way we think about world hunger and the way we eat. The book was a wake-up call for the American public, urging that you can help change the world by changing the way you eat. It has sold more than 3 million copies and is still in print thirty years later.

Diet for a Small Planet—which started out as a one-page handout that the twenty-seven-year-old Berkeley dropout researched and wrote for friends—made Lappé an internationally respected expert on the issue of hunger. *The Washington Post* commented, "Some of the twentieth century's most vibrant activist thinkers have been American women—Margaret Mead, Jeanette Rankin, Barbara Ward, Dorothy Day—who took it upon themselves to pump life into basic truths. Frances Moore Lappé is among them."

In the book, Lappé reveals this troubling fact: there's more than enough food to feed the world's people. Hunger is the tragic result of world food policies that encourage Third World farmers to export the food they grow, while farmers in wealthy countries fill their animals full of food that could feed people. In this upside-down cycle of waste, U.S. farmers feed half the grain they grow to livestock so that Americans can consume twice as much animal protein as they need. Since it takes sixteen pounds of grain and soybeans to produce one pound of beef, the result is a dramatic net loss of food energy. Lappé proposed that we should "eat low on the food chain"—now a familiar concept. Among the other harmful consequences of the "unquestioned rules" of the world food system, Lappé wrote, are overproduction, eroded topsoil, polluted groundwater, and decimation of farm communities.

When the book was published, the medical establishment declared the diet she proposed—lots of vegetable proteins, less meat, fat, salt, and additives—heresy. Today, this diet is being touted by the federal government. Vegetarianism has moved from fringe obsession to mainstream movement. Organic food sales have grown at the rate of 20 percent per year for the last eight years.

It was a long way from the 1950s world of Fort Worth, Texas, where Lappé grew up cheerleading and chowing down steak, to *Diet for a Small Planet*. But engagement in social issues was not new to her. Her parents, "out of step with the dominant culture" in Fort Worth, founded a Unitarian church in the Bible Belt and integrated it years before the civil rights movement.

Lappé recalls lying in bed listening to her parents as they sat around the kitchen table with friends discussing the burning social issues of the day. "I grew up in a family that took for granted that one of life's greatest jobs is engagement," she says. "We assumed that developing one's thinking in lively interchange in order to act responsibly is part of what it means to be fully alive."

Attending Earlham, a Quaker college in Indiana, followed by a special program for community organizing in Philadelphia, made her more radical. She enrolled in Berkeley's graduate program in social work, but then made what she calls "the most painful decision of my life. I dropped out of graduate school and I made a vow to myself that I would never do anything else again in my life until I understood how it related to underlying causes of human suffering. I was moved by this deep intuition that food could become the key to unlock the mysteries of it all. If I could just understand why people were hungry, then I would decode, if you will, the political economy."

She spent hours at Berkeley's agriculture library reading everything she could about the subject. "I was developing my highly honed research technique of following my nose," she says. "I believed that if I just let one question form the next question, and then form the next question, that that would take me somewhere important."

From the results of her research, she wrote a one-page handout that grew into a five-page pamphlet and then a booklet she was going to publish herself, until a friend showed it to Betty Ballantine at Ballantine Books. The stunning success of *Diet for a Small Planet* established Lappé as an authority on the troubling connection between hunger and political policy. Her think tank, the Institute for Food and Development Policy, which she established in 1975 with researcher Joseph Collins, played an instrumental role in raising international consciousness about agriculture and food policy.

In the late 1980s, she went through another period of self-questioning and began to peel away another layer of the onion. "What could possibly be powerful enough to allow us to tolerate and condone as a society what as individuals we abhor?" she wrote in the introduction to the twentieth anniversary edition of *Diet for a Small Planet*. "Few of us would allow a child to suffer deprivation in our midst. Yet as a society we do just that. In the United States, we allow one quarter of our children to be born into poverty. I had come to believe that no program— no matter how 'correct'—could address the problems of our communities and our planet unless many, many more people believed themselves capable of participating in the changes it suggested."

With community organizer Paul Du Bois, with whom she was then married, Lappé moved from California to rural Vermont, where they settled into a converted seventeenth-century barn and wrote *Rediscovering America's Values*. Their goal was to help people "rediscover public life." The book probed why Americans have retreated to their living rooms and shopping malls. "We are social creatures who have an innate desire for a healthy community," Lappé says. "Most of us want to have meaning beyond our individual families, and beyond our own material survival. Then the question is: What's blocking that?" She concludes that we're blocked by a sense of futility, a feeling that we have no power to effect change. "So few people ever feel invited in, ever feel asked, ever feel listened to," she explains. "Shopping is truly the only place where they feel they have choice."

In Vermont, Lappé and Du Bois founded the American News Service to "shine a light" on successful community projects around the country. The stories—on youth violence, workplace issues, schools, community pride and environmental activism, among other subjects— struck a chord with American readers: Within two years, their stories had been published in eighty-four of the one hundred top-circulation newspapers in the country. Lappé is hopeful about signs she sees of an emerging backlash to our consumerist society. "This work puts me in touch daily with people who are engaged in doing things that have nothing to do with market-defined reality," she says. "They're motivated by the desire to have deeper connections with their children or create a better workplace or protect the environment or get together across race lines. That's the reason I have such hope."

SELECTED RESOURCES

Center for Living Democracy
  289 Fox Farm Road, Brattleboro, VT 05301
  802/254-1234
  www.livingdemocracy.org

www.americannews.com
  Due to financial constraints, the site has ceased publishing new articles, but remains online for access to their archives.

World Hunger: Twelve Myths, with Joseph Collins, Peter Rosset and Luis
  Esparza (Grove, 1998; second rev. and updated edition)

Diet for a Small Planet (Ballantine, 1991; twentieth anniversary edition)

Rediscovering America's Values (Ballantine, 1989)

MICHAEL LIND

"In any other democracy, an enraged citizenry probably would have rebelled by now against a national elite that weakens unions, slashes wages and benefits, pits workers against low-wage foreign and immigrant competition—and then informs its victims that the chief source of their economic problems is a lack of high personal diligence."

A T AN AGE when most intellectuals are still jockeying for a corner office in the halls of academe, thirty-nine-year-old Michael Lind is arguably one of the preeminent thinkers of our era, unquestionably one of the most dazzling in his scope of interests. He's published a book-length epic poem about the battle of the Alamo, a novel about power politics in Washington, D.C., a breakthrough political manifesto about how enlightened nationalism could save America, and a controversial treatise defending the Vietnam War.

His byline regularly pops up in the most influential publications, accompanying bright, brash articles that turn the conventional wisdom of both left and right on its head. In *The New York Times Book Review,* he suggested that in the future, as in the past, creative artists will be seen as artisans along the lines of a cabinetmaker, not as Olympian upholders of culture. In *Mother Jones,* he argued that the United States Senate is manifestly undemocratic and that we should carve out new states from big ones to remedy this injustice. In *Harper's,* he pointed out how an arrogant overclass, exercising control over both political parties as well as the media, has "steadfastly waged a generation-long class war against the middle and working classes."

And Lind talks in fascinating detail about a panoply of topics. He forcefully argues that Thomas Jefferson was "a racist, agrarian proto-confederate." He outlines the aesthetic development of the new expansive poetry, which aims "to restore techniques like meter and rhyme to verse." He speculates about how talking computers will bring a new golden age of oral culture. He explains how philan-thropic foundations "sterilized thought on the left." He muses about how American Catholics should have formed their own populist pro-gressive Christian Democratic party after World War II. And he mar-vels about how the German writer Goethe took up the study of Persian poetry in his nineties.

If this sounds like all work and no play, please note that Lind has dined at Henry Kissinger's apartment, sailed with William F. Buckley Jr., and hung out at the White House with Bill Clinton, tossing around ideas for a State of the Union address.

Not bad for a kid from Texas who spent his youth—when he was-n't reading Cicero or writing poetry—chasing armadillos, hunting for fossils, and cruising around in a white Cadillac with an all-girl punk band called the Chickadiesels. Growing up in the Hill Country in and around Austin, thousands of miles from the cultural citadels of the coasts, is what made it possible for him to become an intellectual of such admirable variety, Lind explains: "Back in Texas, it was once taken for granted that if you were an educated person you would be able to write a little poem or write an op-ed article without being a profes-sional op-ed writer. I am constantly taken aback by the specialization I encounter."

Things have gotten so narrow, he notes, that a young woman from the University of Chicago told him at a recent poetry conference that creative writing students are now expected to concentrate on fiction, poetry, or nonfiction, and they are warned that switching tracks might jeopardize their chances of being accepted into a good graduate writ-ing program. He compares this to his great-grandfather, a world histo-ry professor and dean at Southern Methodist University who collected African American literature and delivered his yearly commencement address in free verse.

Although his heart clearly resides in the Hill Country, Lind has lived on the East Coast since he graduated from the University of Texas. While he was in graduate school studying diplomacy and military history at Yale, he launched a conservative campus journal bankrolled by William F. Buckley Jr. From there he was snapped up by the right-wing Heritage Foundation in Washington, going on to serve in George Bush's State Department before becoming executive editor of the neoconservative *National Interest* journal.

Raised in a "New Deal Democrat" family, he was repelled by the cultural radicalism of the left and drawn to the tough anticommunism of the Reagan administration. But in the early 1990s he grew disillusioned with what he saw as the viciousness and oligarchic elitism of the conservative movement, drifted back to his "Rooseveltian" roots, and is now Washington editor of *Harper's* and a fellow of the New America Foundation, a think tank dedicated to forging a new politics of the "radical center."

That term, popularized by Lind in a 1995 *New York Times Magazine* article, sums up his own political values, which, as he admits, offer something to offend hard-core ideologues of every political stripe. While his support of government programs to reverse economic inequality and his articulate denunciation of free trade deals that give corporations the upper hand over workers ought to draw cheers from progressives, he speaks critically of affirmative action, mass-scale immigration, multiculturalism, and dovish foreign policy. "The organized left is essentially brain dead," he declares, explaining that its social agenda alienates the everyday people who ought to be its most fervent supporters. Affirmative action, he notes, was Richard Nixon's divide-and-conquer strategy to keep minorities and the white working class at each others' throats, while "diversity means appointing rich professionals educated in the Ivy League who happen to belong to different races and sexes."

Lind's vision for America's future focuses on reviving the old-fashioned notion of nationalism, which he thinks can be fruitfully adapted to a new century of globalized commerce and information. He sees a strong American culture—distinct from an American government and an American economy—born of the marvelous intermarriage of all our ethnic and racial traditions. "The United States is not going to last forever," he says. "Let's say we're occupied in the twenty-second century and carved up between the Chinese and the European Union. There's no American government, no American constitution, nothing. Do the American people still exist? I hope so.

"I have an optimistic vision of the American people at that time," he continues, "who will be here speaking some identifiable dialect of

English, and culturally there will be this link with us. There may be five or six regional governments, or a world government with a North American division, but they will still be American."

His conception of nationalism doesn't follow in the chauvinistic footsteps of the British or German empires, but rather in those of José Vasconcelos, an early-twentieth-century Mexican philosopher and politician who saw his country's hope embodied in its mixed-race heritage. "I got from him this vision of a new race that arises from racial amalgamation," Lind says. "You actually celebrate mongrelization. This just seems so inspiring to me. The great taboo in North American culture is the black/white divide. Once you get over that, you realize all of American culture from the beginning has been this mongrel culture. There's never been a Euro-American culture. It's always been a transracial culture."

He contends that our unity as a nation depends upon recognizing and celebrating our marvelously mongrel culture, which can be found in everything from break dancing and country music (the banjo's historical roots go back to Africa) to WPA murals in small town post offices. Breaking down snobbery—the old notion that Europe is the only cradle of civilization or the newer idea that it's Africa—is what's needed to better appreciate the strengths of our own culture.

This vision has led Lind to view multiculturalism and identity politics as a step in the wrong direction, a clinging to the outdated framework of racial separateness when it's the mingling of peoples that holds the key to America's vital future. "The last thing I want to do at the end of the twentieth century is say I am a European American and I have this hermetically sealed culture consisting of Beethoven and Bismarck, and these other guys have Father Hidalgo. I don't think that the multicultural left thought this through. What you're doing is legitimizing a separate white tradition."

Regionalism also figures prominently in Lind's conception of American nationalism, and he thinks regional identity will exert as great an influence in American life as ethnic roots. "I think Mexican Americans are not going to be Mexican American in fifty years," he says. "They will be Mexican Yankees or Mexican Southerners or Mexican Pacific Northwest people. This will bring an interesting new richness to the culture."

Lind points to his beloved Hill Country as a miniature example of multiethnic regional culture. Settled more by Germans, Mexicans, Czechs, and Swedes than by the old-line Southerners who dominate the rest of the state, it has unique traditions of its own. These people (Lind himself is fifth-generation Hill Country, with ancestors from Sweden, Germany, and England) created a more politically liberal, live-and-let-live culture (typified by Austin) that makes it different from the rest of Texas and the South.

The Hill Country even has its own distinct landscape, a rolling, rocky prairie dotted with live oak groves. Lind recently bought a fifty-acre ranch along White Oak Creek in Blanco County, complete with a swimming hole. He slips away there as often as his schedule allows and hopes eventually to live there year-round, restoring the prairie landscape with native plants, composing poetry, writing novels, studying new subjects that grab his imagination, and firing off missives that debunk the politics-as-usual of the left and right, East Coast and West Coast.

SELECTED RESOURCES

Vietnam, The Necessary War: A Reinterpretation of America's Most Disastrous Military Conflict (Free Press, 1999)

The Alamo: An Epic (Houghton Mifflin, 1997)

Powertown (HarperCollins, 1996)

The Next American Nation: The New Nationalism and the Fourth American Revolution (Free Press, 1995; 1996)

Up from Conservatism: Why the Right is Wrong for America (Free Press, 1996)

DAVID MORRIS

"There's a widespread yearning for community that the powers-that-be interpret as a yearning for yesteryear— a soda fountain on every corner. They dismiss it as nostalgia. But it's not about nostalgia. It really is about community, something important that's missing from our lives."

"WHEREVER POSSIBLE, we should shrink the distance between those who make the decisions and those who feel the impact," says David Morris, describing the mission of the Institute for Local Self-Reliance, a hands-on think tank with offices in Minnesota and Washington, D.C. that he has helped guide for the past twenty-five years. That sounds so sensible, so indisputable, so all-American—who could be against it? A lot of powerful individuals and organizations, it turns out.

"Right now, society is going the other direction," Morris ruefully notes, pointing to an avalanche of economic and political trends that stamp out the vitality of self-reliant communities, from megamergers that consolidate financial power in faraway boardrooms to international trade deals that take decisions out of the hands of democratically elected leaders and give them to shadowy international bureaucracies.

"Politicians gargle with the word *community*," Morris says, "but they spit it out as soon as they walk offstage. The policies they pursue drive us away from community." As just one example, he cites the success of the Clinton administration and congressional Republicans in exempting

Internet businesses from sales taxes that are applied to Main Street businesses. This amounts to a Washington-mandated bribe for all of us to avoid merchants in our neighborhoods—the people who sponsor local street fairs and softball teams—in favor of faceless firms thousands of miles away.

Yet Morris, a strong-willed optimist, is not ready to throw in the towel. Just looking around his home state of Minnesota, he finds ample evidence of the enduring resilience of small, locally owned institutions. Forty percent of the state's residents own their electrical companies through consumer co-ops or municipal power systems. Credit unions and community banks control one-quarter of all bank assets. More than 30,000 second- and third-generation family businesses are able to compete successfully in the marketplace.

"Small, local enterprises need not simply tap into our nostalgic yearning for a simpler and more rooted yesteryear," he declares. "They can make a powerful case that humanly scaled institutions are the most effective way to go." Always armed with real-world evidence to back up his beliefs, Morris quickly notes that savings and loans that stuck close to home in their lending did not generally need the multi-billion-dollar taxpayer-funded S&L bailout in the 1980s. Small manufacturing firms, which are generally labor-intensive businesses, created 20 million new jobs during the booming 1980s while big Fortune 500 corporations, which are generally capital-intensive and seek to downsize their workforces, lost 4 million jobs. A federal study, suppressed for thirty years, proves that a small town whose economy is supported by family farmers shows significantly more vitality and prosperity in every factor measured than a comparable town dependent on big corporate farms. Family farmers support local businesses and civic organizations while large-corporate farms buy from out-of-town suppliers and ignore local activities.

His indefatigable dedication to promoting the practical vision of local self-reliance is reminiscent of Ben Franklin—whose birthday, Morris once argued in his syndicated newspaper column, should be a national holiday. And like Franklin, Morris is a master of many trades. He delivers dozens of speeches each year for business, government, scientific, agricultural, political, and community groups. He consults for governments and businesses on economic development strategies and policies, and for local governments on economic development and recycling strategies. He has written for publications ranging from the *New York Times* and *St. Paul Pioneer Press* to industry trade magazines and worker co-op bulletins on a boggling array of subjects—sports (why pro teams should be community-owned) to movies (why *Debbie Does Dallas* is more wholesome than the routine Hollywood violence on display at the Cineplex) to history (what we could all learn from Russian anarchist Peter Kropotkin and Pope John XXIII). And from his office—a school building near the University of Minnesota campus in Minneapolis that's been transformed into an incubator for entrepreneurial businesses—he is constantly researching new ideas and new inventions.

An unapologetic promoter of high technology, Morris proves the feasibility of innovations of which Silicon Valley isn't even aware. How about replacing petroleum, which causes global warming and keeps us captive to oil imports, with plant-based fuels and plastics? Outlandish? Not at all, Morris calmly explains. On August 14, 1941, Henry Ford unveiled a prototype of a car made entirely of plant products: a fuel tank filled with ethanol made from corn, a body fabricated from plastic made from soybeans, tires fabricated from goldenrod.

We have stuck with fossil fuels, Morris says, not because of their innate superiority, but rather because of a whole series of decisions that favored petroleum interests. (In Brazil, for instance, most cars and trucks run on ethanol or an ethanol mix.) Studying how choices like these were made propelled Morris into his most recent initiative, the New Rules Project. "We make the rules, and the rules make us," he notes. "Human beings have always fashioned rules to live by. Rules channel entrepreneurship, scientific genius, and economic initiative into the places we want them to go. But today most of the rules promote values most people don't agree with. So what rules would promote the things we want to see?"

The two premises of the New Rules Project—that citizens are well prepared to make the decisions that affect their lives, and that a prosperous society can be created by applying information from around the world to produce things from local materials—illustrate the kind of radical common sense that characterizes Morris' thinking.

He credits the space program, in part, with launching his passion for local self-reliance. "In the late 1950s, after the Russians shot off Sputnik, every eight-, nine-, ten-, and eleven-year-old in America was supposed to want to be an astronaut. I was part of a special science program in the New York City schools. You were studying either how to get the rocket into space or how to keep the people in the spacecraft alive. It was the second that intrigued me. From that point on, I've been thinking about how systems work to support life. Actually there is a direct link between the space program and local self-reliance—solar power. The first commercial applications of solar power were for orbiting satellites in the 1960s. That helped to bring down the price of solar power so that communities could think about using it."

After earning a degree in labor and industrial relations from Cornell and a master's degree in Latin American studies from the University of Florida, Morris moved to Chile in 1970 to study the newly elected socialist government led by President Salvador Allende. He was struck by Allende's ambitious plans to break free from domination by foreign economic interests. "If Chile, a country about the size of New York City in population and far less wealthy, could think about controlling its own destiny, why couldn't regions in the United States?" he asks.

Allende's dreams were thwarted by an American-backed coup in 1973, on the day that Morris' book about Chile, *We Must Make Haste Slowly,* was published. But Morris didn't give up hope for the idea of local control as a path to the good life. He was living at the time in Washington, D.C., which was undergoing interesting political changes on the local level. Since the civil war it had been an American colony ruled almost completely by Congress, but beginning in the 1970s a movement arose to press for more local say in municipial affairs. Morris and neighborhood activists Neil Seldman and Gil Friend, who all saw potential in local self-reliance as a way to lift up a poor and demoralized city, founded the Institute, which first concentrated on Washington and then branched out to work in more than a hundred cities. Morris found himself doing so much work in Minneapolis-St. Paul that he finally moved there and established the Institute's Minnesota office.

While increasing economic globalization seems to run counter to his own deeply felt views, Morris can nonetheless claim several substantial victories. In 1974, he drafted a paper on how city governments could jump-start the solar power industry through bulk purchasing of solar cells—an initiative that has begun to bear fruit in the last several years. In 1982 he published a book, *The New City-States,* in which he argues that metropolitan regions could boost prosperity by creating their own economic structures independent of national or global economies. That is exactly what's happening now in places like Barcelona, Milan, Singapore, and Stuttgart, and the business world is using his phrase "new city-states" to describe it. So it would be unwise to count out others of his seemingly utopian ideas—substituting grain fields for oil wells or thoughtfully redesigning society's rules to enhance community, for example—as too radical to exert an influence on the course of our civilization in the next century.

SELECTED RESOURCES

Institute for Local Self-Reliance
 1313 Fifth St. SE, Minneapolis, MN 55414
 www.ilsr.org

The New Rules, quarterly magazine of the New Rules Project,
 published by ILSR www.newrules.org

Self-Reliant Cities: Energy and the Transformation of Urban America
 (Sierra Club, 1982)

The New City-States (Institute for Local Self-Reliance, 1982)

Neighborhood Power: Returning Political and Economic Power to Community Life,
 with Karl Hess (Beacon, 1975)

HELENA NORBERG-HODGE

"Decentralization is a prerequisite for the rekindling of community in Western society. Mobility erodes community, but as we put down roots and feel attachment to a place, our human relationships deepen, become more secure. . . . A trend toward smaller-scale political and economic units would help us develop a broader worldview—one based on interconnectedness. Instead of narrowing our vision, an intimate connection to community and place would encourage an understanding of interdependence."

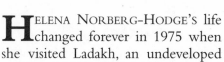

HELENA NORBERG-HODGE'S life changed forever in 1975 when she visited Ladakh, an undeveloped corner of India high in the Himalayas, as part of a German film crew documenting the region's traditional Buddhist society. For Norberg-Hodge—a linguist and painter living in Paris who had been born in New York, raised in Sweden, and educated in Germany and Austria—it felt like coming home for the first time in her life.

"What was so transformative," she recalls, "was that these people had the most remarkable joie de vivre and an amazing tolerance and harmony. They seemed to be so at peace with themselves. It was also a magnificent landscape. When you looked across a vista or at a village, if you ever encountered anything ugly it was new and from the outside."

She had planned to visit for just a few weeks but stayed more than a year, happily joining a project group compiling the first Ladakhi/English dictionary. Although the people of Ladakh endured a harsh climate (frigid temperatures eight months of the year) and what would seem to us primitive living conditions (no indoor plumbing, and dried animal dung as the chief source of heating and cooking fuel), Norberg-Hodge was struck by how content they seemed.

"Despite the lack of labor-saving devices, the Ladakhis had an amazing abundance of time," she says. "They worked at a gentle pace and had an amount of leisure time unknown to working people in the West. Indeed, they spent most of the winter at festivals and parties. Even during the summer, hardly a week passed without a celebration of one sort or another."

Returning to Ladakh almost every year since then, Norberg-Hodge has seen profound changes—the abundance of smiles giving way to anxious ambition and grim-faced insecurity. A new highway linked Ladakh with the rest of India and the modern world at about the time of her first visit, and Westerners have poured into this once isolated region, altering both the traditional culture and the people's sense of themselves. "Young children I had never seen before used to run up to me and press apricots into my hands," she says. "Now little figures, looking shabbily Dickensian in threadbare Western clothing, greet foreigners with empty outstretched hands. The films they see and the tourists they meet make their lives seem primitive.

"Ladakhis started thinking that their culture was backward, stupid," she adds. She noticed that the young men in particular were dazzled by Western wealth and technology; they were the first to adopt Western clothing and to start hungering for fancy consumer goods. They learned to scorn anything old or slow. Now, traditional agriculture, family life, clothing, architecture, and crafts—all are being abandoned in favor of modern methods. "I've witnessed the breakdown of people's connection to the land," says Norberg-Hodge. "People are being pulled away from the rural village economy into the city and to paid employment. Very soon, they get the impression that the only thing that matters is money."

Many Ladakhis see modern civilization as a utopia that has found high-tech solutions to human problems, from disease to boredom. Yet evidence to the contrary is visible all around them. Crime, once almost unheard of, has become a problem in the capital city of Leh, including the first murder that anyone can ever remember. The population is exploding—a perilous situation in an area with such fragile farmland—now that traditional polyandry (one woman marrying a number of brothers) is being replaced by the nuclear family. Ethnic tension with the small Muslim population has flared as people fight over scarce jobs in the cash economy. Worst of all, says Norberg-Hodge, is that these once proud and happy people now feel inferior to other cultures.

While it is true that the modern world can bring benefits to this ancient people—alleviating health problems caused by burning animal dung as fuel is one example—Ladakhis need not abandon their own culture, says Norberg-Hodge. In 1978, she founded the Ladakh Project, a group dedicated to helping Ladakhis understand that they can choose which of the Western ways they want to adopt and which of the traditional ways they want to keep. The project has also introduced sustainable technologies that take less of a toll on the fragile desert ecosystem than typical development. Trombe Walls, for instance—an inexpensive solar heating system that takes advantage of the region's 325 sunny days each year—have been installed in many homes, allowing families to avoid costly and polluting fossil fuels from outside the region.

Each time she returns to North America or Europe from Ladakh, Norberg-Hodge watches in dismay as people rush to make a living and struggle to find meaning in a civilization that measures the value of everything by its price tag. As the globalization of the economy marches on, things grow harsher for people everywhere: less economic security, less free time, less community and connection to natural rhythms, more stress, more microwave dinners, more feelings of inadequacy about our income and physical attractiveness. Like the villagers of Ladakh, we are being psychologically impoverished, she says. "The destructive global economy can exist only as long as we are prepared to accept it and subsidize it. We can reject it."

The International Society for Ecology and Culture, a new organization founded by Norberg-Hodge—with offices in Berkeley, Ladakh, Dartington, England, and Frankfurt, Germany—has campaigned against international trade agreements that lock us tighter into globalization. Globalization, she explains, is not an inevitable fact of human progress, but a jerry-built economic system created by corporate-friendly politicians and paid for with our tax money. Toys from China, butter from New Zealand, and clothes from Central America are cheaper than what's made just down the road because of enormous public expenditures in highways, deep-water ports, energy production, global communications networks, and high-tech research—as well as the military power that keeps oil cheap and developing nations subservient to wealthy ones.

Revitalization of local economies and a swing back in the direction of small-scale, geographically rooted businesses and culture is Norberg-Hodge's alternative vision of development. "The local becomes much more competitive than the global when you stop subsidizing the global," she says. "And suddenly you have a proliferation of smaller businesses, many more mom-and-pop shops, many more small farmers, smaller producers of all kinds, much more actively engaged, much more stimulated to produce in a healthy way, and having fun doing it, in flourishing communities.

"If you want to start doing something right now, start with food. The apples on your table have traveled perhaps 10,000 miles. We can start today to build a local food movement and enjoy the wealth of benefits from reconnecting farmers and consumers. Fresh, local food for all may be one of the most rewarding—and delicious—ways to save the planet."

The proliferation of farmers' markets and community-supported agriculture, where households contract with a local grower for regular deliveries of fresh organic produce, is one sign Norberg-Hodge sees that modern people are yearning for a different kind of life. "There are a multitude of microtrends in virtually every field. People are again making the kitchen the center of their homes, rather than walling off the place where food is prepared from where it is eaten as was done in the industrial era. This is happening all over the world. People are reviving regional cuisine and culture; planting their gardens with native species where it was once fashionable to have only exotic species; incorporating local materials and styles into architecture.

"These trends are often labeled new," she adds. "In an important sense they are very old. All these things a part of a deeper pattern of returning to nature and the local." While offering economic and environmental advantages, a shift to using more local resources also offers psychological benefits—we feel more at home in the world when we know the farmer who grows our food and can see the place where the stone in our home was quarried."

Ironically, spreading the message about the benefits of local ties keeps Norberg-Hodge on the road many months each year. Her home is at Totnes, a town near the moors of southwest England that has become a center for people interested in sustainable living. She tends a small garden and with her husband, John Page, cooks up big dinners for friends, which are usually followed by a piano recital of Page's latest classical composition and then several more hours of conversation.

"I am not advocating asceticism. I'm advocating wealth, richness, joy, culture," she says. "We are spiraling back to an ancient connection between ourselves and the earth. The process is often an unconscious one. Our mainstream culture encourages a linear view of progress, one in which the goal is to free ourselves from the past and the laws of nature. The modern-day mantra 'we cannot go back' is deeply ingrained in our thinking. Of course we couldn't go back even if we wanted to, but our search for a future that works is inevitably bringing us back to certain fundamental patterns that are in greater harmony with nature—including our own human nature."

SELECTED RESOURCES

The Ladakh Project
  International Society for Ecology and Culture
  Box 9475, Berkeley, CA 94709
  www.isec.org.uk

From the Ground Up: Rethinking Industrial Agiculture,
  with Peter Goering and John Page (Zed, 2001; second rev. edition)

Ancient Futures: Learning from Ladakh (Sierra Club, 1991)

JOHN PAPWORTH

"I see every neighborhood governing its own neighborhood affairs, like law and order, and having its own bank and insurance system so the economic surplus of the neighborhood is not being drained away to remote boardrooms. And as far as possible, I see every neighborhood providing its own food and basic necessities—at least being very close to the sources of these things rather than being dependent on a vast and intricate structure of global markets that has the effect of impoverishing both sides of the world."

The phrase "small is beautiful" has entered our vocabulary as a reminder of the disasters frequently created by gigantic projects such as high-rise public housing and eight-lane urban freeways. And no one could be more happy about this than John Papworth, a longtime advocate of small-scale projects that fit the scale of our natural landscape, our democratic values, and the needs of human beings. Indeed, as founder of the English magazine *Resurgence,* he played a part in promoting the phrase by publishing many of the essays later incorporated into economist E. F. Schumacher's best-selling book, *Small Is Beautiful,* which popularized these three words of wisdom and the ideas behind them.

But for Papworth, a charmingly gruff Anglican priest with a long mane of white hair that reinforces his role as a prophet, beauty is only the beginning of the story. Small is intelligent. Small is powerful. And small is absolutely necessary if our civilization is to survive the battery of crises that face us.

"There surely has never been a time in all history," he comments, "when a readiness for change has been so widespread and when a clear sense of the directions toward which change should move has been so conspicuously lacking."

People in great numbers are seeking solutions to global pollution, climate change, nuclear weapons, ethnic wars, and species extinction. But "unless these concerns are related in some way to a concern for a human-scaled perspective," Papworth says, "many of them may just as easily leave things as they are or even make them worse."

Recycling admirably preserves natural resources but makes little difference overall because the total volume of our garbage keeps mounting. Human rights crusaders draw attention to ethnic atrocities, but large countries continue to lay claim to the land and resources of minority groups. "The crisis of giant power of many kinds now out of control can only be answered by the deliberate localization of power in people's hands at the level of the human-scale neighborhood or village," he says. "There is surely reason to suppose that local people running their own neighborhood are far more likely to do what is decent than government ministers trapped in the entrails of power mongering on a mass scale."

Well aware that such views brand him as a radical far beyond the scope of Karl Marx or even the most outspoken of today's Green activists and cyberanarchists, Papworth digs back twenty-four centuries for an influential ally: "To the size of a state there is a limit as there is to plants, animals, and implements, for none of these retain their natural facility when they are too large." Aristotle's words, says Papworth, express a basic truth that the modern age ignores in its rush to do more and more, bigger and bigger, faster and faster.

Our blindness to this truth has vast consequences: Neighbors don't know each other. Communities are devastated by decisions made in distant boardrooms and government offices. And we are surrounded on all sides by sheer ugliness, from hulking skyscraper boxes to endless swarms of strip malls to foul-smelling corporate farms.

These are themes Papworth explores in *Fourth World Review,* the idiosyncratic and witty newsletter he has published since 1982. He defines the Fourth World as communities that don't have the power of a state or multinational corporation behind them: indigenous people,

ethnic minorities, rural towns, urban neighborhoods, small businesses—
in other words, almost everyone on the planet who is not a mover and
shaker in the megaglobal economy. Subscription rates reflect his bottom-up allegiances: The sliding scale starts with "shirtless ones and
musical buskers" ($20) and moves up through "students, 2nd hand car
owners & false teeth flashers" ($40), then "jet-setters, dishwasher own-
ers, those with wall-to-wall carpeting, taxi users, opera fans, regular
wine drinkers, cigar smokers, experts, consultants & specialists" ($100),
and, finally, "company directors, presidents, royalty, europlotters, bank
managers, mediums, gurus, archbishops, pop stars & media personalities" ($1,000). Millionaires and lawyers have to negotiate a price direct-
ly with Papworth.

Besides thinking globally in *Fourth World Review,* he acted locally
in the St. John's Wood neighborhood, where he lived for many years
with his family. At hearty meals around the big wood table in his
kitchen, neighbors and visitors from all over the world exchange ideas
between bites of his famous home-baked bread. He founded the
neighborhood football club, the local magazine, the gardening club,
and a social committee. He staged a sit-in at the famous Abbey Road
crosswalk (featured on the Beatles album cover) a few blocks from his
home to protest "car madness."

But with the death of his wife, Marcelle Papworth, a French journalist he met on a peace pilgrimage to Cuba in 1964, and the
departure of his three grown children, Papworth sold his house in 1998
and moved to a village west of London for a quieter life. Yet, one can't
imagine things staying too quiet with Papworth in the community.
He has a way of stirring up excitement, as when he made headlines as
"The Shop-lifting Vicar" for suggesting at a neighborhood meeting that
stealing from a locally owned shop is both illegal and immoral, while
stealing from a chain store is illegal but no more immoral "than picking up seashells at the beach." Locally owned shops, he reasons, are an
integral part of any community, while outside owners suck wealth out
of community and give little back: "Jesus said love thy neighbor; he
said nothing about loving Marks & Spencer"—the giant British chain
of stores. This bit of biblical interpretation failed to impress church
superiors, who have threatened to revoke his clerical privileges.

"If you take responsibility for local things away from local people," he says, "you make them irresponsible." No one assumes responsibility for what goes on in most communities today; the concerns of
people on a city block or country village don't matter to the people

with real power—at city hall, in corporate boardrooms, in the nation's capital, at international summits. The breakdown at this local level, happening a million times over, adds up to the giant crisis of our time. And it's a moral crisis as well as a political one, Papworth says: "Gandhi was right: You cannot have morality without community. And community is a social unit in which the personal relationships of the members are the strongest force in determining its character. You can't say that of a mass society.

"We're all living like currants in a bun, you know, we're not related to each other at all," he exclaims. "You can only have a moral society—even a cultural or artistic one—if people are related to each other. But we now relate to distant power centers. So instead of having moral relationships, we've got power relationships."

Papworth's small-is-beautiful vision goes back to 1955, when he ran for Parliament as a member of the Labour Party. Raised in an orphanage, sent to work in a bakery at age fourteen, attending college only after serving in the Royal Air Force during World War II, he had always been drawn by the party's championing of the working class. But the campaign was a disillusioning experience, not because he lost but because he saw how the party's central committee—not the members—called the shots. This seemed a mockery of Labour's egalitarian values, and when the party later asked him to run again in a district where he was sure to win, he declined.

He got involved in ban-the-bomb protests and at the same time pursued his interest in the perils of large institutions through informal discussions with renegade economists E. F. Schumacher, R. H. Tawney and Leopold Kohr. Tawney, a distinguished professor, pinpointed the genesis of the mass-scaled society we now see all around us: abolishment of laws prohibiting usury during the reign of Queen Elizabeth I. This made conquest of the New World economically feasible and established the precedent of financiers dictating what happens in a place to which they have no real ties. "The question is not whether usury is bad," Papworth notes. "The question is how do you control it? The way to control it effectively in democratic terms is by keeping it local. I think each neighborhood should be controlling its own bank and economic arrangements."

Papworth founded *Resurgence* magazine in 1966 to promote the peace movement and the principles of human-scale development. He left the magazine (which is still published today) in the early 1970s to become personal assistant to Kenneth Kaunda, president of Zambia.

They had met years earlier when Papworth was involved with an organization promoting independence for colonial nations. "Somebody rang me up," Papworth recalls, "and said there's this black chap to whom no one will rent an apartment. Could I put him up at my house?" The two soon became friends, sitting up late at night discussing politics. Papworth and his family spent nine years in Zambia, where he launched the Village Industry Service, an agency that still operates today promoting education, health care, and locally run businesses in rural areas. The idea is to improve the quality of life, largely through creation of small-scale enterprises, so that fewer villagers feel compelled to move into overcrowded cities.

Even with an accomplishment like this—and his distinguished record of raising a ruckus about these ideas around England—he realizes he's fighting a losing battle, at least right now. The scale at which our world operates keeps getting bigger and bigger. At eighty, how does Papworth keep going—how does he stay hopeful and happy? "One has to spread a fair amount of doom and gloom about our prospects in order to wake people up," he answers. "That doesn't mean one's life is full of doom and gloom. I try to enjoy myself. I go to theaters and concerts. I love poetry. I love reading detective novels. I love going on walks. I love good food and wine. I'm generally jiving it up.

"I think the capacity of human beings to love and to laugh is still very powerful. And I'm encouraged by the way in which multitudes of people across the world are instinctively turning to the small, to the local: things like local-based currencies and organic farming."

SELECTED RESOURCES

Fourth World Review
    The Close, 26 High Street, Purton, Wiltshire SN5 4AE United Kingdom
Small Is Powerful: The Future as if People Really Mattered (Praeger, 1995)

ANDRES DUANY & ELIZABETH PLATER-ZYBERK

"Is there an alternative to sprawl? There is, and it is close at hand: the traditional American town. Americans have shown over and over again that they will pay premium prices to live in the relatively few traditional towns that remain, places such as Marblehead, Massachusetts; Princeton, New Jersey; and Oak Park, Illinois."

SEVERAL GENERATIONS of Americans have watched in silent sadness as our landscape has been ravaged beyond recognition: green countryside bulldozed into unsightly strip malls, spirited small towns transformed into drab suburban agglomerations, bustling city neighborhoods drained of life and left for dead. And it seemed there was nothing we could do about it. Soulless sprawl was an unalterable fact of life, like tornadoes in Kansas and humidity in Houston. Real towns, offering vibrant street life and inviting public places, became something many of us experienced only on vacation: in the French Quarter, Provincetown, or Europe.

Then along came Andres Duany and Elizabeth Plater-Zyberk, partners in both architecture and marriage, who created Seaside, a brand-new resort development on Florida's Gulf Coast that captures what is best about classic old southern towns like Savannah, Charleston, and Key West: narrow streets, second-story porches, and a lively town center within easy walking distance. A strong feeling of connectedness has arisen among residents (and even visitors) thanks to all the impromptu socializing that happens when people meet on the sidewalk, see each other on their front porches, or gather in the public squares. It feels like home—or at least how home used to feel before the advent of freeways, Wal-Mart, and four-car garages.

Seaside was an immediate hit; property values increased tenfold in just a few years after ground was broken in 1980. Duany, Plater-Zyberk, and their firm (now with offices in Miami, Charlotte, Washington, D.C., and Manila, Philippines) have since launched 140 projects, from a pedestrian-oriented mobile home park in Arizona to Prince Charles' celebrated Poundbury village in England, all of them designed to offer the charm, conviviality, and convenience of traditional towns.

Time magazine hailed Seaside as one of the ten great design achievements of the 1980s. Vincent Scully, a Yale professor and one of America's leading architecture critics, calls Duany and Plater-Zyberk's work "the most important contemporary movement in architecture." At the same time, they've earned the scorn of many fellow architects, who say they want to turn back progress or—worse—that they indulge in sappy nostalgic Disneyfication. "They were brave enough to acknowledge that we used to do architecture right in America," counters Scully, "and now we were doing it wrong."

Despite the controversy their work inspires, what they do is far from radical. They simply make the case, both in blueprints and in speeches around the country, that "there are two models for growth in America. One is the traditional neighborhood pattern and one is suburban sprawl. The old neighborhoods still work, and we would like to make them an option for people again."

In some cases, this means revitalizing an existing urban district, such as they did in the downtowns of West Palm Beach and Naples, Florida. Sometimes it means creating a new town from scratch, like Mashpee Commons on Cape Cod, a pedestrian-oriented downtown created from the parking lot of an old mall, or Middleton Hills, a community with Prairie-style architecture that rose from farm fields outside Madison, Wisconsin. Often, they rework zoning codes for cities and counties, making it possible once again to build the kinds of classical communities that Americans still love.

"It is actually illegal in most places—literally against the law—to build the kind of communities that human beings have favored for centuries," Duany says, revealing the showmanship and indisputable common sense that make him a compelling public speaker. He's made this case at hundreds of public meetings around the country, often riling up the crowd to demand changes in their own hometowns. Bureaucrats steadfastly opposed to any zoning variances or new codes often change their tune when confronted by citizens with a passionate new vision of what their communities can be.

Suburban sprawl is not the product of natural urban evolution, Duany and Plater-Zyberk explain. It's the direct result of post–World War II zoning codes that dictate wide streets, huge lots, attached two-car garages, and the absolute separation of houses from shops and workplaces. The result is that the typical suburban family now makes a dozen automobile trips every day because their home is cut off from stores and schools by impassable rivers of roaring traffic. Kids can't wander down to the park or the candy store on their own. People too old to drive comfortably are placed under house arrest. Middle-class families are strapped with the considerable expense of owning and maintaining two or three cars, at an average annual cost of almost $6,000 per car. Even affluent households can easily spend two hours a day commuting, which adds up to eight weeks a year away from loved ones and favorite pastimes.

"Communities are designed today to make cars happy, not people," Duany says. "Elizabeth and I are not asking for people to sacrifice. We're offering people the pleasure of walking to work and shopping. We're not taking their cars away. They just don't have to use them all the time. It's about having choices."

The traditional town that Duany and Plater-Zyberk advocate (which can be either a freestanding "village" in the open country or a neighborhood in the heart of a city) brings back into one place the basics of people's lives: groceries, day care, schools, parks, cafés, and maybe a health club, ice cream parlor, moviehouse, or bookshop. "It's a fundamental civic right, for God's sake," says Duany, "to have daily needs available within walking distance." Not only is there less need to jump in your car every time you want a carton of eggs, there's a greater sense of community. You talk with neighbors on the street or at the coffee shop rather than waving to them from behind a windshield.

Besides these personal advantages, traditional towns help solve the problems of traffic congestion, sprawl, air pollution, affordable housing, and urban decline. Driving is reduced and public transportation boosted, since a central shopping district makes bus and train connections more convenient. Apartments for young people, retired couples, and other lower-income households can be blended in with single-family homes—above the stores, in granny flats behind houses, in multifamily units near the bus stop or train stop.

As the popularity of traditional town planning grows, it boosts the prospects of inner-city neighborhoods, where in many cases these qualities already exist. "We have an underlying goal to change the way we build and destroy cities," Plater-Zyberk says. "We want to make and rebuild places that are so good people won't want to tear them down in twenty years. And there is a social aspect to it, which is about creating a physical environment that fosters social connectedness."

Duany and Plater-Zyberk have not been alone in promoting a new vision for American communities; a number of architects—Peter Calthorpe and Daniel Solomon in San Francisco, among others—arrived at the same conclusions around the same time, and these ideas have now blossomed into a growing movement called New Urbanism. New Urbanist projects are now under way in thirty-four states, ranging from Disney's famous town of Celebration near Orlando, which will eventually encompass 8,000 homes and a downtown, to a block of attractive retail shops with affordable apartments upstairs in the hard-hit neighborhood of South Central Los Angeles.

"One thing that excites me," says Plater-Zyberk, whose style is cerebral compared to her husband's passionate tone, "is how prominent the physical environment—both natural and built—is in the concerns of the average citizen. From the kids on campuses protesting to save historic buildings to the everyday residents participating in public meetings, there is a great deal more engagement with these issues than there was just a few years ago."

The reason for all this, according to Duany and Plater-Zyberk, is that people have grown tired of high-concept modernism and are paying closer attention to the basic elements that make a place comfortable, functional, and beautiful. Both of them make a point of noting that they grew up in congenial traditional towns. Duany lived in Santiago, Cuba, and then, after Castro's revolution, Barcelona, Spain, which he loved to wander around even as a kid. Plater-Zyberk was raised in Paoli, Pennsylvania, a town on a commuter rail line near Philadelphia that proves suburbs can have all the qualities of real towns. "We would walk to shops, walk to school, walk to our friends," she remembers. "We would also walk to the train station, and we could go into the city for music lessons or to the dentist, which was two towns down the line. You could get everywhere by train."

Each gravitated toward architecture because of family ties. Duany's father was a developer—who, ironically, developed the first Levittown-style suburb in Cuba. Plater-Zyberk's father, who fled communist

Poland in 1947, was an architect who designed both modernist buildings and historic restoration projects.

The two met at Princeton's architecture school, attended graduate
school together at Yale, and then moved in the mid-1970s to Florida,
where they gained notoriety as founding partners of the Arquitectonica
firm, whose flashy modernist high-rises were featured in the opening
credits of *Miami Vice*. At that time they also helped found the
Architectural Club of Miami, which sponsored lectures by interesting
figures in the field. One of the speakers they brought to town, Leon
Krier, a Luxembourg architectural theorist who argued that modern
architects ignore centuries of proven wisdom about cities, totally capi-
tavated them. "He said that what has been done to European cities since
World War II was more destructive than what happened during the
war," Plater-Zyberk recalls, "and that cities were really just made up of
quarters, and that we need to pay attention to how those quarters function for a city to really work."

This struck a chord with their own deep feelings about what made
great architecture, and they abandoned glitzy modernism in favor of a
small Miami residential development that drew on the feel of historic
Charleston. That soon led to the Seaside commission.

Duany and Plater-Zyberk live in Coral Gables, a vintage 1920s suburb near the University of Miami (where Plater-Zyberk is dean of the
architecture school), laid out according to the principles of traditional
town planning. Their office, a stylishly renovated airplane engine factory, is in Miami's Little Havana neighborhood, which pulses with street
life. Things pulse inside the office, too, where dachshunds Teddy and
Chrissie yap at the 20 or so designers who regularly rush out for cups
of amazingly thick Cuban coffee at the Ayestaran Market down the
street. An espresso machine works nonstop at the back of the office.

A cup of coffee is one of the measures of culture, Duany once told
Esquire magazine, because it stimulates companionship, public life, and
ideas. But when life at the office becomes overstimulating, Duany and
Plater-Zyberk like to take off for one of those great places that inspire
their work. Plater-Zyberk counts New Orleans, Charleston,
Manhattan, Havana, old Warsaw, Rome, villages in Provence, Forest
Hills in Queens, and Mariemont, a suburb of Cincinnati, as favorites.
Duany favors Antigua in Guatemala, Trinidad in Cuba, and a number of
small towns in Turkey, Switzerland, and Germany.

Duany admits to a passion for reading military history, which he
sees as directly applicable to his work. Fidel Castro, ironically, is one of

his models as a strategist. "In the Cuban Revolution," Duany explains, "you have small skirmishes, small victories, but you have six or seven radio stations that transmit the news. Castro created just enough action to have something to talk about." Duany and Plater-Zyberk, in the same vein, know they can't beat the entire planning profession head-on. But through highly regarded model projects like Seaside and regular speaking tours—their version of Castro's radio strategy—as well as guerrilla attacks on zoning codes, they deploy the principles of traditional town planning against the mighty forces of suburban sprawl. And they're showing it's possible for traditional town planning to win.

SELECTED RESOURCES

Duany Plater-Zyberk & Company (DPZ)
 1023 SW 25th Ave., Miami, FL 33135
 www.dpz.com

Congress for the New Urbanism
 Hearst Building, 5 Third St., Suite 500A, San Francisco, CA 94103

New Urban News
 Box 6515, Ithaca, NY 14851
 www.newurbannews.com

Suburban Nation: The Rise of Sprawl and the Decline of the American Dream,
 with Jeff Speck (North Point, 2000)

The New Civic Art, by Andres Duany and Robert Alminana (Rizzolli, 2000)

The Lexicon of the New Urbanism (DPZ, 1999)

The New Urbanism: Toward an Architecture of Community,
 by Peter Katz (McGraw-Hill, 1994)

Andres Duany and Elizabeth Plater-Zyberk: Towns and Town-Making Principles,
 essays by Alex Krieger et al, ed. Krieger with William Lennertz (Rizzoli, 1991), a catalog for an exhibition of work by Duany and Plater-Zyberk, fall 1990 at Gund Hall Gallery, Harvard University Graduate School of Design

VIRGINIA VALENTINE

"When you are caught up in a good book, it is one of life's most satisfying things. But it's about more than being satisfied. It exposes you to a whole range of philosophies and experiences. When you read, there's nothing that separates you from someone else's life—that's wonderful."

A NEW YORK CITY woman was invited to join a book club, and on the appointed evening strolled over to the Upper West Side building where it met. Once she was in the lobby, she realized that she'd forgotten the apartment number. Making a calculated guess, she rang an intercom button and explained that she was looking for the book club meeting. She was buzzed in and soon was in the thick of a discussion about a new book—actually the book she thought they would be discussing the following week. The food was good and so was the company. Yet it seemed strange that the friend who had invited her wasn't there. Finally, it dawned on her that she was in the wrong place. The book club she meant to visit was meeting at the same time on the same night in the same building to discuss the same kind of books—but in a different apartment.

Virginia Valentine, book club coordinator for Denver's Tattered Cover bookstore, passes along this story (first recounted by writer Mary Cregan in the *Chronicle of Higher Education*) as her vision for the future: book clubs so numerous that there's one behind almost every door. Book clubs can remake American culture, she says: "Amazing things happen when people start talking about books."

Books are Valentine's bread and butter. She has worked for almost twenty years at Tattered Cover, one of the most venerable and successful independent bookstores in the country. But skyrocketing book sales are not the only reason she's thrilled at the recent book club boom. "I don't think this is just a fad, inspired by Oprah," she says, adding quickly that she's grateful Oprah has rekindled so many people's interest in reading. "Book clubs offer people the chance for philosophical give-and-take. They are the human embodiment of culture. They connect people to one another, and they encourage people to grow. It's amazing to see what a club reads the first year and what they're reading ten years later. Clubs really boost people's literary tastes and intellectual reach."

And book clubs are community centers, she adds: "I get five, six, seven calls a day on voice mail from people—mostly professional women in their twenties and thirties—asking me to steer them to a book club. Book clubs answer an intellectual need of people who are working alone in their cubicles or on the Web." Offering support and practical guidance to more than 300 book clubs through the years, Valentine has seen friendships flower, romances take root, and new ideas sown in fertile ground. This coming together of people—once a natural occurrence of everyday life—is crucial in maintaining a connected culture as we enter an entirely new era of information exchanges, she says. Isolation increases as people privately pursue their interests and obsessions, apart from other influences. While the Internet has become for Valentine an indispensable tool to uncover background on new authors, she's concerned about the changes it may bring to the world in which her grandchildren grow up.

"Children live now in a world that is so sophisticated," she observes. "They can instantly be in the midst of almost anything they want, whether it's pornography or violence or whatever. It's accessible at their fingertips. It's not filtered by any other influences. That's my greatest fear." Though she makes no claim that book clubs can solve the world's problems, she believes young people would benefit from more opportunities for public engagement—not just bookclubs, but other ways of mixing with people from the broader community.

Besides making matches between solo book lovers and lively reading groups, Valentine conducts seminars on how to start a book club, gives talks about authors that clubs might want to explore, and compiles a tip sheet of smart, stimulating titles—which resembles *Publishers' Weekly* (an industry trade magazine) more than a simple reading list. A recent edition numbers twenty-two pages with seventy-eight recommendations fleshed out in pithy, heartfelt opinionizing—from best-sellers like *Memoirs of a Geisha* and *Birds of America* to worthy novels in danger of falling through the literary cracks.

As Tattered Cover's fiction buyer, Valentine was encouraged by owner Joyce Meskis to nurture the reading groups that were beginning to meet at the store and elsewhere. "It's the perfect job," Valentine volunteers, sounding a little bewildered at her good fortune. And she's perfect for it, according to her colleagues. A profile in the bookstore's newsletter describes her as "a cross between Carol Channing and Edith Wharton: With an irrepressible sense of humor and commanding knowledge of books, she has won the hearts of customers and coworkers."

Valentine's passion for reading goes back to her Depression-era girlhood in Cleveland Heights, Ohio. "My grandmother read to me as a baby, and I started to read early, and always loved it," she recalls. "We would think nothing of going to the library once a week and bringing home ten books, things like *The Hunchback of Notre Dame,* which I never thought of as a literary book, and read them all, many times under the covers with a flashlight."

At Vassar she studied—what else?—literature, philosophy, and the classics, and kept reading at an impressive clip after she quit school to marry Yale English major Bruce Valentine. She studied alongside him as he finished his senior thesis, then combed the shelves of libraries in the small towns where they were stationed during his years in the military. "I read right through Faulkner trying to understand the South," she recalls. They eventually settled in Denver, where Bruce joined his family's lumber business. While raising a son and daughter, she would talk with other mothers at the playground and the grocery store, and the subject would turn to what they were reading. Valentine was always full of suggestions, and it seemed natural to take a job at a bookstore when her youngest child left for college.

After more than two decades in the business, she still buries her nose in books, several at a time, every free moment. This adds up to two or three books a week. (When we spoke she was raving about *Summer at Gaglow* by Esther Freud and *The Last Life* by Claire Messud.) "I read a couple of hours before I go to sleep, which is easy since I watch very little television," she says, "and then if I wake up in the middle of the night, which I have taught myself to do, I can read another hundred pages. Isn't that terrible?"

SELECTED RESOURCES

Tattered Cover
1628 16th St., Denver, CO 80202
www.tatteredcover.com

SOCIAL ACTION

DISCUSSIONS ABOUT saving the world and reforming society always seem to begin—and often end—with thoughts of the 1960s. So many public issues—from abortion to zoning—are inextricably linked to that decade in the same way big band music is linked to the 1930s. It doesn't matter that feminism, environmentalism, gay liberation, multiculturalism, and other significant social changes actually took root in the 1970s. Most political movements and altruistic impulses arising today are judged in the eyes of the media (and participants) by standards set years ago in Selma, Berkeley, and Chicago's Grant Park.

Everyone profiled in this chapter, indeed in the entire book, was shaped by the events of that era—or the fallout from that era, in the case of Geoff Mulgan and Ted Halstead, who weren't yet in first grade when students rose up at Columbia University and in the streets of Paris. It may not be an exaggeration to say that political debate ever since has been a heated referendum on the 1960s. The religious right and Reaganite neoconservative movements were forged out of fear and loathing of the excesses of the era. Liberals and activists, meanwhile, have been trying to rekindle that rebellious, uplifting spirit.

But do the 1960s cast too large a shadow on current campaigns for social change? While the legacy of those years inspires people to stand up for what they believe, it can also stifle fresh thinking about where we need to go as a society and the best way to get there. Some of the opinions of that era haven't stood the test of time. No one, for example, argues these days that everyone who's in jail is an oppressed political prisoner, and some progressive activists openly question whether affirmative action and identity politics remain good ideas for the twenty-first century. And it's becoming clear that a protest march is not always the most effective way to raise public awareness, especially when all-important media coverage depends on people being arrested.

The visionaries here, in distinct ways across various fields, embrace the values of the 1960s—peace, love, justice, ecology, liberation—but are committed to new outlooks and strategies to translate those values into action. Andrew Kimbrell, founder of the Washington, D.C.–based Center for Technology Assessment, declares that while it was once a radical's duty to smash any limit he or she came up against, our collective future now depends on our learning to accommodate limitations. Ted Halstead, the early-thirties founder of another Washington think tank, the New America Foundation, sees the smartest solutions for social problems coming from the radical center of the political spectrum that's emerging among young people. Muhammad Yunus, an economist from Bangladesh, prescribes small-scale capitalism as the best way to end poverty, and has proven his beliefs by making tiny loans to desperately poor people and seeing the prosperous businesses they create.

MIT linguist and foreign policy expert Noam Chomsky charts the accumulating power of corporations and their woeful effect on people around the world. Colin Greer, an English immigrant who heads a New York charitable foundation, sees a firm commitment to progressive principles as the only way to fulfill America's promise of liberty and justice for all. Gary Delgado, an Oakland organizer and social scientist, urges leftists to get strategic about spreading their message to everyday people. Feminist and African American activist bell hooks sounds a similar note among her many delightfully outspoken opinions. Jim Hightower, a radio host and former Texas commissioner of agriculture, predicts a coming political shake-up as people realize that "America's true political spectrum does not run right-to-left, but top-to-bottom—and most people aren't even within shouting distance of the top."

Riane Eisler, author of *The Chalice and the Blade* and founder of a California think tank, takes the long view with ideas about transforming our culture of domination and competition into a richer society based on partnership and cooperation. Geoff Mulgan, a policy adviser to British prime minister Tony Blair, thinks such a change is already under way as information technology and global commerce prove that we're all interconnected. Winona LaDuke, an Anishinabe activist from Minnesota and the 1996 and 2000 Green Party vice presidential candidate, says a brighter future depends not just on closer ties to people around the globe, but also on deeper bonds to the places where we live.

While these visionaries line up in different spots along the ideological spectrum, they share a common belief that politics as usual cannot solve the acute problems of our world: rising economic inequality, continuing human rights abuses, mounting environmental tragedies. Meaningful and lasting social change will occur only with a shift in the dynamics of power, one in which more people—ideally, everyone—can have a say in the decisions that affect their lives.

—Jay Walljasper

NOAM CHOMSKY

Donna Coveney: MIT

"Our society is not really based on public participation in decision making in any significant sense. Rather, it is a system of elite decision and periodic public ratification. Certainly people would like to think there's somebody up there who knows what he's doing. . . . But also, it is an important feature of the ideological system to impose on people the feeling that they really are incompetent to deal with these complex and important issues: They'd better leave it to the captain. . . .That means you have to establish the pretense that the participants of that elite know what they are doing and have the kind of understanding and access to information that is just denied the rest of us. So that we poor slobs ought to just watch, not interfere."

MARX. LENIN. SHAKESPEARE. Aristotle. The Bible. Plato. Freud. *Chomsky*. Hegel. Cicero.

MIT linguist and political analyst Noam Chomsky ranked as the most quoted living thinker, according to a 1980–1992 tabulation of sources in the Arts and Humanities Citation Index. He also comes out on top among current intellectuals in a survey of the Social Sciences Citation Index done by the MIT library.

Chomsky's intellectual output and influence are so vast, reports Michael Albert, editorial writer and columnist for *Z Magazine,* that when Albert visited Poland in 1980, people he met thought two scholars named Noam Chomsky were at work in America—one in linguistics and one in politics.

So why is it that we rarely hear from him on television, op-ed pages, or any other mainstream source of news and opinion? We don't even hear *of* him. Chomsky stands out not only as America's most quoted intellectual but also as our leading political dissident. What he says so boldly challenges conventional thinking about America's role in the world that it's far safer for mainstream TV producers and newspaper editors to ignore him than to answer him.

Chomsky turned the linguistics field upside down with his revolutionary theory that human language skills are innate, not learned. We are all born with an ability for language, he says, which is then shaped by the sounds we hear as toddlers to become English, or Finnish, or Kurdish. His theory helps explain why you can immediately understand sentences (like this one, for example) that you've never encountered before. Chomsky's work also suggests that humans have a natural instinct for creative expression. His impact on the field is so immense that the years prior to the publication of his 1957 book, *Syntactic Structures,* are looked upon by some linguists as B.C.—Before Chomsky.

In the 1960s, outraged by the Vietnam war, Chomsky began to broaden his study to include foreign policy. He blasted the usual liberal line that Vietnam was a tragic mistake committed by well-meaning but misguided policy makers. In Chomsky's view, the war amounted to a U.S. invasion of South Vietnam, done not in a spirit of democratic idealism but out of naked self-interest. Our politicians and business chiefs, Chomsky says, feel entitled to use military force anywhere in the world to protect their perceived interests—whether it's oil supplies, cheap labor, or simple revenge.

Chomsky's became one of the most prominent opponents of the war, making the case for why we should withdraw in the pages of the *New York Review of Books* and *The Boston Globe* as well as earning a slot on Richard Nixon's enemies list. But when the war wound down, Chomsky did not. He continued to condemn U.S. actions in the Middle East, Latin America, and the Caribbean, as well as the propaganda system in place at home to justify them. And it was at this point that Chomsky disappeared from mainstream public debate. His political books went unreviewed and his articles were accepted only by small alternative publications. An odd fate for a man who is quoted almost as often as Freud.

But Chomsky has risen to the challenge of being a dissident. Now in his seventies, he continues to write at least one book each year on foreign policy (in addition to his steady load of linguistics research) and undertake lecture itineraries that might hobble someone half his age. Chomsky's lectures are not lightweight affairs and he usually fields questions from the audience until university or church hall janitors plead with him to stop so they can go home. His breadth of knowledge is breathtaking; he can speak at length about the political economy of London journalism in the 1960s and then detail the history of Indonesia's brutal attack on East Timor. Despite charges from critics on the right and center that he's grown increasingly caustic, Chomsky has gained a large and loyal following, especially among young people, whose enthusiastic attendance at his lectures belies stereotypes about the political apathy of Generation X.

In assessing the state of American democracy today, Chomsky goes back to the 1930s, when "the United States more or less joined most of the advanced industrial societies in providing some kinds of rights for working people," he says. "There was real fury about this in the business community."

Business, especially the labor-intensive manufacturing sector, counterattacked New Deal reforms with a massive propaganda campaign that hit its stride in the 1950s. "It targeted everything," he says, "the entertainment industry, the media, the churches, recreation programs, there was just nothing left. They were quite clear about what they were doing—fighting the everlasting battle for the minds of men and seeking to indoctrinate people with the capitalist story. By the end of the 1950s, unions had been severely weakened, the media had been very much weakened."

Then along came the protests and social reforms of the 1960s, and the business sector grew "concerned over what was called the crisis of democracy. The crisis was that democracy was beginning to function." Another corporate counterattack on workers' rights and social programs was launched in the 1970s and, aided by economic changes like the globalization of the economy and the spiraling increase in speculative capital, it has continued to the present.

"This is a long-term process," Chomsky says. "It basically never changes. The United States is more of a business-run society than others. The United States is extremely weak in health care, in day care, in allowing parental leave. Right across the board, the United States has very weak social support systems. They have been declining sharply for the usual ideological reasons. Business is very class-conscious, so they are always fighting a class war. People just won't face the fact that the society is run by private tyrannies."

But the lessons of history aren't all grim. "In the 1920s, it also looked as though the business victory was total," he says. "Labor was practically destroyed." Then came the 1930s, the rise of labor unions, and the social reforms that Chomsky feels Americans must now fight vigorously to save.

How do we do that? "The answer is to rebuild civil society," Chomsky replies. "American society is now remarkably atomized. Political organizations have collapsed.

"People here," he adds, "should do what they did in the Haitian slums, where it was possible to construct grassroots organizations that enabled the democratic system to function. They forged a very lively and vibrant civil society. To talk about bringing democracy to Haiti is a joke. We should look there and find out how it worked. It works when people get organized and are willing to work together and have a sense of solidarity and are willing to put aside their own immediate personal issues for a broader concern.

"As far as the left is concerned," he continues, "I think we should listen to what the right is saying. One of the major congressional initiatives has been what they call 'defunding' the left." And guess who that is: Catholic Charities, because of priests and nuns working in poor communities, and the American Association of Retired People, because it had a small program to help elderly people get jobs. "That's the left," Chomsky says. "In fact, anyone who's trying to do anything for human beings is the left. Well, that's sort of right when you think about it."

Chomsky's been an ardent student of political affairs since his boyhood, when he used to take the train from his home in Philadelphia to New York City, where an uncle ran a newsstand. He would hang out there all day, reading current affairs magazines and listening to his uncle and customers talk politics, until it was time to grab the last train home. Although it was never his formal field, he stayed atop political developments around the world even while he was launching his academic career and raising three children in suburban Lexington, Massachusetts.

He and his wife, Carol Schatz Chomsky, stopped entertaining at home years ago so their dining room could become a repository for the files, books, and clippings he combs through in researching his own books. Although his schedule is booked years in advance for speeches and guest professorships, he is a legendarily generous correspondent: He stays in touch with hundreds of people, writes lengthy replies to short thank-you notes, and congratulates new mothers and fathers by sending parenting tips gleaned from his own experience. For years, he and Carol took care of grandchildren on Saturday nights to give their own kids a break.

How does one man do so much intellectual work and at the same time stand as an exemplary friend and father? An iron constitution and steel-trap mind help, but Chomsky's secret is a long break each summer to garden and relax at a vacation home on Cape Cod. A few weeks of digging around in the sandy soil and feeling the ocean breezes, he says, recharges him for another round of duty as America's leading dissident.

SELECTED RESOURCES

You Are Being Lied To: The Disinformation Guide to Media Distortion, Historical Whitewashes and Cultural Myths, ed. Russ Kick (Rasorfish Studios, 2001)

Propaganda and the Public Mind, with David Barsamian (South End, 2001)

Chomsky on Miseducation, ed. and intro. Donaldo Macedo (Rowman & Littlefield, 2000)

A New Generation Draws the Line: Kosovo, East Timor and the Standards of the West (Verso, 2000)

Fateful Triangle: The United States, Israel, and the Palestinians (South End, 1983, 1999)

The New Military Humanism: Lessons from Kosovo (Common Courage, 1999)

Profit Over People: Neoliberalism and Global Order (Seven Stories, 1999)

Class Warfare: Interviews, with David Barsamian (Common Courage, 1996)

Manufacturing Consent: Noam Chomsky and the Media: The Companion Book to the Award-Winning Film, by Peter Wintonick and Mark Achbar (Black Rose, 1994)

Year 501: The Conquest Continues (South End, 1993)

Manufacturing Consent, a film by Peter Wintonick and Mark Achbar (1992)

What Uncle Sam Really Wants (Odonian, 1992)

GARY DELGADO

© Kathy Sloane

"As people of good intent, as progressives, as family members, as citizens of the world—how do we do the right thing? Do we even know what the right thing is? . . . To find solutions to social problems and to envision a desirable future, we must take into account shifting racial realities, the complexities and inequities of an unregulated global market, and the normalization of political conservatism."

A S AN AFRICAN AMERICAN who grew up in Brooklyn's Bedford-Stuyvesant ghetto, as the son of immigrants from Jamaica, and as a community organizer who has spent the past thirty years helping poor people push for, "as corny as it sounds, a just society," Gary Delgado has plenty of reasons to keep a wary eye on the activities of right-wing groups. His deeply felt vision of a multicultural society in which people of all races, incomes, and ethnic origins live together in prosperity and mutual respect collides with zealous conservative efforts to slash social programs, dismantle equal opportunity initiatives, and expand the power of big business.

But Delgado, founder of several influential activist organizations in the San Francisco Bay Area, is thinking about more than self-defense as he studies the techniques and impact of right-wing movements. He believes that progressives, low-income community activists, and people of color can learn practical lessons from corporate lobbyists and the religious right about how to achieve political change.

"If you look at the right over the past ten years," he says, "you'll see that they have opened up over two hundred research institutes. They've also built a number of grassroots organizations that use exactly the same kind of techniques that progressive social activists used in the 1960s and 1970s. On campuses, they have training organizations for student journalists. They have various organizer training institutes.

"Look at their infrastructure and their ability to do research and propaganda," he continues, with deepening exasperation, "their ability to develop new leaders, their ability to place people in key positions."

Grassroots campaigns for social justice are often overwhelmed by the sheer political firepower of conservative opponents, he says, even when public opinion might initially favor the progressive side. Delgado was awed by the right's political muscle and media wizardry while working with activist organizations in California in 1994 to stop a ballot initiative, Proposition 187, that scaled back public services for immigrants. "The immigration question was framed in people's minds exactly the way the backers of Proposition 187 wanted it framed," he notes. "In meetings we'd hear people say 'They're taking our jobs,' that kind of stuff. And these were progressive leaders from progressive community organizations. Half the people in the room were second-generation immigrants and they were complaining about immigration."

With the support of many black and even some Latino and Asian voters, Proposition 187 passed, ushering in a new era of resentment toward and repression of foreign-born Americans. For Delgado, it was a loud and clear sign that progressive movements desperately need to rethink their strategies. That's long been the focus of two key organizations he launched: the Oakland-based Center for Third World Organizing, which trains leaders from minority communities in organizing for social change; and the Applied Research Center (ARC), also based in Oakland, which monitors the latest research coming out of universities and think tanks for new ideas about how to boost the prospects of the movements for social change.

He now concentrates his energies at ARC, which he consciously modeled after the right-wing think tanks that have provided ideological ammunition for successful conservative movements over the past twenty years. Delgado understands the power of reliable research both in planning politicial strategies and making the case to the public. After years of organizing for the National Welfare Rights Organization and ACORN (Association of Community Organizations for Reform Now), of which he was the first organizer, he went back to school for a Ph.D.

in sociology at Berkeley so that he could be more effective in challenging the stubborn persistence of racism and economic inequality in our society.

One ARC study examining race relations in the Bay Area contradicted conventional wisdom that outright racism is a thing of the past. The report substantiated "employment discrimination, especially toward 'foreign-looking' immigrants; racial tensions between police and residents in communities of color; mortgage redlining; and across-the-board nonenforcement of housing discrimination laws."

"Racism," Delgado wrote in the report, "was not just alive and well. It [is] a potent force in the lives of Latino hotel workers, African American bus drivers, and Asian women working in high-tech computer-related production plants of Silicon Valley."

In studying the changing contours of America's political landscape, Delgado has shifted his own thinking about how best to realize the American dream of liberty and justice for all. "Progressive social change was never an easy task. And it is getting harder," he notes. "On the one hand, working with surgical precision, political conservatives have reshaped the terrain of possible political discourse. On the other hand, they have wantonly destroyed for many any hope of participating in society."

Part of the right's stunning success on issues ranging from the military budget to "so-called welfare reform," he says, can be blamed on progressives' unwillingness to take firm political stands. Conservatives outline their beliefs in direct ways, calling affirmative action or bilingual education, for instance, unfair. The left hems and haws, never offering a heartfelt or convincing case for their side of the issues. "I contributed to that, and now, if you'll excuse the expression, it's turned around to bite us in the ass," he says. "For a very long time, I believed that one should not be ideologically attached, that one should be able to figure out what was appropriate in every situation and do what made sense.

"That was a mistake," he says ruefully. Progressives now appear to be afraid to say what they really believe—a surefire way to alienate the average American. Delgado's chief mission today is helping progressive organizatons identify and articulate basic values. "Our vision cannot simply be a warmed-over lowest-common-denominator notion of Jeffersonian democracy," he says.

As an example he points to several antigay initiatives on the ballot in Oregon in recent years. Gay rights activists did not craft a cautious response to the measures; they were very direct in denouncing the groups supporting the initiatives as homophobic and unfair. Voters rejected the initiatives each time.

"How do we arrive at a vision that takes into account and combines our own political beliefs, values, aspirations, and experiences with those of our constituents?," he asks, and then answers: "Very slowly. In finding ways to build our vision, we don't have to agree on everything. However, if we have any hope of affecting larger societal issues and continuing to be relevant to our own constituents, we have to create space for discussing and developing a collective vision."

Ideas, of course, aren't the only thing the right has in abundance. Conservative research institutes are lavishly funded by wealthy individual and corporate benefactors—funders who think nothing of taking a planeload of grassroots activists to Washington for a week of training sessions, or bankrolling studies whose conclusions might be useful to their cause. The Applied Research Center, by contrast, constantly hustles for foundation grants just to pay rent and meet payroll. Delgado is always thinking about ways to even the sides in this war of information. "We are going to have to get public universities accountable on this stuff," he says, noting that as tax-funded institutions they have an obligation to serve the public good. "Right now they absolutely do not provide any information on a variety of issues that helps anybody in a given community understand how a particular policy proposal is going to affect their lives.

"I see a day when organizations of poor people and people of color have the benefit of not just the best thinking of the people in their community but also information from some of the experts about the economic and political impact of certain kinds of decisions."

Delgado's intense, patient, and unwavering commitment to improving the lot of low-income communities and people of color stems from his own upbringing. His mother, a public health nurse, was a staunch advocate for the underprivileged. "As a kid I was at the freedom schools of the civil rights movement, I was at antiwar rallies. I didn't call it politics then, it was just responding to what I saw around me." He attended the State University of New York at Old Westbury, an experimental college that offered him extensive college credits for working off-campus to help welfare recipients gain dignity and better benefits. "I was working for the National Welfare Rights Organization," he recalls, "knocking on doors in the suffocatingly humid summer of 1970. My turf was a small black neighborhood in northeast D.C. In preparation for the first organizing meeting,

I 'door-knocked' sixty-one families; fifty-nine people came to the meeting."

Later, during a demonstration at a Washington welfare office, police took Delgado aside and pulled out their batons to beat him when an older woman, Mrs. Bailey, stepped in to say, "Don't you hurt that boy, he's my organizer." Delgado says she may have saved his life, and he counts that moment as when he decided to commit his life to helping people fight for a better life.

"The truth is, the times were on our side," he remembers. "The black-led civil rights movement had just won hard-fought but heady victories. The tide had turned against the Vietnam War. The government felt obligated, if often reluctant, to address the inequities of poverty and racial discrimination."

Times have changed, and so must the tactics we use to gain a better life for millions of disadvantaged Americans. But Delgado understands that the victories of thirty years ago didn't just happen overnight; they were the product of long years of often frustrating work on the part of countless grassroots activists. That's the kind of work he's engaged in today, testing new tactics in pursuit of the same long-term goal: "a multiracial movement of poor people to redesign, reset, and implement a vision for a just society."

"I see a day when we decide again there is a role for government in ensuring there is equality in society. Some of that we can get through legislation. Some of it throught regulation. But for some of it you just need to organize. It will come about through our willingness to engage with the American public in a direct conversation about justice and fairness."

SELECTED RESOURCES

Applied Research Center
   3781 Broadway, Oakland, CA 94611
   www.arc.org

Deliberate Disadvantage (Applied Research Center, 1996)

Beyond the Politics of Place: New Directions for Community Organizing (Chardon, 1997)

RIANE EISLER

"I believe that the core of all the major religious traditions—be they Hindu, Muslim, Buddhist, Hebrew, Christian, or Taoist—are the partnership values of sensitivity, empathy, caring, and nonviolence. . . . However, we also need to recognize the "dominator" elements in religious teachings: elements that have served to justify and maintain domination and oppression—for example, the biblical justification of holy wars and control of men over women."

David Loye

"**W**HY IS OUR world so full of man's infamous inhumanity to man—and to woman?" asks Riane Eisler, a social scientist, former military researcher, lawyer, feminist activist, and author of a sweeping revisionist look at human history, *The Chalice and The Blade*. "What is it that chronically tilts us toward cruelty rather than kindness, toward war rather than peace?"

While these are questions of universal importance, Eisler's own life story adds a personal poignance. Born into a Jewish family in Austria, Eisler experienced horrible heights of inhumanity firsthand. "I went from being a little girl who people on the street patted on the head to being an enemy of the state."

She watched as her father, a prominent businessman in the cutlery trade, was dragged away one night by a Nazi gang. Her mother recognized one of the thugs as a former employee to whom the family had been kind, and angrily shouted at him to release her husband. The gang did—but only after demanding a large sum of money. The family then fled to Cuba, where they were among the last groups of refugees allowed to enter. Later ships with Jews fleeing Nazi terror were turned back. Even as a little girl of seven, Eisler wondered, "How could people really have so little empathy, so little caring? What happened?"

These experiences left her with a drive to accomplish big things in the world—"to justify that I had been spared." And from an early age, she says, "I saw something important as being the kind of thing that men did. Because women's work of caring for family and people's health and children was not considered important work."

Moving to the United States in 1946, she eventually did marry and raise a family, but also graduated from UCLA with a degree in anthropology and sociology. She was hired by the RAND Corporation in the 1950s to work on sophisticated Pentagon war game projects before going back to UCLA to earn a law degree. The first ripples of 1960s feminism drew her in and soon Eisler was in the midst of the movement—helping found the Los Angeles Women's Center, campaigning for the Equal Rights Amendment, writing a legal column for a feminist newspaper, teaching college courses on women's studies, drafting legislation for the California legislature, and contributing to a key U.S. Supreme Court case furthering the cause of women's rights under the equal protection clause of the Fourteenth Amendment. She wrote the *Equal Rights Handbook* (1978) and *Dissolution: No-Fault Divorce, Marriage, and the Future of Women* (1977), which predicted the feminization of poverty that became such a critical problem in the 1980s and 1990s.

Eisler also pursued her own anthropological and historical study, spending long hours in college libraries absorbing everything she could about early civilizations, mythology, and ancient mystery cults. In a way, she was searching for answers to her childhood questions about human nature.

In the 1970s, she grew particularly intrigued by the work of several archaeologists, who uncovered evidence of goddess-worshipping cultures in prehistoric Europe. One of the archaeologists, Harvard and UCLA professor Marija Gimbutas, who did extensive excavations in the Balkans, theorized that women in these cultures enjoyed equal status with men.

Continuing her own study of the Neolithic culture that flourished sometime between 6000 B.C.E. and 2500 B.C.E., Eisler formulated a new theory of human civilization in *The Chalice and the Blade* (1987)—which has been translated into sixteen languages and was praised by Princeton anthropologist Ashley Montagu as "the most important book since Darwin's *Origin of Species*." According to Eisler, whose book incorporated groundbreaking research from a new generation of feminist scholars, the Neolithic Age was a time of relative peace when many of the inventions we depend upon today were created: agriculture, metals, architecture, writing, weaving, sanitation. These societies worshipped the Great Goddess—a symbol of fertility, the Earth, and regeneration—but were not matriarchies. Men and women, leaders and followers, wealthy and poor, lived with a general sense of equality. Because cut-throat competition was not seen as the key to advancement, rigid hierarchies never took hold.

Eisler calls this model of society the "partnership" way, and stresses that the ease of relations between men and women is at the core of what sets it apart from later civilizations, which she calls "dominator" societies. From the subjugation of women comes a similar pattern of domination over nature, children, the poor, the powerless, and outsiders—a paradigm that shapes every institution of human culture today.

These two cultural systems are not mutually exclusive; "partnership" thinking sometimes makes inroads into a dominator society, which Eisler believes happened in the time of Jesus, the Renaissance, and in present-day Scandinavia. She analyzes current conservative, fundamentalist trends around the globe as a reaction to newly arising movements that promote partnership values like ecology, feminism, and economic fairness. "We are in the midst of massive dominator regression right now precisely because on the grassroots level, the system is threatened and that is manifesting itself in violence and in the widening gap between haves and have-nots, the push to get women back in their traditional place and, of course, in the insane arsenal of weapons the world has become."

Yet, despite this backlash, Eisler foresees a continuing momentum in the direction of partnership. She's launched the Center for Partnership Studies in order to research and promote these ideas through schools, in the media, and within political and business associations. One of the center's projects, The Alliance for a Caring Economy, works on practical solutions to the serious problems arising from how little our culture values the day-to-day work of caring for people—the disparity between "important" work and "women's" work that Eisler noticed as a small child. The Alliance spotlights creative programs, such as governments covering health insurance for childcare workers to help well-qualified people stay in the field. It also lobbies for paid parental leave, which is the norm in almost every other advanced industrial nation except the United States.

"We need to move toward a system that affords real value and real reward to the essential work of caring and caretaking," Eisler declares. We pay less to childcare workers than we do to parking lot attendants. That's lunatic." Partnership is not just an abstract goal for the center but an intimate fact of life; Eisler works side by side with her husband, social psychologist and futurist David Loye, at the organization's office on California's Monterey peninsula. Setting out to shift the course of fifty centuries of human history must feel like a daunting assignment, but Eisler, Loye and the rest of the staff try to keep a sense of proportion about their mission. Particularly hectic days are remedied with walks on the nearby beach. And Eisler says that paying attention to breathing, which allows her to center herself, helps in sorting out sometimes intimidating amounts of work.

Devising a partnership model of education is Eisler's current mission. The Center is helping to develop and test a curriculum in a Seattle high school, in which the values of gender fairness, multiculturalism, ethics, and environmental consciousness are incorporated into all subjects and school policies. She also has helped to create new education prototypes in partnership with the Institute for Research on Learning, with the University of Kansas, and with *New Moon,* a national magazine edited in Duluth, Minnesota, by and for girls ages eight to fourteen. Eisler's recent book, *Tomorrow's Children,* outlines how schools could become places where "both boys and girls will be aware of the enormous range of their human potentials . . . equipped to cultivate the positives within themselves and others . . . joining together to build a world where chronic violence, inequality, and insensitivity will no longer be 'just the way things are,' but 'the way things once were.' "

SELECTED RESOURCES

Center for Partnership Studies
  Box 30538, Tucson, AZ 85751
  www.partnershipway.org

*Tomorrow's Children: A Blueprint for Partnership Education in the
  Twenty-First Century* (Westview, 2000)

The Partnership Way: New Tools for Living and Learning,
  with David Loye (Harper, 1990; rev. ed., Holistic Education, 1998)

Sacred Pleasure: Sex, Myth, and the Politics of the Body
  (HarperSanFrancisco, 1995)

The Chalice and The Blade: Our History, Our Future (Harper & Row, 1987)

COLIN GREER

"To have a democratic future means actually trying to live in a democratic present. You build staging grounds for a larger democracy. There isn't a lot of point being involved in activities that are simply means/ends conflicts. You have to find ways in which your idea of what you're after is on some level achievable in the present."

COLIN GREER, you might say, went into the family business. While it's a long way from a candy store in London's East End, where Greer was raised upstairs, to an art deco office on New York's West End Avenue, where he now serves as president of the New World Foundation, the work is in many ways the same.

"My parents were really the social workers of the neighborhood," he recalls. "There was a hospital across the street and the doctors would come in and buy candy, and my parents would connect them to people in the neighborhood who needed medical care. And my grandfather was, amazingly, a respected figure in a neighborhood that could often be anti-Semitic. He was nearly blind and couldn't work much, but he founded the local synagogue and wandered around the neighborhood being kind to everyone, listening to what was going on in their lives."

Greer continues this family tradition, albeit on a broader scale. He and his colleagues at New World help social justice, environmental, and youth activist groups across the United States by giving them millions of dollars in grants to work in their communities. He is involved in

choosing who to fund and helping develop them as effective forces for
social change, as well as trying to influence broader political trends by
supporting key researchers and strategists in the progressive ranks.
Applying lessons learned from his grandfather, Greer always makes
time to listen closely to the people he meets: from neighborhood
organizers from South Central Los Angeles and environmental activists
from Louisiana, to Senator Hillary Rodham Clinton (whom he
advised on the potential of government-foundation partnerships on
social issues while she was First Lady) and Minnesota's Senator Paul
Wellstone (whom he advises on public education).

Growing up in a poor neighborhood, and one where he sometimes was taunted for being Jewish, instilled in Greer a vision of
fighting for fairness. He distinctly remembers one day when Nellie, a
neighbor struggling with an alcoholic husband and a houseful of kids,
walked into the candy store and told him, "You're bright, Colin.
You're going to get out of here, and you're going to become a lawyer
and a judge and you're going to bring justice back to us." Although
he eventually chose education, journalism, and foundation work
instead of law, Greer says, "I always feel, even though I am in a very
different place in a very different country, that I am trying to bring
justice back to Nellie."

The New World Foundation—one of America's biggest funders of
progressive causes—exists thanks to an endowment from heirs of nineteenth-century farm machinery manufacturer Cyrus McCormick.
Greer was appointed president in 1986 by Hillary Rodham Clinton,
then board chair, who overcame her initial misgivings that he was too
leftist for the position. Although holding little experience in the phil-
anthropic field, he impressed foundation officials with his record as an
education professor at City University of New York, where he established a successful university-without-walls program for working-class
students, and ran the innovative multidisciplinary Institute of
Contemporary Studies. He tackles projects in a flurry of hard-driving
energy and insistent intellectual probing balanced with a shining smile
that puts people at ease.

In addition to his New World work, Greer writes regularly on
political and ethical issues. He has interviewed Billy Graham, Mikhail
Gorbachev, Tipper Gore, and Archbishop Desmond Tutu for *Parade*
magazine, as well as writing a special report for the magazine that
cracked stereotypes about poor people in America. "When Americans
think of starving people, they think of Third World countries," he

wrote. "Millions endure hunger right here at home: Parents are going to bed without food so they can feed their children. Baby formula is mixed with water to make it last longer." While that might not be news to progressive policy analysts and social activists, it caused a stir when it appeared as the cover story of a magazine that arrives as part of tens of millions of Sunday newspapers.

Greer also writes columns for *Child* magazine about how parents can teach morals and values to kids, a subject that he elaborated upon in two recent books. *A Call to Character* and *The Plain Truth of Things* (both edited with fellow educator Herbert Kohl) gather stories from scores of people—Frederick Douglass to Mary Poppins, Lao-tzu to Annie Dillard—with insights for families facing the complicated moral universe of our time. "Many families don't find time to sit down and read and talk with children, especially as they grow away from bedtime stories and the first few years of school," Greer and Kohl write. "Too often TV commands the attention of children and parents, and threatens to overwhelm their imaginations. Regular reading when your children are eight to thirteen years old is just as important as it was when they were younger."

Unlike many contemporary commentators, Greer doesn't use *values* as a code word for maintaining traditional social arrangements. Just the opposite. "Moral decisions are difficult and often involve risk and daring; they can lead to discomfort, just as they can lead to the deepest kind of comfort when you feel that you're an upright person, a person of integrity," write Greer and Kohl, who invoke Gandhi as an inspiring model of honor: "For him, moral living is not about being right, but about being awake—awake to suffering in the world and aiming to reduce it."

Like many immigrants, Greer is deeply attached to his chosen home. His love affair with America began in 1965 as a shipboard romance, when he was fresh out of The London School of Economics and headed for graduate school at Columbia University. "I couldn't believe two things," he recalls. "First, there were faculty and students on the boat coming back from various schools' semester-abroad programs, and I couldn't believe how engaged the students were and how open the faculty was to arguing with them. That would never happen in an English university. Then, when we got within radio pickup of New York, there was enormous emotion among everyone about coming home that was very powerful to me. I didn't have that sense of England as home."

Greer remains hopeful about America's future in spite of dismaying political and economic trends. "Many of the ideas I think of having been part of the left are really built into the American value system now," he says. "Public schools are regarded as the engine of American democracy, but they are underfunded. We talk about community as the basis of social cohesion, but we undermine community with our economic development. It's not that these values are challenged, it's that we don't look hard enough at how what we do diminishes the possibility of achieving these values."

That's his mission at the New World Foundation and all the other projects he pursues: to push America to live up to its ideals of freedom, equality, and justice. His experience as part of the 1968 generation—he protested against the war in Vietnam, fought for civil rights, and embraced feminism, with its important message that the personal is political—makes him careful not to let hierarchical divisions shape relationships at the foundation or with citizen organizations. And he's conscientious about commitments to his family and community. He and his wife, Franny LeBarre, a psychoanalyst, rent an apartment in Manhattan and spend weekends at a small house in upstate New York, where Greer revives his imagination by writing poetry. In the city, theater is his creative outlet. He helps the Lark Theater, a small company that produces the work of new playwrights. "I help them read and select plays, and hope to spend some time in their directors' training program."

SELECTED RESOURCES

New World Foundation
   100 E. 85th St., New York, NY 10028-0997

The Plain Truth of Things: A Treasury of the Role of Values in a Complex World,
   with Herbert Kohl (HarperCollins, 1997)

*A Call to Character: A Family Treasury of Stories, Poems, Plays, Proverbs, and Fables
   to Guide the Development of Values for You and Your Children,*
   with Herbert Kohl (HarperCollins, 1995)

Choosing Equality: The Case for Democratic Schooling,
   with Ann Bastian et al (Temple Univ. Press, 1986)

The Great School Legend: A Revisionist Interpretation of American Public Education
   (Basic, 1972; Penguin, 1976)

TED HALSTEAD

"Today's young adults will be remembered either as a late-blooming generation that ultimately helped to revive American democracy by coalescing around a bold new political program and bringing the rest of the nation along with them, or as another silent generation that stood by as our democracy and society suffered a slow decline."

TED HALSTEAD, the thirty-three-year-old president of the New America Foundation, showed an entrepreneurial flair while he was still a student at the international high school in Brussels. He and a few friends would regularly rent a warehouse, buy kegs of beer, hire a DJ, and throw a big dance party that attracted hundreds of young people from the school. Not only did it make him a few francs, but it helped forge a sense of kinship among foreign kids like him who were living in Belgium.

You might say that he's still at it with New America, the Washington think tank he founded in 1998. There's not much beer around the comfortable DuPont Circle office, and even less dancing, but New America still aims to bring outsiders together in an atmosphere of convivial support—in this case, young people alienated from America's political system. As Halstead pointed out in a 1999 *Atlantic Monthly* cover story, half of all eighteen- to twenty-four-year-olds voted in the 1972 presidential elections; in 1996, it was 32 percent. "Why are so many young people opting out of conventional politics?" he asks. "And what does this mean for the future of our democracy? Might it be that today's political establishment is simply not addressing what matters to the young?"

Generation X's political sensibility is different from that of the baby boomers and the World War II generation, Halstead explains. They're wary of government and political parties, because they don't see those institutions effectively addressing the issues that matter to young people: growing economic insecurity, continuing environmental degradation, breakdown of community, decline in public schools and other services, and escalating levels of personal and public debt. But that doesn't necessarily translate into apathy. As a generation, they are more likely than baby boomers to volunteer at local charities and boycott products from disreputable sources, Halstead notes. The typical young American, Halstead reminds us, is not an Internet prodigy making six-figures a year, but a service worker with lousy benefits and fading hopes of matching his or her parents' middle-class comforts. Halstead notes that a full two-thirds of his generation will never get a bachelor's degree.

"At the very heart of the Xer worldview is a deep-seated economic insecurity," he declares. "But whining will do no good. The only way for Xers to reverse their sad situation is by entering the political arena that they have every reason to loathe. After all, collective problems require collective solutions. Xers cannot reasonably expect the political establishment to address, let alone fix, the sobering problems they are to inherit unless they start participating in the nation's political process and learn to flex their generational muscle."

Halstead launched the New America Foundation to create and promote a fresh political agenda dedicated to improving prospects for young Americans. Knowing that young voices are as rare in national policy debates as senior citizens at a rap concert, Halstead named a number of under-40 thinkers as fellows. Candidates were selected on the basis of originality of their thinking, writing ability, and commitment to broadening the political debate. He offered them a nice office, steady pay, and lots of encouragement to get their ideas out in leading publications. Early results of this innovative attempt to influence the zeitgeist are promising; in the first five months of operation, New America fellows—including Debra Dickerson (then 39), Margaret Talbot (37), Michael Lind (36), Gregory Rodriguez (32), and Jonathan Chait (26)—published nine articles on various topics in *The New York Times,* ten in the *Los Angeles Times,* as well as others in *The Washington Post, , USA Today, Newsweek, Newsday,* and *Slate.*

As the new kid on the block in Washington's think tank world, New America has earned notice even though old-timers like the archconservative Heritage Foundation, conservative American Enterprise Institute, and centrist Brookings Institute spend far more money. New America's direct-market approach—producing articles rather than policy papers and news conferences—is a new tactic on the intellectual battleground of American politics. Halstead has also enlisted some key allies. Respected journalists James Fallows, Walter Russell Mead, and Fareed Zakaria are on the board alongside former Clinton cabinet member Laura D'Andrea Tyson, and funding comes partly from a heretofore untapped source: the cyber industry. Eric E. Schmidt, chairman and CEO of Silicon Valley's Novell, explains his involvement: "Here is a place in which new ideas can flourish which are not aligned with any partisan view. A large number of people out here are tired of the left-right debate, which exists largely because it makes for good television."

Making a clean break from the conservative-liberal bickering of mainstream debate is the central theme of Ted Halstead's vision of a new political synthesis, which he believes will benefit not only young people but also millions of other everyday Americans who feel politicians are unresponsive to their wishes and ideas.

"Look at the Democratic Party," he says. "I see it as a combination of right-wing economics, which is basically Clinton, with a left-wing social agenda: identity politics, multiculturalism, affirmative action. That's the exact opposite of where most of the country is. I think the majority of Americans are somewhere between the fundamentalism and social Darwinism of the right and the permissiveness of the left."

The hope for American politics, in Halstead's view, lies in creating a new "radical center," a concept popularized by New America fellow Michael Lind. The two of them are working on a book outlining this new political stance, which borrows ideas from all across the philosophical spectrum and applies them in bold ways to looming economic, environmental, and social problems. The focus is on results, not ideological consistency, which fits squarely with the pragmatic sensibilities of what Halstead calls the "fix-it generation."

Affirmative action, for instance, which understandably enrages low-income whites, might be eliminated in favor of more equitable class-based opportunity programs. Proportional representation, which would give voters a choice between three or four candidates in most elections, might replace the "winner-take-all" electoral system that leaves us stuck with two political parties that are more similar than not.

The foundation is dedicated to introducing and promoting new ideas in America's political debate, through the fellows program as well as other projects like the Next Generation of National Leaders—an annual forum for young leaders from the worlds of politics and technology to exchange visions and policy proposals.

A number of New America initiatives advocate embracing the fiscal restraint championed by conservatives as a way to make sure today's young people are not crushed by an avalanche of government debt in the future, but at the same time heed progressives' calls to remedy economic inequality. That can't be done, snicker conventional political pundits: You can't tax less and spend more at the same time. But that's where the radical part of Halstead's "radical center" kicks in. He has mapped out a fiscal plan he calls balanced-budget populism: spending money to improve schools and other public services and at the same time saving money by curtailing corporate welfare and reordering our tax system. "The government should take roughly a constant share out of GDP, so the question shouldn't be how much to tax, it should be what to tax, who to tax, and who gets the benefits," he says.

Halstead points out that 70 percent of Americans—the least wealthy 70 percent—lose more of their paychecks to payroll taxes like Social Security than to federal income taxes. That's where he'd start the shift in economic policy, "replac[ing] payroll taxes with pollution taxes, thereby boosting wages, promoting jobs, and cleaning up the environment, all without raising the deficit. Taxing waste instead of work is precisely the kind of innovative and pragmatic proposal that could help to galvanize the members of Generation X, who have been put to sleep by the current tax debate."

"Universal capitalism" is another idea he touts. Every American child would become a trust fund baby, with a nest egg of, say, $40,000 from the government to invest in college, a business, or a house after she or he turns eighteen. ("One of the requirements would be that they can't piss it away," he notes.) This would help remedy injustice by giving everyone at least a small stake in the economic system. To pay for it, Halstead proposes another fresh idea, common assets, by which he means all the undervalued resources owned collectively by the American people: grazing, mining, and timber rights on public lands, the electromagnetic spectrum, and so forth. "We the American people ought to get just compensation when they are used," he says. "So many of these publicly owned resources are being given away for free or at greatly subsidized costs. By reclaiming those assets we could raise literally trillions of dollars in the coming years, which could more than fund this idea."

You'd expect a thirty-three-year-old bursting with so many detailed policy proposals to have spent most of his life holed up at home reading back issues of the *National Journal* and watching C-Span. But Halstead honed his political talents in a remarkable self-directed apprenticeship all over the world. He grew up in Belgium, worked for a headhunting firm in Japan, studied philosophy and ecology at Dartmouth, traveled around Southeast Asia, worked on environmental and land reform projects in Guatemala, organized Ohio communities around environmental issues, joined the staff of a small Washington think tank, founded the environmental and economic think tank Redefining Progress in San Francisco at age twenty-five on a modest $15,000 grant, enlisted 2,500 prominent economists (including eight Nobel laureates) to sign a statement explaining that measures to curtail global warming would actually be good for our economy, and earned a master's degree from Harvard's Kennedy School of Government—all before he was thirty. Each of these experiences gave him something to think about and helped shape the work he's now pursuing with the New America Foundation.

He credits growing up in Europe, where his family moved when he was just three months old, with igniting his precocious interest in social policy. "I had friends from all over the world," he says, "and there was that sense of appreciation of culture, history, differences, politics, and so forth, which you miss growing up in America because America is so big and powerful that you get insulated by the American way. But I always knew that America was where I would end up. I spent every summer here."

Recently he underwent that most American rite of passage: buying a house. After years of exploring the world, chasing dreams, and undertaking new causes, he says he's ready to settle down, get involved in his community, and generally find a little more balance in his life. His new house even has a hot tub, he admits sheepishly, and it's a terrific way to escape the manic pressures of the Washington political scene. "I go in there for twenty minutes in the morning by myself and just sit back and think. Quiet time is when your inner wisdom can come out. We have most of the answers we need in our heads. It's just that we don't spend the time to listen."

SELECTED RESOURCES

www.newamerica.net

"A Politics for Generation X," Atlantic Monthly, August 1999

JIM HIGHTOWER

© Alan Pogue

"I am an agitator, and an agitator is the center post in a washing machine that gets the dirt out."

WITH A BEST-SELLING book and a radio show with millions of listeners across the heartland under his belt, Jim Hightower surely counts as one of America's most influential progressive voices. He leads the charge against economic inequality, political corruption, environmental despoilment, and all manner of prejudice with hard-hitting opinionizing like this: "Some say we need a third party. I say we need a second one."

And: "We ought to pass a law that says the board of directors and top management of a company that wants to build a polluting facility—anything that spews or burbles—would have to live within one hundred yards of that facility."

And this: "If Paul Revere were to make his midnight ride now, it is not an invasion by redcoats he would warn us about, but the astonishing assault global corporate powers are making on our liberties, economic fortunes, way of life, and sovereignty."

That's pretty strong stuff, especially in a political climate in which wishy-washy Bill Clinton has been hailed as a crusading idealist, and tepid centrist Michael Kinsley represented the left on TV's *Crossfire*. (Hightower has described these two, respectively, as "a man who campaigns as FDR and governs as Herbert Hoover" and "Tweety Bird sent into a cockfight.")

But you wouldn't easily recognize Jim Hightower as a progressive activist—at least not the kind of progressive we are accustomed to. He wears a cowboy hat, speaks in an unreconstituted Texas twang, and hangs out at burrito stands and honky-tonk taverns, peppering his commentary with one-liners instead of the rhetorical abstraction we've come to expect from leftists. He's more Will Rogers than Ralph Nader, more Willie Nelson than Warren Beatty, more Main Street than Harvard Yard.

Hightower's political education was acquired not in college courses but at home in Denison, Texas: around the kitchen table, at Methodist church services, and listening to country-western music. He's more apt to quote Western swing fiddler Bob Wills ("Little bee sucks the blossom / but the big bee gets the honey / Little man picks the cotton / but the big man gets the money") than Gandhi, Che Guevara, or Rachel Carson.

"My daddy ran a newsstand and all the other downtown merchants and delivery guys and clerks would come in to stand around his soda pop machine and I would listen to them solve all the world's problems in the fifteen minutes they had before they needed to go back to work," he recalls.

If anyone asked those guys to describe their political beliefs, Hightower says, they would all say *conservative*—especially if the only other option was *liberal*. But if someone got them talking, "they'd hear about how out-of-state bank-holding giants are coldly squeezing the life [out] of little guys like them and little towns like Denison; about how both political parties have become whores to the Wall Street crowd and don't really give a rat's ass about Main Street folks; about how the tax laws are written by and for big corporations and the privileged at the expense of the working man and woman; about how the oil and chemical companies are run by a gang of greedy polluters who'd just as soon piss in your Dr. Pepper as say hidy to you."

One lesson Hightower learned from the impromptu political forums was the importance of humor. "Whatever topic was in the news of the day, those guys would get off to giggling about it," he recalls. "There was just a natural sense of goosey fun that I grew up with. And later I discovered that people absorbed what I was saying in large part because of the jokes. Humor gives us a way to communicate without totally depressing people. You can talk about how the bottom 80 percent of our society got only 1 percent of the $12 trillion generated in new wealth recently, but you can also say, 'Sure, Wall Street is whizzing—it's whizzing on you and me.'"

This is the spirit of good-natured political subversion that boosted sales of Hightower's book, *There's Nothing in the Middle of the Road
but Yellow Stripes and Dead Armadillos* (a phrase he first heard from a
farmer in Deaf Smith County, Texas). In addition, he issues daily radio
commentaries that inject a dose of political playfulness into the day's
news on more than fifty stations. For example: Quoting an ad executive who bragged that "as long as the consumer accepts the intrusion
of advertising, there is no limit as to where it will go," Hightower
quips, "It won't be long before your church altar is adorned with a
flashing neon sign hustling St. Joseph's aspirin."

While he didn't acquire his political beliefs at North Texas State
University (where he worked as assistant manager of the local chamber
of commerce to pay his tuition), Hightower did learn in political science class that there was a better word than *conservative* to describe his
political views: *populist*. It's a word he still uses with pride, making a
connection with the Populist uprising of the late nineteenth century—
a ragtag army of dirt farmers, sharecroppers, factory workers, and small-
business owners who laid the groundwork for most of the progressive
reforms of the twentieth century.

Taking a cue from the Populists, who sent 10 thousand organizers
across the South, Midwest, and Great Plains to spread their message of
economic fairness, he feels that progressive activists today need to ven-
ture beyond college campuses and liberal urban enclaves to engage
middle America in discussions of economic fairness. The time is ripe for
a progressive resurgence, he says.

"The powers that be have overreached. They have stomped on too
many people," Hightower says. "Our leaders are well-practiced at holding down the poorest one-fifth of our population, labeling them 'welfare
cases,' riffraff, or worse, and hiring ever more police with ever more police
power to contain them in their own neighborhoods or in prisons. But
we're talking now about four-fifths of the American people. . . . They
know about the productivity gains U.S. companies are enjoying, the
unprecedented new wealth that has been created, the corporate profits
and stock values that have soared—because they helped produce all this.
Yet practically all the economic benefits generated by the many have
been forklifted to the top, leaving them stewing in the realization that
their families' middle-class opportunities are being stiffed."

Hightower sees stirrings of a new progressive populist movement all
across the countryside. He points to the work of citizen groups like
ACORN, Clean Water Action, the Green Party, the Institute for Local

Self-Reliance, and the re-energized organizing efforts of the AFL-CIO, along with the efforts of creative politicians like Senator Paul Wellstone (Minnesota), Senator Byron Dorgan (North Dakota), Representative Bernard Sanders (Vermont), Representative Marcy Kaptur (Ohio), and Representative Lane Evans (Illinois).

And he's no armchair observer when it comes to either activism or politics. For five years in the 1970s, Hightower ran the Agribusiness Accountability Project, which documented how government and land-grant colleges favored big, agro-industrial interests over family farmers, with disastrous results not only for rural America but also for the safety and taste of the food on everyone's table. The project was closely connected with Ralph Nader, whom Hightower cites as one of his chief influences—along with farmworker leader Cesar Chavez, revolutionary agitator Thomas Paine, abolitionists Frederick Douglass and Sojourner Truth, novelist Upton Sinclair, and Socialist Party presidential candidate Eugene V. Debs.

Hightower put his populist principles into practice in the 1980s, when he was twice elected Texas commissioner of agriculture. He and his longtime partner, agricultural economist Susan DeMarco, who worked for a yearly salary of one dollar, established a slew of innovative programs to help small farmers, develop new crops, and promote sustainable agriculture. They doubled the number of farmers' markets across the state, boosted livestock exports from $6 million to $77 million, and, in the words of *The New York Times,* "turned [a] once-obscure, $20-million-a-year, 580-person agency into a national center for reforming American farm policy."

These experiences left him with the belief that liberalism-as-usual is not enough—not enough to boost the prospects of the 80 percent of Americans left behind by the financial spree of the past two decades, and not enough to win the hearts and minds of the majority of Americans who don't vote. These people, most of whom probably would back liberals if they did turn out, don't vote because they don't find anything worth voting for.

"The liberal response is to say, 'Oh my God, the farmers are losing their farms, workers are losing their jobs—let's find a way to get 'em some money or a program for 'em,'" Hightower says. "The populist approach is to say, 'There's something wrong with the system. We gotta redesign the system.'

"America's true political spectrum does not run right to left, but top to bottom," he continues. "Right to left is theory; top to bottom is experience. And most people today know they are no longer even within shouting distance of the powers at the top, whether those powers wear the masks of Republicans or Democrats, conservatives or liberals."

SELECTED RESOURCES

www.jimhightower.com

If the Gods Had Meant Us to Vote They Would Have Given Us Candidates: More Political Subversion from Jim Hightower
(HarperCollins, 2001)

There's Nothing in the Middle of the Road but Yellow Stripes and Dead Armadillos
(HarperCollins, 1997)

BELL HOOKS

"If black folks are to move forward in our struggle for liberation, we must confront the legacy of . . . unreconciled grief, for it has been the breeding ground for profound nihilistic despair. We must collectively return to a radical political vision of social change rooted in a love ethic and seek once again to convert masses of people, black and nonblack."

Donna Dietrich

GLORIA WATKINS—better known by her great-grandmother's name, bell hooks—first gained prominence with her 1981 treatise, *Ain't I a Woman: Black Women and Feminism,* which castigated the white racial bias of the feminist movement. Since then, she's published a tide of books and articles in which she tackles a range of subjects; love, race, and religion are recurrent themes. Hooks is a radical thinker, never content to take on easy targets. She's a complex critic, postmodern in the best sense of the word, a penetrating analyst of America's racist dilemmas and also an optimist—about race relations, creativity, and love.

Hooks was born in 1952 into what she calls the "working-class, black, Southern, Christian culture" of Hopkinsville, Kentucky, a small, segregated town. When she was a child, her grandmother died in the next room. She watched as her mother closed the dead woman's eyes, and afterward as the men from the funeral home took the body out of the house on a stretcher. "I see this as a moment in time that shaped who I became," hooks recalls. "I saw this and thought, 'Wow—if this is death and it can be looked at and faced, then I can do anything I want to in life. . . . That [experience] allowed me to be the rebellious child I was—daring and risk-taking in the midst of my parents' attempts to control me." Daring and risk-taking have become an intellectual imperative for hooks. She decided to become a writer at the age of ten, despite a father who thought she was "ruining [her] chances" with her books and her big ideas. "Men did not like a too-smart woman," she discovered.

As a Stanford University undergraduate and a University of Wisconsin master's degree candidate in the 1970s, she faced similar attitudes, even as that decade's incarnation of feminism opened new horizons to women. "Our feminist women professors were encouraging their promising, brilliant students to be daring, to explore our minds and our bodies to the fullest," she continues. "I vividly recall the heated debates we had about whether or not women would seize this new day and write our hearts out."

Hooks seized the day. *Ain't I a Woman,* her first book, offered a scathing critique of the 1970s-era women's movement for failing to include black women in its ranks. Since then, hooks has written twelve books of critical theory, two memoirs, and a book of poetry. Along the way, she has thoroughly rethought and reshaped her ideas on her central concerns: race, feminism, and the politics of power.

Her early work reflects the influences of her intellectual coming-of-age. She earned a Ph.D. in 1983 from the University of California, Santa Cruz, during the heady excesses of postmodernism and political correctness.

But over time hooks has expanded the limitations of postmodernity in both substance and style. A complex thinker and talented writer, she demands a rare level of accountability from her fellow intellectuals. In a stinging assault in the journal *Postmodern Culture,* for example, she assails academics who merely "appropriate the experience of 'otherness' in order to enhance its discourse or to be radically chic." Instead, she challenges her colleagues to make their work relevant to the everyday lives of people at the margins—or at the very least, to write works that are accessible to readers who aren't members of their professional clique.

This command to be accessible is evident in her own writing. Unlike the work of many of her postmodernist peers, hooks' critical writing always lies somewhere between polemic and personal tale. She invariably illustrates her positions with personal experience and details of her own life and history. Only two of her books are designated "memoirs," but all of her works contain the memoirist's urge to understand the world by understanding the self.

Perhaps because she stays so close to personal truth, hooks frequently takes unconventional positions. She blames racial desegregation, for instance, for the downfall of black education. Before desegregation, she writes in *Teaching to Transgress* (1994), all her teachers knew her family and were essential members of her immediate community. They "believed that to educate black children rightly would require a political commitment." Both the sense of community and this active approach to learning were lost when her school was desegregated: "Bused to white schools, we soon learned that obedience, and not a zealous will to learn, was what was expected of us. . . . For black children, education was no longer about the practice of freedom."

Likewise, in the title essay of *Talking Back* (1989), hooks launches a critique of mothering. In the composition, she moves fluidly from personal narrative (describing the beatings she received from her parents for "talking back") to pro forma feminist critique ("Silence is often seen as the sexist . . . sign of woman's submission to patriarchal authority") to a radical—indeed, a taboo—rethinking of her subject (in this case, censure of parents, especially black mothers, for responding to creativity with violence).

Time has not mellowed her iconoclastic vision. A recent essay titled "Penis Passion" praises the explicit joys of heterosexual sex in the age of ready access to birth control: "We could go down between male legs," she writes, "abandon ourselves to mystery, and rise up satisfied and pleased with the knowledge that we could give and receive sexual delight." Hooks is sympathetic to "anti-sexist women [who] feel there is no way to engage the penis that does not reinforce male domination," but does not number herself among them. Instead she insists that "when women and men can celebrate the beauty and power of the phallus in ways that do not uphold male domination, our erotic lives are enhanced."

Hooks has recently turned to Buddhism. Raised a Christian, she is drawn to Buddhism in part because it answers a primary call of her writing life. "Spirituality has always been the foundation of my experience as a writer," she explains. "Most writers know that our visions often emerge from places that are mysterious." She says that Buddhist practice brings a "certain quality of mindfulness and stillness" to her daily activities that complements the writing life.

Buddhism has also offered hooks a "path out of blame," she says: "I was seeking a way out of that whole notion of wrongdoing, blame, and punishment. I wanted something that actually had a promise that one would not have to inhabit the space of blame." That's less a departure from her scathing critique of the "sexist, racist patriarchy" than one might think. All along, the most radical components of hooks' message have been her unflagging hope and her fealty to love in all its forms.

"In this society, there is no powerful discourse on love emerging either from politically progressive radicals or from the left," she writes. "The absence of a sustained focus on love in progressive circles arises from a collective failure to acknowledge the needs of the spirit and an overdetermined emphasis on material concerns. Without love, our efforts to liberate ourselves and our world community from oppression and exploitation are doomed."

In *Killing Rage: Ending Racism* hooks articulates her hopeful vision of an "interracial circle of love" made up of individuals committed to "anti-racist struggle." In the face of cynicism and hopelessness, hooks maintains optimism. She challenges "those of us who know the joy of being with folks from all walks of life, [and] all races" and who are "fundamentally antiracist in their habits of being" to "give public testimony." Only then, she writes, can the "interracial circle of love that I know can happen" conquer hatred.

SELECTED RESOURCES

Salvation: Black People and Love (Morrow, 2001)

Happy to Be Nappy
  (Hyperion, 1999; Jump at the Sun, 2001), a children's book

Where We Stand: Class Matters (Routledge, 2000)

Feminism is for Everybody: Passionate Politics (South End, 2000)

All About Love: New Visions (Morrow, 2000)

Wounds of Passion (Henry Holt, 1997)

Bone Black: Memories of Girlhood (Henry Holt, 1996)

Reel to Real: Race, Sex and Class at the Movies (Routledge, 1996)

Killing Rage: Ending Racism (Henry Holt, 1995)

Art on My Mind: Visual Politics (New Press, 1995)

Outlaw Culture: Resisting Representation (Routledge, 1994)

Teaching to Transgress: Education as the Practice of Freedom (Routledge, 1994)

Talking Back: Thinking Feminist, Thinking Black (South End, 1989)

Ain't I a Woman: Black Women and Feminism (South End, 1981)

ANDREW KIMBRELL

"It's very difficult to challenge the dogma of modernity. This is particularly true for the media and public policy makers. I can't go into court and talk about the sacredness of a river. I have to say *'efficient use of natural resources.'*"

ANDREW KIMBRELL, a Catholic convert who unapologetically lists "faithfulness to family and society" as his greatest source of hope for the future, nonetheless relishes his role as a heretic.

In our time, there's no greater heresy than challenging the modern ideal of always pushing the limits. To question the value of breaking new ground, even in controversial fields like genetic engineering or biological weapons, is to find yourself called a crank, and far worse. Yet Kimbrell—a lawyer, writer, and former concert pianist—has made a career of doing just that, blasting away at high-tech orthodoxy in books and articles, in courtrooms and public addresses, in lobbying efforts and public education campaigns.

"This is the century of the technological imagination," he said in 1999. "We think we can do anything with enough research & development—even find the genes that control aging so that we can achieve immortality. But most spiritual traditions say that limits are important, limits bring transcendence. When we are playing music, holding a baby, making love, pitching a great fastball—those moments are meaningful and beautiful in and of themselves.

"The idea of limits becomes for me the central vision of the twenty-first century. Sure, we want to keep pursuing cures for diseases, but not destroy all limits. Technology cannot replace transcendence."

That's what drives Kimbrell—the belief that, although technology is a useful tool, we cannot allow it to replace our ethical philosophies, moral judgments, and spiritual teachings. "The religion that really controls our time is modernity," he explains, diagramming the new Holy Trinity that rules the world with a firmer and more far-reaching hand than any pope in history: science (the "all-knowing" Father), technology (the "all-doing" Son), and market economics (the "all-consuming" Holy Ghost). "These are the new deities," reverentially worshipped by modern-day priests in the cathedrals of government, universities, the media, and corporations around the world, says Kimbrell.

A wide smile, an infectious laugh, and a keen curiosity about almost everything under the sun help make Kimbrell a truly effective heretic; no one can dismiss him as a negative, sour-on-life personality. Indeed, he credits love—his love for the Beaverkill River in the Catskill Mountains of New York—as the reason he embarked on a career as an activist. He and his brother started visiting the river as young men, hurrying there after work on Fridays to squeeze in some fly-fishing before dusk. When they learned of plans for a huge condo development, which not only would ruin the scenery but also flush sewage into the river, they helped organize an opposition movement that successfully blocked the project. That campaign, which involved legal action, influenced him to go to law school.

"I reversed my hobby and my profession," he says, noting that until that time he made a living as concert pianist and music teacher in New York City. Introduced to classical music in the crib by his Czech immigrant grandparents, he's always been absorbed by music and studied piano and composing in Vienna. He still plays for fun, and is now writing music for six of Shakespeare's sonnets—an idea that struck him while he was watching the movie *Shakespeare in Love*.

Politics had always been a big part of his life. Kimbrell grew up attending civil rights and anti–Vietnam war demonstrations in New York City with his mother, an actress and Czech immigrant. (His father, a colonel in the U.S. Army, died in an auto accident when Kimbrell was two.) In high school and at conservatory, he helped run the organization Music and Art Students Against the War in Vietnam.

"It's amazing that a generation got together and helped stop a war as an act of conscience," he says. "The antiwar movement gave me a real sense of pride to be part of something that changed the world."

As founder and president of the International Center for Technology Assessment (CTA), which operates out of a brick rowhouse just blocks from the U.S. Capitol, Kimbrell taps that rebel spirit to question the consequences of new technologies. He's not bent on ousting all new contraptions; the office buzzes with clicking computer keyboards and whirring fax machines. CTA research, political organizing, and lawsuits target genetic engineering, the internal combustion engine, cloning, animal patenting, food irradiation, and industrialized agriculture and forestry.

In many years of work—first with Jeremy Rifkin's Foundation on Economic Trends and later with CTA—Kimbrell filed successful legal briefs against forcing a surrogate mother to give up her baby in the famous Baby M case, against the Pentagon's biological warfare programs, and in favor of stronger health labeling on meat and poultry. On Capitol Hill, he's written legislation with members of Congress all over the political spectrum, from archconservative Henry Hyde (outlawing the commercialization of surrogate motherhood) to liberals like Mark Hatfield and Barbara Boxer (on animal patenting and genetic privacy).

His book *The Human Body Shop* marshals powerful moral, medical, and spiritual evidence against the emerging commercialization of the body. In addition to exposing the chilling details of a new global marketplace trading in human organs, genetic material, and reproductive capacity, he calls for a "body revolution" that would tie traditional beliefs about the body's sacredness with new insights drawn from holistic views of wellness and alternative medicine.

His next book, *The Masculine Mystique,* is a manifesto urging the men's movement to expand out from inner mythopoetic work to embrace a broad political program that could bring a new perspective to issues like militarism, economic inequality, family breakdown, environmental degradation, and social alienation. Praised by both men's movement founder Robert Bly and feminists, the book brings fresh ideas to the raging debate about gender issues. It sold more than 15,000 copies in hardback and earned Kimbrell a warm welcome at many men's meetings across the country.

Kimbrell's wide-ranging focus takes in everything from wilderness preservation to workplace stress, to the empty values we bestow on teenage boys—a constellation of concerns. "When I talk about technological society, I mean systems, not just machines," he says. "A corporation's structure is a technology, and so is an assembly line. They were created the same way machines are created: to perform a particular function without much thought to other consequences of their existence."

He attributes this view to his training as a classical pianist. "My teacher, Kurt Appelbaum, taught that the technique of playing actually creates the emotion of a piece of music—in contrast to many teachers who say that you adopt a technique and add the emotion later. Years later it struck me that it's the same with technology. We create it to perform a function and then try to add our values—and that doesn't work. Technology creates its own values. We need to be aware of that any time we implement a new technology."

SELECTED RESOURCES

International Center for Technology Assessment
   666 Pennsylvania Ave. SE, Suite 302, Washington, DC 20003
   www.icta.org

The Human Body Shop: The Engineering and Marketing of Life
   (HarperSanFrancisco, 1993; rev. ed., 1997)

The Masculine Mystique: The Politics of Masculinity (Ballantine, 1995)

WINONA LADUKE

"I believe the challenge we all face is making a home, restoring, building, investing in, and reclaiming a community, a destiny, a way of life. I believe we all need to choose some ground and stick to it. There are no more frontiers and no greener pastures. This is what we are fortunate enough to have."

AFTER graduating from Harvard, a year's study at MIT, and a master's degree from Antioch, Winona LaDuke—who was born in Los Angeles and grew up in Oregon—decided it was time to move home to White Earth in northern Minnesota, a place where she'd never actually lived before.

"The thing about being an Indian person," LaDuke explains, "is that you feel most at home with your own people. I'm best suited for Indian country. Sure, I could go out and get a job in a boardroom. But that's not going to help anyone else on my reservation."

While she was growing up on the West Coast with an Anishinaabe father who worked as an actor in Hollywood westerns and later became an author and lecturer on Native spirituality, and a Jewish mother who taught art and was involved in the civil rights movement, LaDuke always felt a strong tug from the direction of White Earth, the ancestral lands of the Anishinaabeg (Ojibwe people). She reveled in stories of the place: about the forests and lakes, about ceremonies and feasts, about gathering wild rice and preparing herbal medicines, about stolen land

and struggles to win it back. "People back there kept asking me when I was going to come home," she recalls.

So in 1982, after finishing graduate school and working on environmental and land issues on the Navajo Reservation in the southwest and the Pine Ridge Reservation in South Dakota, LaDuke moved home to become principal of the White Earth Reservation school. She quickly found herself involved with a lawsuit to recover lands promised to the Anishinaabeg by an 1867 federal treaty. When the case was dismissed in court four years later, she founded the White Earth Land Recovery Project to continue the effort to regain the lost lands. More than 90 percent of the original 837,000 acres covered in the treaty are now in the hands of non-Indians. Using foundation grants and a $20,000 human rights prize awarded to LaDuke by the Reebok company, the group has bought back a thousand acres and hopes to acquire thousands more in the next ten years through purchases, gifts, and legislation. The project sells wild rice and maple syrup harvested at White Earth to raise funds.

Besides working in her own community, LaDuke is involved in an array of other Native and environmental issues. She twice ran for vice president on the Green Party ticket with presidential candidate Ralph Nader, in 1996 and 2000. In elections characterized by empty sound bites, she won rave reviews for her frank message: "I believe that decision making should not be the exclusive right of the privileged," she declared. "Those affected by policy—not those who by default often stand above it—should be heard in the debate. It is the absence of this voice which unfortunately characterizes American public policy and the American political system."

In 1985, LaDuke founded the Indigenous Women's Network, which she represented at the 1995 U.N. Women's Conference in Beijing, and has served on the national board of Greenpeace USA. Her leadership has been critical in the successful fight to stop flooding of Canadian Native lands by a massive complex of hydroelectric dams near James Bay. "If you beat a uranium mine, dam project, or timber company, they're just going to move on to Saskatchewan or James Bay or somewhere else," she says. "You have no choice but to work on the international level.

"But in order to do that, you have to have sound footing in one place. If you work on the international level but your community doesn't know what you're doing, then what's the point? The more you're an isolated intellectual, the more you're out of touch."

LaDuke is the first to admit that it's far from easy to follow her advice. She has encountered vast resistance around the White Earth reservation, not just from white people, but also from Indians, even on an issue as innocuous as building a ceremonial roundhouse. And when protesters from the Land Recovery Project blockaded a truck owned by a lumber company that was clear-cutting in their community, the White Earth tribal council gave the truck permission to use reservation roads.

Most Indian reservations are divided, LaDuke explains, between members who see salvation in jobs in the mainstream economy and those who want to maintain traditional culture. "The wage workers look toward more jobs in government and resource development, while the traditional class looks more toward preservation of the land, water, and traditional structures on the reservation. These dynamics constantly come in conflict."

At White Earth, the pro-development tribal chairman and other tribal officials were convicted of election fraud, mail fraud, and embezzlement. "I need to deal with the tribal council because it affects other people where I live," she says. It's the same with the power structure in any other community: "You've got to take them on. You've got to change them. And you've got to work with them."

At forty-two, LaDuke's commitment to White Earth stretches beyond her own lifetime. "When I speak at Rotary Clubs in towns around here," she says, "I tell them that 150 years from now we [Indians] are going to control most of the land here around White Earth. It took eighty years for things to get this bad, and it will take time for things to get better."

Looking ahead, she envisions a White Earth where the Ojibwe language is heard on the streets, in the schools, on radio and television. The lakes are clean, the forests are replenished, and the local economy sustains itself in part on maple syrup, buffalo, deer, and wild rice. Traditional religious rituals flourish. The Anishinaabe Nation is independent of the American government and runs its own college. "I see non-Indians as well as Anishinaabeg on this reservation, sharing common land, values, and language," she says.

The mother of a thirteen-year-old daughter, a ten-year-old son and a baby, LaDuke cites the intergenerational nature of Native culture as a key element that nurtures people through long years of adversity. "We tell our stories to the children," she says. "It's incumbent on us to offer oral history because no one else will. At our ceremonies we have an elder who prays for us all. We make sure the kids are part of everything."

Traditional Anishinaabe religious practices are another source of power and sustenance. "Spirituality is the foundation of all my political work," she says. "We just had the changing of the seasons feast. The land, the water, and all that is around me, ceremony and community—these are the things that restore me. I go to every single powwow I can. I dance as much as I can.

"For a lot of people in this country, religion carries a lot of baggage— 'the opiate of the masses' and all that. But I think that's changing. You can't dismiss the significance of Eastern religion, earth-based religions, and Western religions on political work today. What we all need to do is find the wellspring that keeps us going, that gives us the strength and patience to keep up this struggle for a long time."

SELECTED RESOURCES

White Earth Land Recovery Project
  32033 E. Round Lake Rd., Ponsford, MN 56575

Honor the Earth
  2801 21st Ave. S., Minneapolis, MN 55407
  www.honorearth.com
  LaDuke is program director of this national Native grant making and
  political advocacy organization sponsored by the Indigenous
  Environmental Network and the Indigenous Women's Network.

All Our Relations: Native Struggles for Land and Life (South End, 1999)

Last Standing Woman, (Voyageur,1997), a novel

GEOFF MULGAN

"What is the biggest difference between our lives and those of our great-great-grandparents? We might answer in terms of technologies, big cities, material wealth, television, or women's rights, and all of these have indeed transformed the way we live. But for me what stands out is something else: the connectedness of life, the ways in which our lives are now bound up with each other. . . . Our lives are connected through the environment and our shared dependence on the atmosphere and the oceans. . . . They are connected through the global economy, which makes the livelihood of a town in northeast England dependent on capital from Korea and markets in Germany; and through communications systems that now connect nearly a billion places through the telephone; and through the myriad images broadcast by television stations."

YOU WOULD hardly expect that a lad who at fourteen joined Britain's militant left-wing movement and at seventeen was living in a Sri Lankan monastery would by age thirty-four be working at 10 Downing Street as an adviser to the Prime Minister. That's Geoff Mulgan's résumé in a nutshell, but don't presume this to be a case of another 1960s radical abandoning his youthful ideals for a seat at the banquet table of prestige and privilege: Mulgan was *born* in the 1960s, and he's always favored a pragmatic brand of radicalism that has guided him both inside and outside the corridors of power.

After a period of traveling through Asia, including five months of intense meditation study at the Sri Lankan monastery, he headed off for Oxford and then went to work at the Greater London Council—an umbrella government for the independent municipalities that make up London—organizing street fairs and multicultural festivals, with the aim of bringing more people into the political process as well as having a little fun. Then he helped found Red Wedge, an effort to bring young people into the Labour Party through rock concerts and political rallies. The results of both of these experiences—Margaret Thatcher vengefully abolished the Greater London Council and Labour Party politicians failed to connect with the kids—taught Mulgan some hard lessons. "I could see that politics was pretty much in disrepute," he says. "People saw it as a cynical domain of self-serving people who made promises they never kept. . . . Instead of being at the cutting edge, it is an odd characteristic of our times that all too often politics today feels like a backwater, a declining industry struggling to keep up, rather than a place of imagination and energy."

Weary and a little discouraged, Mulgan moved to the United States to study new information technology at MIT's famed Media Lab, then went home to teach communications at the University of Westminster before winding up on the Parliamentary staff of Gordon Brown (now Chancellor of the Exchequer). Throughout this time, Mulgan was wondering what could be done to reconcile the mistrust between people and the political system that ostensibly belongs to them. "I really believed that politics can be, at its best, the source of many of the things that make life good—public health, education, or even equality or peace or freedom," he says. "Yet I thought politics was completely moribund in Britain—on all sides of the political spectrum. Social democracy and Thatcherism alike have bitten the dust."

After the Labour Party was defeated in a 1993 election everyone thought was in their pocket, Mulgan launched Demos, a nonpartisan think tank dedicated to blowing some fresh air into political and social debates. *Demos,* the root word for *democracy,* is Greek for "people gathered together," which is precisely how the think tank operates: Young staff members spend as much time talking with scientists, entrepreneurs, and grassroots activists as with the usual crowd of politicians, economists, and professors. They focus on politics in the broadest sense of the word.

Demos was soon the talk of England. While others were wringing their hands about the intractable problems of unemployment, Mulgan outlined how the vigorous informal economy of barter and unpaid services—often viewed by governments as a problem, not a solution—

could be tapped to increase work and prosperity for everyone. When others were giving up on the inner city, Demos issued several reports, *The Freedom of the City* and *The Creative City,* pointing to the immense reservoirs of creativity bottled up in every city and how uncorking it is the key to urban revitalization. And as leftists were denouncing the concept of evolutionary psychology, Demos devoted an issue of its journal to this controversial new field, and to what feminists and social justice activists can learn from it.

Tony Blair, the young and ambitious new leader of the Labour Party, was one of the people keeping an eye on Demos. Like Mulgan, he had grown suspicious of ideological abstractions and wanted to focus instead on the tangible things—sprucing up parks, creating jobs—that improve people's lives. When he was elected Prime Minister in 1997, Blair brought Mulgan to 10 Downing Street as a policy adviser to work primarily on children's and poverty issues. Mulgan was surprised to find himself deep inside the power structure, but he relishes the chance to put ideas into action. "For all the defects of politics," he says, "there is still no other dominant source of leadership in modern societies. Power may have passed to the media, to global finance, even to individual consumers, but often their influence turns out to be a negative—a capacity to block things . . . rather than a positive capacity to achieve change.

"You have to be careful not to stay inside power structures too long or you become part of the problem," he cautions. "But if you have nothing to do with the power structure, you become negatively oppositional, without ever offering any ideas about how to do things differently."

Mulgan believes that the very nature of power is undergoing a transformation to what he describes as a more Taoist approach: "We're moving away from the era of strong power systems, formal structures, hierarchies, and classically defined authority to structure more defined by thought and relationships. This is partly because of information technology, partly because of people not willing to be bossed around." Another aspect of this shift from "hard" to "soft" power, he notes, is a willingness to let life organize itself naturally and spontaneously, rather than imposing structure from the outside. ABB, a prominent international engineering firm, exemplifies this new thinking about management, Mulgan notes, with its successful "leadership through mission" model rather than the old leadership by hierarchy structure.

He also foresees a growing recognition of what he calls the "invisible hand of altruism"—the partner of the invisible hand of the market that early capitalist economist Adam Smith hailed as the instrument that turns private self-interest into public good. Governments all over the world are now dedicated to promoting the invisible hand of self-interest, but they don't always understand the importance of the other hand, of public interest. "One of the things we're trying to do," Mulgan says of the Blair government, "is to find the twenty-first-century structures to allow people to give a few hours a week to volunteering or mentoring or being active in the community, as opposed to giving more and more time to the formal economy, which is what has been happening over the past decade or two."

Admitting that he's an optimist (it "releases energy, whereas pessimism leads to a closing in"), Mulgan disputes the notion that we are headed toward a "*Blade Runner* version of the future, with rich people in their gleaming skyscrapers, and down below in the streets, an underclass. I don't think there is anything inevitable about that, but it will take a huge effort of will on the part of societies to make sure it doesn't happen." One bright spot he sees is the continuing evolution of information technology, which he believes will follow the path of industrial technology—first disempowering workers by taking away their traditional livelihoods and forcing them into lower-wage employment, but then improving their lives by shortening the workweek, facilitating collective action, and creating material abundance. There is nothing automatic about this, Mulgan cautions. People must stand up to challenge current trends toward inequality and devise creative solutions to combat it—actions that seem more likely now that even well-educated workers see their livelihoods threatened by new technological and organizational structures. He sees education as a key issue. Developing lifelong education programs are as important to the prospects of today's workers as universal education was in boosting the fortunes of industrial workers of the late nineteenth century.

Much of his optimism rests in the hope that we can find a balance between our historic urge to grab ever more personal freedom and an emerging realization that interdependence is equally important to a happy, fulfilled life. In his book *Connexity*, he eloquently makes the case that "our challenge is to develop new forms of connection, and new shared institutions that draw on our innate sociability and our instinctive disposition to act ethically. If we don't, we face a future where individualism will lead not to richer lives and diversity, but rather to an atomized society of people fearful of strangers, who hide behind locked doors and impersonal screens."

This marks a sharp shift in Western values, he acknowledges: "Our attitudes have been so shaped by the centuries-long battles to win freedoms from kings and the church, and to liberate the powerless from the oppressive orders, that it is hard to acknowledge that what was once the solution may now have become the problem."

In industrialized societies today, he notes, the most pressing social problems no longer stem from an absence of freedom, but rather from too much freedom that leads to antisocial and self-destructive behavior: crime, environmental degradation, drug abuse, violence, alienation, overeating. In our quest for freedom, we've ignored our equally basic need for interdependence and the comfortable social order that it creates. "For people brought up in a liberal culture, the question of order inevitably appears to look backward: it is about returning to a traditional hierarchy in which everyone knew their place," he says. "But the questions really look forward: It is about how do we create the conditions for a fuller freedom?"

Modern culture is like adolescence, he says. We have succeeded in breaking away from the helpless dependency of childhood, and now prize our freedom above all else. The next step is to embrace a more mature sense of interdependence, a step that new information technology and a global economy allow us to take. A society's acknowledgment of its responsibility to take care of the environment and people all over the world is the equivalent of a person making a commitment to partners, children, family, and friends. "The tragedy would be if our fixation on a narrow idea of freedom blinded us to how freedom could develop into something more," Mulgan says.

And to prove this isn't just dreamy theorizing, he points to his own North London neighborhood, where Turkish, Kurdish, and Greek immigrants "live happily together," even though they violently oppose one another in their homelands. It's not the most fashionable address for a young man on the way up, but Mulgan loves it because "it's a place where you feel connected to the rest of the world—it's the most multiethnic neighborhood in Europe."

RESOURCES

Demos
  The Mezzanine, Elizabeth House, 39 York Road, London SE1 7NQ
  United Kingdom
  www.demos.co.uk

Connexity: How to Live in a Connected World
  (Harvard Business School Press, 1997; 1998)

Politics in an Antipolitical Age (Polity, 1994)

MUHAMMAD YUNUS

© Salahuddin Azizee

"The number of poor people increased from 1.3 billion in 1996 to 1.5 billion in 1998. Yet with the creation of wealth proceeding faster than ever before in our history, there's no reason why anyone should be poor. If we pay attention to the problem, we can create a poverty-free world—not in the distant future, but in the very near future."

BANGLADESHI banker Muhammad Yunus has a bold vision: eliminating economic misery from the planet. But don't make the mistake of dismissing this good-humored, humble man as a dreamer. With the quiet, methodical approach of the economics professor he once was, Yunus has set about proving just how possible his dream is. Along the way, he has earned the respect of Bill and Hillary Clinton, the World Bank, and *Asia Week* magazine, which named him one of "Twenty Great Asians." He has also exploded our notions about the intractability of poverty and the limits to what one person can do to change the world.

Grameen Bank, which Yunus started in 1976, lends small amounts of money—sometimes as little as one dollar—to the world's poorest people, considered unworthy of credit by traditional banks because they lack collateral. Grameen currently makes unsecured loans to 2.3 million poor borrowers, more than 94 percent of them women, in 39,000 villages in Bangladesh. It boasts an impressive 97 percent repayment rate. According to one study, half of Grameen's longtime borrowers have pulled themselves out of poverty. Hundreds of thousands of other people around the world have benefited from the more than 200 programs in fifty-eight countries that replicate the Grameen model—including ones in inner-city Baltimore, and in Pine Bluff, Arkansas.

Yunus had just finished a Ph.D. in economics on a Fulbright scholarship at Vanderbilt University, and had just returned to Bangladesh to teach in 1974 when a great famine hit. "I saw a lot of people dying of starvation," he says. "That shook me up. Why should they have to die from hunger?" The experience made him increasingly disillusioned with the "elegant theories" he was spouting to his economics classes at the university: "I felt absolutely incapable of dealing with the massive poverty and hunger that existed in the villages around the campus," he says. "I soon realized that in a major way economics is responsible for creating the world that we live in."

Adopting an approach seldom taken by academics and international development institutions, he talked to poor villagers and asked them what they needed to make their lives better. "I was shocked to see how people suffered for lack of access to tiny amounts of money, as small as one dollar," he says. "I was surprised to see how much hard work each poor person is putting in just for mere survival. Their poverty was not a personal problem due to laziness or lack of intelligence, but a structural one: lack of capital. Poverty is not created by these poor people. It's created by the institutions and policies that we have made for ourselves."

Yunus started out by making a loan out of his pocket to a group of bamboo stool makers. When he saw what a difference such a small amount of money—just $27 total—could make in their lives, he decided that this kind of microlending could make a difference in a poor nation like Bangladesh. Although local bankers initially turned a deaf ear to his plea, he eventually convinced one bank to let him start a pilot program in a nearby village. The idea worked. Poor borrowers repaid their loans at a rate equal to or better than conventional bank clients, and Yunus took a leave of absence from the university to devote himself full-time to building this new enterprise.

Recruiting female borrowers was a formidable challenge in an Islamic culture in which women are discouraged from handling money or even leaving their homes. But despite the challenge, the number of people enrolled as members in the bank leaped in three years from 290 to 24,128. In 1983, Grameen finally became an independent bank. Yunus and his hardworking young staff built the bank through a slow process of trial and error. Yunus studied the mistakes of conventional loan operations and decided that the large repayments they required often led to borrowers missing payments and eventually defaulting. He determined to make repayments so small—an initial system of daily repayments has now been modified to weekly—that his clients would barely miss the money. He also decided to base his transactions on human trust rather than the complicated legal contracts relied on by traditional banks. "Grameen would succeed or fail depending on the strength of our personal relationships," he says.

One of the most important innovations, though, was his requirement that clients organize themselves in small groups. The group must approve the loan requests of each member, so peer pressure and support keep individuals from falling into a problem situation. A clear vision of unlimited human capacity—and the good that can come of empowering women—made him the hero of the 1995 U.N. Conference on Women in Beijing. His work transformed the lives of people like Anwara, a mother of four who struggled to feed her family on her husband's meager day-laborer wages. She used her $50 Grameen loan to buy a cow, sold milk to repay the loan, then bought another cow, raised a calf, and sold it. Continuing like this, she eventually made enough money to buy a small farm. Anwara has managed to educate all her children and is sending her daughter to college.

Whereas others trying to solve the problems of poverty target the evils of capitalism, he wants "to face the issue as it is rather than be biased by one kind of philosophy or doctrine." In his view, the free-enterprise system "is most conducive for eliminating poverty. Each human being has the potential of unlimited capacity. Once you tap that, you bring enormous energy and ingenuity into the marketplace. The more people who are better off, the more they demand. It's good for business." Yunus believes that traditional approaches to poverty—socialism, welfare, charity—sap human ingenuity. Excited by the potential of information technology to bring much-needed improvements to the poor villages of the world, he now lends some of his longtime customers that indispensable tool of the modern entrepreneur: the cell phone. In a country where less than 1 percent of the population has access to telephones, possession of a cell phone is not just a status symbol but an important source of power. A person with a cell phone "is no longer isolated. She receives respect from other people because now she's in control of information," he says. Internet access for local villagers—tying them to ideas, education, and jobs—is another of Yunus's goals.

Yunus lives modestly with his wife, Afrozi (chair of the physics department at a local university), and daughter in a three-room apartment just a short walk from his office, in the Bangladeshi capital city of Dhaka. Born to relatively prosperous parents who worked hard to ensure that all of their nine children got a college education, Yunus saw his mother help the poor people who came to their door. He was also profoundly influenced by India's independence movement in his early childhood and later was caught up in the idealism accompanying Bangladesh's independence from Pakistan. "We in the movement looked forward to changing the lives of extremely poor people," he says.

Ironically, the man who has offered millions of people a hand out of poverty attributes his success to an ability to think small. "I avoid grandiose plans," he says. "I start with a small piece that I can do. I go to the root of the problem and then work around it. It's building brick by brick. I try not to throw away any ideas in the beginning because they seem silly or ridiculous. Maybe later those ideas will become more relevant and important."

RESOURCES

www.grameen-info.org

Banker to the Poor, with Alan Jolis (Public Affairs, 1999)

The Price of a Dream: The Story of the Grameen Bank and the Idea that is Helping the Poor to Change Their Lives, by David Bornstein (Univ. of Chicago Press, 1997)

Give Us Credit, by Alex Counts (Times, 1996)

Grameen Bank and Muhammad Yunus, ed. Muhammad Badrul Ahsan (Mowla Brothers, 1996), a collection of interviews given by Yunus to the national and foreign press in Bangladesh.

SEEING GREEN

ENVIRONMENTAL ACTIVISM has been a fact of American life since the first Earth Day in 1970, when millions of people—from kindergartners to nursing home residents—proclaimed their commitment to protecting the planet. Through the years we've seen spectacular improvements—waterways cleaned up, smog reduced, new wilderness areas and national parks established. Yet many ecological problems stubbornly persist. While recycling programs have blossomed across the land, our production of garbage increases every year. While Lake Erie and the skies above Los Angeles are clearer, we now face a daily bombardment of chemicals in our air, water, and food.

Government, industry, and many environmentalists have focused on the easiest challenges, the ones that can be remedied with new technology or stepped-up enforcement of existing laws. These are considerable achievements, and they were accomplished over the objections of many who argue that clean air and water aren't worth the cost. But now we must tackle the more difficult dimensions of the environmental crisis—the problems that demand changes in how we run our economy, produce our food, live our lives, and think about the world. Global warming , for example, can't be reversed just by putting scrubbers on a few smokestacks. The solution depends upon worldwide efforts to develop safer sources of power, curtail our use of cars, and address inequalities between rich and poor nations.

The men and women profiled in this chapter urge a shift in thinking about the natural world, moving from just fixing particular environmental problems to a broader ecological perspective that recognizes the world as a web of connections, all of which affect each other. The fix-it approach, still touted by some environmental organizations and most political leaders, focuses on symptoms, while ecological or green thinking zeroes in on root causes. Trying to solve environmental issues in isolation from the whole fabric of nature and society often means transferring problems from one spot to another or ignoring important dimensions of the problem.

Take automobile pollution as an example. For many, the answer is new gizmos to minimize auto emissions, along with more research on electric cars. To the green way of thinking, this misses the point. Reducing emissions is little help when the number of miles North Americans drive each year races ahead. And the manufacture and use of electric cars create twice as much hazardous waste as that produced by conventional ones. Plus, cleaner engines will not affect some of the automobile's most vexing side effects: sprawling cities, unsafe streets, proliferation of pavement.

The real solution is to rethink transportation. Better bus and train service is an obvious necessity, but so is careful attention to how our communities are shaped. Fostering compact neighborhoods, where we can meet most of our needs within walking distance, would not only reduce air pollution but also bring more conviviality into our lives. Who knows?—this might be a step toward slowing down the frantic pace of our society.

That's a common theme in this chapter: The big changes necessary for the Greening of America will improve the quality of our lives—not condemn us to the grim future of scarcity that is often portrayed by journalists and politicians.

"It doesn't work to just tell people to get out of their cars," notes Bill McKibben, author of *The End of Nature.* "Instead, we need to encourage them to ride a bike. It's elegant. It's fun. It makes you feel better." Theodore Roszak, a Berkeley novelist and historian, takes this view one step further with his pioneering work in the field of ecopsychology, postulating that living in harmony with nature is a key element of human contentment.

Author and activist Charlene Spretnak makes a compelling case for the importance of a spiritual dimension to green thinking. Physicist Fritjof Capra believes that a basic understanding of ecological wisdom is as important to children as reading or math, and he has devised an ecoliteracy curriculum now used in numerous Northern California schools. Virginia architect William McDonough also finds profound lessons in the natural world, which he draws upon for his award-winning buildings and industrial products. Californian Paul Hawken, a founder of the Smith & Hawken garden tool company, believes that paying attention to the ecological dimensions of commerce could radically transform business into a force for preservation rather than exploitation. Meanwhile, Santa Fe-based activists Kenny Ausubel and Nina Simons have launched the bioneers movement based upon the idea that natural living systems can be a model for a whole new generation of earth-friendly technologies and public policies.

Technology of a different sort captures the attention of San Francisco activist and former ad man Jerry Mander, who documents the way we welcome questionable inventions into our world with little thought of their long-term consequences. Theo Colburn, a zoologist with the World Wildlife Fund in Washington, D.C., raises similar questions about the thousands of untested chemicals that are released into our environment, some of which she believes disrupt our reproductive and endocrine systems. Hazel Henderson, who has established a research center in St. Augustine, Florida, is a longtime advocate of alternative technologies, as well as new economic models that take environmental destruction into account. Edward Goldsmith, an eminent English environmentalist, believes stopping the globalization of our economy is the most important step in protecting the environment. The late Donella Meadows, a biophysicist and environmental studies professor at Dartmouth, took a hard look at economics, too, pointing out that the earth cannot sustain current levels of industrial growth much longer.

A common theme among all these thinkers is that nature itself can provide lessons in healing the Earth, and in overcoming problems that we may not immediately think about as environmental concerns. Careful attention to how an ecoystem works—the vital network of links between disparate species—offers insight into how human organizations develop and also how they break down. Recognizing that interactions within a company or a community resemble the dynamics of a rainforest or backyard garden lets us break out of the modernist mentality that the world functions like a machine. Instead of reducing everything to the smallest possible parts in order to understand how a system works, paying attention to how the parts as a whole connect with each other brings fresh insight to numerous fields. The importance of a diversity of voices and ideas in an organization, for instance, becomes clearer when we realize that diversity is a key component of a thriving ecosystem.

Whether it's William McDonough's award-winning office buildings or Fritjof Capra's management seminars or Theo Colburn's breakthroughs in public health, this ecologically inspired approach to understanding our world may yield more positive and enduring results than all the high-tech breakthroughs and market miracles touted in the headlines each week.

—Jay Walljasper

KENNY AUSUBEL &
NINA SIMONS

"We face an extraordinary opportunity for the restoration of our home, the earth, and with it our spirit. As the Age of Biology beckons, it is not only the threat of destruction that propels us forward. Instead, the bioneers show, it is the inspiration and magic of life that will finally prevail. As we gaze in the mirror of history, we find ourselves facing the inescapable knowledge that we inhabit one planet, indivisible and imbued with intelligence and spirit. . . . What the bioneers seek is nothing less than a new covenant with nature, the "re-enchantment of the earth". . . . The signs are everywhere, when you know where to look. Like grass sprouting through the pavement, the force of life is reclaiming the earth and infiltrating culture the moment the machines go silent and their guards fall asleep. As environmental restoration emerges as a major global industry, the bioneers act as beacons guiding the dynamic transition to a future environment of hope."

YOU WOULDN'T expect an ecological restoration movement to be led by two New York City natives, where dirt is something you wipe off your apartment windows, not where food is grown. But Kenny Ausubel and his wife and business partner, Nina Simons, both found their way from the streets of New York to the high country outside

Santa Fe. In that rich, back-to-the-earth atmosphere, they emerged as social entrepreneurs and founders of the bioneers movement, which brings "biological pioneers" together to share ideas for restoring ecological balance to the earth.

Ausubel and Simons want to explore the interconnectedness of nature and cultures to restore what biologist E. O. Wilson describes as an affinity of life for life. These bioneers—a term they coined for those people working in such diverse fields as restorative agriculture, social activism, anthropology, and medicine—call for "a declaration of interdependence," a new Age of Biology based on the principles of kinship, diversity, interdependence, cooperation, and community. "To make the successful transition to a restorative, just, and healthy world, we need to understand ourselves as biological creatures at one with the diversity of all life," says Ausubel. "When we can truly see this unity and interdependence, we will find nature to be forgiving, generous, and resilient."

The annual Bioneers Conference in San Rafael, California, which Ausubel and Simons started in 1990, brings together people like John Todd, an expert in using plants and microbes to clean up toxic sites, master organic gardener Gabriel Howearth, environmental writer Bill McKibben, and Mohawk Indian healer and midwife Katsi Cook to discuss issues like heirloom gardening, global warming, and restoring indigenous herbalism and midwifery. The conference's positive atmosphere is an antidote to the hopelessness that sometimes paralyzes environmental activists.

"I don't think that the world will be saved by a sense of threat," says Ausubel. "Each of us has a spark of life inside us, and our highest endeavor ought to be to set off that spark in one another. Most environmentalists have come to the movement out of reverence, not fear. Actually, what we have to learn is to hold the reverence and the sense of threat in our minds at the same time." A serious, mysterious illness that could never be diagnosed but gave him symptoms of a stroke struck Ausubel while in college at Yale. He moved out West to try to restore his health. As he slowly healed, Ausubel started to write and to study filmmaking. "[The illness] sent me off in a whole other direction with my life," he says. "It's like a lightning tree: If the lightning doesn't kill the tree, then it grows in another direction."

Some time later his mother called to tell him that his father had cancer. Within six months, his father was dead. It was a traumatic and shocking experience—one that made him take notice when he came across an article about a man named Harry Hoxsey, who for twenty-five years was attacked by the American Medical Association for offering what he claimed was an herbal cure for cancer. Intrigued by the story, Ausubel went on to produce an award-winning feature-length documentary called *Hoxsey: How Healing Becomes a Crime.* Around this time he met Simons socially, and she became interested in the project and helped promote the film.

"It was a very challenging sell," says Simons, "being a documentary, the *D* word, about cancer, the *C* word. We were actually very successful at it. We went back to New York and promoted the film at several major film festivals, and several of the New York critics gave it favorable reviews. Somehow Hoxsey was just a magical glue for us, so we began really collaborating there."

Another film project, about a Native American planting project at New Mexico's San Juan Pueblo, introduced them to people who were collecting heirloom seeds to help preserve biodiversity. "I thought I was at San Juan Pueblo to make a film," Ausubel says. "As it turned out, I was there to found a seed company." In 1989, he cofounded Seeds of Change, a company that sells seeds from heirloom and traditional native plants, many of them threatened with extinction, to tens of thousands of backyard gardeners across the United States and Canada.

"Some 27,000 species a year are being lost," Ausubel says. "Experts predict that, within the next fifty years, we will lose at least a quarter of the 250,000 known plants. Just in the brief period of the 1970s and 1980s, a thousand independent seed companies have been purchased by giant chemical and pharmaceutical corporations," which then drop the plants from commerce because they can't be patented. Simons devised a marketing campaign for the fledgling company and helped make it the biggest mail-order organic seed company in the country.

For Ausubel and Simons, the business was a way to preserve not just biodiversity but also the irreplaceable cultural record that seeds represent. "Some indigenous people believe that the voices of the ancestors speak through the seeds," explains Ausubel. "In turn, each time you plant a seed, you become an ancestor for the generations to come. It's a very profound spiritual transmission."

Ausubel and Simons left Seeds of Change in 1994 due to a different vision from the firm's other owners, but they're continuing to promote native foods, most recently with a project to market Iroquois white corn with native American leader John Mohawk. Ausubel, who works with many progressive companies and nonprofit endeavors, continues to set an example of socially responsible entrepreneurship. "It seems to me that the real culprit in the imbalance of wealth and destruction of the environment is the corporate model," he says. "Corporations have been taking and taking, and there is no concern about giving back anything."

Simons is co–executive director of the Collective Heritage Institute, which conducts public education, creates model environmental restoration projects, and produces the Bioneers Conference. She recently introduced into the conference an emphasis on "restoring the feminine"—a spirit "that has been suppressed for, depending on the culture, anywhere from five hundred to five thousand years," she says. "The worldview that I hope for and believe in is that we can all learn to hold a balance of the masculine and the feminine within ourselves, learn to develop better relationships between men and women, and demonstrate that balance in terms of our power structures and how we govern ourselves."

For her, too, the move from New York, where she studied theater and then mysticism at the Arica School, to Santa Fe was a life-changing decision. "I began to connect with my own idealism about my work," she says. "What has emerged as my vision involves the profound sense of gender imbalance in the world. If we could change this one thing, it would have an impact on everything that's wrong. Not only in the external world but within each one of us and the masculine and feminine energies we carry." In Simons view, our culture's rediscovery of the marvels of nature and the basic life-giving properties of heirloom plants represents a revival of the long-suppressed feminine force in the universe.

Today Ausubel and Simons get energy and inspiration from daily walks with their two dogs in the woods around their Santa Fe home. "It's easy to get bogged down in the circumstantial and mundane, but if we connect to our passion, that in itself will be regenerative. We won't have to wait for the energy; it will be there," says Simons. "But how do we connect to that passion? We need to pay 'exquisite attention,' as a friend of mine says, to our responses to things—we need to notice what makes our flame glow brighter. Then we'll be able to catch the flame and feed it."

SELECTED RESOURCES

Bioneers,
  Collective Heritage Institute
  901 W. San Mateo Rd., Suite L, Santa Fe, NM 87505
  www.bioneers.org

When Healing Becomes a Crime: The Amazing Story of the Hoxsey Cancer Clinics and the Return of Alternative Therapies (Healing Arts, 2000)

Restoring the Earth: Visionary Solutions from the Bioneers (H J Kramer, 1997)

Seeds of Change: The Living Treasure (HarperSanFrancisco, 1994)

Hoxsey: How Healing Becomes a Crime (Realidad Productions, 1987), video

FRITJOF CAPRA

"The environment is no longer one of many 'single issues': it is the context of everything else—of our lives, our businesses, our politics. The great challenge of our time is to build and nurture sustainable communities—social, cultural, and physical environments in which we can satisfy our needs and aspirations without diminishing the chances of future generations."

Dharma World

IN A SURPRISINGLY high-profile career as a scientist and ecological philosopher, Fritjof Capra has boldly questioned many fundamental assumptions of our civilization. Nothing should be automatically accepted as accurate, he maintains, not even our "belief in the scientific method as the only valid approach to knowledge." He refutes the prevailing views that the universe functions like a mechanical system, that society is a competitive struggle for domination, and that human advancement is the outcome of economic and technological growth.

For a trained theoretical physicist—with a Ph.D. from the University of Vienna, postdoctoral work at the University of Paris, and research positions at Berkeley and Imperial College in London—such ideas are almost unthinkable. But Capra is not your average physicist. Physicists seldom write best-selling books like Capra's *The Tao of Physics,* an investigation of the common ground between scientific breakthroughs and Eastern mysticism. Physicists seldom make movies, as Capra did with *Mindwalk,* an exploration of social and scientific values starring Liv Ullmann, John Heard, and Sam Waterston. And physicists almost never admit that fields other than physics are more central to our understanding of the universe.

"I found that the paradigm of physics was not appropriate to discussions of social phenomena, economics, or even biology," he says. "The study of living systems—ecology—is really the appropriate concept for talking about broader issues. Ecology is a more practical framework. It's the principle underlying all subjects.

"The essence of an ecosystem is that all things are interconnected," he continues. "Understanding ecosystems, therefore, leads us to understanding relationships. Understanding relationships is not easy for us, because it runs counter to the traditional scientific enterprise in Western culture. In science, we have been taught to measure and weigh things. But relationships cannot be measured and weighed; they need to be mapped."

Adopting ecology rather than physics as the central model of scientific inquiry leads to an entirely different view of the world. Because ecology is the only branch of science that focuses on relationships, Capra says, it can help us understand a forest, a city neighborhood, and even global problems in new ways. Instead of breaking things down to examine their most minute parts, we can study how these parts work together as a whole: the relationships between different species, between activity on the street and crime, between the status of women and birth rates.

Capra explores the far-reaching implications of this thinking in his best-selling book, *The Turning Point,* which became the basis for *Mindwalk*. Both book and movie make the case that an emerging paradigm is replacing—or at least competing with—the view of the universe that has guided our civilization since the days of Sir Isaac Newton and René Descartes. Rather than believing our universe is an inert chunk of matter, this new view looks upon it as a living system that resembles an ecosystem more than a machine. In *Mindwalk,* these ideas are at the heart of an invigorating debate between a fictional physicist, politician, and poet who bump into each other at a French monastery, at a time when all three are searching for answers to the confusion in their lives.

Capra made the film with his brother, Bernt, a Hollywood production designer whose credits include *Baghdad Cafe* and *What's Eating Gilbert Grape?* Nine years after its theatrical release, *Mindwalk* still does a brisk business in video stores—a sign that such seemingly abstract ideas strike a chord with many people.

But the audience Capra seeks now is the preteen set. The Center for Ecoliteracy, which he founded in 1995, is working in twenty schools throughout Northern California, training teachers and administrators both to teach ecology "and to orient the whole school curriculum around the principles of ecology," he says. "You can make a link between ecosystems as communities of animals and human communities. In fact, the principles of ecology can be seen as the principles of community."

Hands-on experience of nature is emphasized, with each school growing its own garden or working to restore a local creek. Capra says surveys of students show these activities to be one of the most popular school activities—second only to field trips.

In management seminars, he brings a similar message to business and civic leaders: "We live in a time of unprecedented technological and social changes. And yet, our business organizations seem to be incapable of dealing with change. CEOs have reported that up to 75 percent of their organizations' efforts to change did not yield the promised results. I have come to believe that one of the main reasons for this paradox lies in our outdated perceptions, our mechanistic view of the world."

Human organizations need to mirror natural organisms, Capra counsels. He points to the work of Chilean neuroscientists Francisco Varela and Humberto Maturana, who define organisms as living networks that respond to disturbances in their environment. "This insight contains profound lessons for how to facilitate organizational change," Capra says. "In the mechanistic model of management, a lot of energy and money are spent on trying to sell new organizational structures, designed by outside experts, to the people who work in the organization, and this very often creates resistance."

Resistance is simply a natural response to outside disturbances, says Capra. It's not a problem; it's actually the source of creativity. The lessons of living systems suggest that if people within an organization participate from the very beginning in plans for change, their natural creativity—applied through the networks of relationships and spontaneous cycles of conversation and feedback that form the real core of any organization—might be directed toward making improvements, not resisting someone else's vision of change.

This all seems a long way from the rigorous scientific training Capra underwent as a student in the 1960s. What happened? A lot of things, he replies in a calm voice with traces yet of an Austrian accent.

His imagination was expanded as an undergraduate by reading Werner Heisenberg, the Nobel-laureate founder of quantum physics, who was pondering many of the same questions in the 1920s and 1930s. Then, while teaching in California, he met Gregory Bateson, Margaret Mead's husband and a seminal figure in establishing new paradigm thinking. He also cites the 1960s themselves as influential in pushing him to look beyond the narrow confines of physics to probe the inner workings of the universe. "My first postdoctoral job was in Paris in 1968," he recalls, "and I got very much politicized. I was a research physicist by day and sort of a hippie by night. I was hanging out with artists, writers, and filmmakers, and many of them were interested in Eastern mysticism. That struck me as a whole new way to understand the world."

He also points to his childhood in wartime Austria, when both of his parents were Nazi supporters, as another influence on his thinking. The remorse his family felt when they discovered the full extent of Nazi horror instilled in him a deep lesson about questioning authority. During the war, his family moved from Vienna to his grandmothers' farm near the Slovenian border. The economic hardship of the war years meant they had to raise most of their food themselves—a firsthand experience of the principles of ecological sustainability. But Capra recalls that he and his brother had an oddly bucolic existence—running barefoot all summer, gorging themselves on fresh fruits and vegetables, learning the names of trees.

The natural world remains a source of solace and joy for Capra, and with his family he often hikes through the hills near his home in Berkeley or heads to nearby beaches or mountains. He also finds inspiration and relaxation in meditation, and in another passion not generally associated with ecological philosophers: jazz. "Charlie Parker, Thelonious Monk, Miles Davis, John Coltrane, Horace Silver—that's what gives me goosebumps," he says.

Jazz may be the perfect metaphor for Capra's view of the universe: The improvisations of a jazz performance—one player picking up the thread of another's notes and making something entirely new of it while at the same time keeping in sync with the whole band—echoes his ideas about living systems.

SELECTED RESOURCES

Center for Ecoliteracy
  2522 San Pablo Avenue, Berkeley, CA 94702
  www.ecoliteracy.org

The Tao of Physics (Shambala, 2000; fourth edition)

Mindwalk (Paramount, 1990), video

The Web of Life: A New Scientific Understanding of Living Systems
  (Anchor, 1996)

The Turning Point: Science, Society, and the Rising Culture
  (Simon & Schuster, 1982; Bantam, 1983)

THEO COLBORN

Maclean's Magazine

"Every one of you is carrying at least five hundred measurable chemicals in your body that were never in anybody's body before the 1920s. We have dusted the globe with manmade chemicals that can undermine the development of the brain and behavior, and the endocrine, immune, and reproductive systems—vital systems to assure perpetuity. We are just beginning to understand how these chemicals can affect our children's ability to learn, to socially integrate, to fend off disease, and to reproduce."

WORLD WILDLIFE FUND senior scientist Theo Colborn has been called the Rachel Carson of the 1990s. Just as Carson sounded the alarm about pesticides' effects on wildlife in her 1962 book, *Silent Spring,* Colborn brought to the world's attention in her 1996 book, *Our Stolen Future,* an alarming message about the threat of endocrine disruptors—synthetic chemicals that imitate or block hormones and are linked to a range of health problems in animals and humans. The book, which was translated into eighteen languages, gained wide media attention with its warning of a threat to human health and reproduction.

Colborn's groundbreaking work challenges the fundamental assumption that has long guided public policy: the assumption that there's a level of exposure to environmental toxins that is safe. "All it takes is a tenth of a trillionth of a gram of free hormone to change how the individual develops in the womb," she warns. "That's equivalent to one second in 3,169 centuries. Anyone who can say that low-dose exposure is not harmful doesn't understand how natural systems function."

Endocrine disruptors are found in PCBs, dioxins, furans, and some of the billions of pounds of pesticides and plastics that are produced each year. PCBs and dioxins have been strongly linked to diminished IQ, learning problems, and attention deficit in children of mothers who have been exposed. Some scientists think endocrine disruptors may also play a role in the alarming increase in breast cancer (up 4 percent per year from 1982 to 1987) and prostate cancer (up 126 percent from 1973 to 1996)—although Colborn is quick to point out that proper studies to prove or disprove that link have not yet been done. And some suspect a link to lowered sperm count: Danish researchers have found a 50 percent decline in sperm count between 1938 and 1990—a period that coincides with the dawn of the chemical revolution.

Colborn, tall, thin, and energetic even in her seventies, made her discovery while she was working for the Conservation Foundation (later to merge with the World Wildlife Fund) on a book about the Great Lakes. "Project coordinator Richard Liroff whipped in front of me this proposal for a book on the Great Lakes and asked me to do the science," she says. "As I read the proposal, I knew there was a story there." She began poring over hundreds of studies indicating wildlife and human problems around the Great Lakes. Eagles were failing to reproduce or were giving birth to chicks with beaks so deformed they couldn't eat. Minks were having smaller litters and then would practically stop reproducing altogether. Women who lived in the region were having children with neurological development difficulties.

Colborn began to synthesize the work of hundreds of studies from such diverse fields as zoology and toxicology, and noticed a pattern that others had overlooked. The affected people and animals had regularly eaten Great Lakes fish contaminated with PCBs, pesticides, and dioxins. Yet there was no evidence of the increased cancer that most researchers had expected to see in such cases. "Within eight to ten months, I had tripped on something I couldn't believe—and didn't want to believe— was true," she says.

Her startling discovery was evidence of a pattern of problems not in exposed adults, but in their offspring. Scientists researching herring gulls nesting in polluted areas had found male gulls with feminized sex organs. In 1991 Colborn and zoologist John Peterson Myers brought together twenty-one scientists to compare notes at a conference in

Racine, Wisconsin. It was the first time most of them had talked to each other, and as they shared their respective pieces of the puzzle, they came to an inescapable conclusion: Hormone-disrupting chemicals were affecting unborn humans and wildlife.

Although scientists and the chemical industry agree that the evidence raises serious questions and merits study, funding has been a struggle. "There's been no money and no research directed toward this because it's not cancer," Colborn says. "It's very difficult to get funding for endpoints as ephemeral as intelligence and behavior. Yet if you look at these studies and the number of children who are exposed, you realize this is not a rare event. It isn't like cancer, where maybe one in a thousand or a million will get cancer. This is a population-wide event."

What is needed, says Colborn, is to phase out production of these chemicals to keep them out of our air, water, food, and household products. Two months after *Our Stolen Future* was published, Congress passed the Food Quality Protection Act and Safe Drinking Water Act, which require the Environmental Protection Agency (EPA) to develop measures designed to test chemicals for endocrine effects. The EPA appointed Colborn and thirty-eight other scientists, including industry representatives, to draw up a list of synthetic chemicals for which screening tests should be devised. The scientists named fifty-one chemicals. Colborn, who has a direct, disarming manner, is working hard to convince the chemical industry to pay to develop these standardized screening tests. She is also trying to get companies that use endocrine disruptors in their products—such as computers, cars, home products, clothing, and toys—to help foot the bill.

Colborn's unlikely projectory from mother and pharmacist to world-renowned scientist was launched by her decision to go back to school while middle aged, earning a Ph.D. when she was fifty-eight. After years of running three pharmacies in northern New Jersey, she and her husband had moved to a Colorado farm. Colborn became active in local debates over water pollution and use of limited water resources, which were heating up in the West. "There were a lot of people in Washington making decisions about water in the West with a vision of rivers like the Hudson or the Potomac as what the Colorado River looked like," she says. "But where I lived, you could wade across it." She decided to go back to school in order to be a more effective activist. Although she intended to return to her Colorado home and work as a pharmacist, she discovered a love of research that lured her to the University of Wisconsin at Madison to pursue her Ph.D.

"The moment I decided to go back to college and learn more about water quality and what we were doing to our natural systems, everything just seemed to fall into place," Colborn says. "Hundreds of people befriended me, gave me a bed when I was traveling across the country, gave me the encouragement I needed to keep going. My children told me, 'You can't quit now just because you're having trouble with your thesis committee.' There was always someone there, facilities there, support there—things just kept coming out of the woodwork."

Today she divides her time between a simple apartment in Washington, D.C., where she works at World Wildlife Fund, and a small house in the tiny Colorado town of Paonia. "I walk out my back door and go to the library, the post office, the grocery store, the doctor's office," she says. "Everything's there." She spends her free time listening to classical music and jazz, reading, and watching birds in the Colorado mountains.

Considering the dire consequences of her findings, she's amazingly upbeat. "The hopeful thing is that this is not genetic damage," she says. "Even people who have problems because of their mothers' prenatal exposure can have normal children themselves. The beauty of it is that we can turn this thing around"—she pauses for a moment, then continues thoughtfully—"but unless our funding for research shifts in the early part of the next century from remediation and cures into the mode of prevention and precaution, we're not going to make much progress."

The challenges are great. But with Theo Colborn on the case, bringing scientists together and talking reason with legislators and industry leaders, they seem somehow surmountable.

SELECTED RESOURCES

Our Stolen Future: Are We Threatening Our Fertility, Intelligence, and Survival?: A Scientific Detective Story, with a new epilogue by the authors, Theo Colborn, Dianne Dumanoski and John Peterson Myers (Dutton, 1996; Penguin, 1997)

EDWARD GOLDSMITH

Robert Barber

"Nearly everyone today seems to accept the preposterous view that modern man is actually 'improving' the world—making it a better place to live in—against all the evidence to the contrary that is accumulating by the minute."

PROTESTS IN EUROPE against genetically engineered food imports and McDonald's-ization of their food traditions are dismissed by U.S. officials as displays of "irrational fear." But to British ecology activist Edward Goldsmith, the articulate son of a wealthy hotelier and brother of the late billionaire financier, Sir James Goldsmith, they are a rare act of rationality in an age of senseless ecological destruction. While other environmentalists work with McDonald's to develop more earth-friendly packaging, Goldsmith decries the ecological abuse committed by powerful multinationals and calls for no less than their destruction. "You can't share this planet with colossal transnational corporations," he says. "There is not even the remotest possibility. They control the USDA, they control the FDA, and they control your government and ours. We have got to get rid of them. We have got to break them down."

Uncompromising language is a trademark of the charming, Oxford-educated founding editor of the influential British journal *The Ecologist*. He inspired activists to launch the Green Party in Britain with the 1972 publication of his manifesto, *Blueprint for Survival*. In a special issue of *The Ecologist* (September/October 1998), he took on genetically modified food and its number one purveyor, Monsanto Corporation. The British printer, fearing a lawsuit by the chemical giant, destroyed the entire print run—an event that only served to underline Goldsmith's vision of corporate power run amok. Two articles in the issue went on to win citation in Project Censored's "Ten Most Censored Stories" awards.

The next big battle, says Goldsmith, will be against the creation of a unified world economy. In a 1996 book he edited with Jerry Mander, *The Case Against the Global Economy,* he warned against the dangers of global economic agreements like those pursued by the World Trade Organization. These trade agreements, which promised wealth and prosperity for all, have instead unleashed unprecedented power for the faceless, pro-corporate World Trade Organization to override local and national regulations—laws, Goldsmith points out, that were designed to protect the "interest of labor, the unemployed, the poor, and, of course, the environment." What's more, the globalists' goal of transforming 5 billion Third World citizens into Western-style consumers is "totally unsustainable."

What should we do? In his 1992 book, *The Way: An Ecological World-View,* Goldsmith holds up ancient and indigenous societies "as models of the principle of living in harmony with the natural world." Whether it was the worldview of the Hindu Dharma, the ancient Chinese Tao, or Native Americans, traditional cultures have "emphasized two fundamental principles that necessarily underlie an ecological worldview," he writes. "The first is that the living world or ecosphere is the basic source of all benefits and hence all wealth, but will only dispense these benefits to use if we preserve its critical order. From this fundamental first principle follows the second, which is that the overriding goal of this behavior pattern of an ecological society must be to preserve the critical order of the natural world or the cosmos that encompasses it."

Goldsmith argues that the only answer to ecological dilemma is a dramatic reform of industrial civilization: "The environmental problems we face today, such as the destruction of the world's forests, the drainage of its wetlands, the pollution of its groundwaters, rivers, estuaries, seas, the erosion, the chemicalization of just about everything, and of course global climate change—the problem that dwarfs them all—are not unrelated. They . . . are the inevitable consequences of the policies that we apply, all of which are designed to contribute to the overriding policy of promoting the massive, uncontrolled economic development that we identify with progress. Unfortunately, we believe quasi-religiously in

economic development. It underlies the worldview of modernism—of
the secular religion of today—which is unfortunately the source of all
our problems."

Unless a drastic reversal of this trend occurs, he predicts an imminent end to life as we know it: "If current destructive trends persist for
long enough, and they do not have to persist for very long—forty, fifty,
sixty, at the most one hundred years—our ever more degraded world
will have ceased to be capable of supporting complex forms of life,
including man. Fortunately, it is unlikely that these trends will continue that long. Something will bring them to an end. But, let us be
realistic: that something, whatever it is, will almost certainly not be an
intelligent and responsible decision taken by politicians anywhere in
the world. . . . In effect, we have delegated the solution to our problem to disasters of different sorts: economic disasters, social disasters,
and of course ecological and climatic disasters, if the others do not
occur first."

Few people speak out about this impending ecological cataclysm,
Goldsmith writes in *The Way,* because it threatens our deeply
entrenched way of life: "This general human tendency to regard the
only world we know as normal is reflected in just about all the disciplines that are taught in our schools and universities."

To restore our relationship with the natural world, he advocates a
return to local, self-sufficient communities—something Goldsmith
himself practiced for seventeen years when he lived on a small farm in
Cornwall with five to six colleagues and their families. "If today's policy is to create a global economy totally controlled by vast,
uncontrollable, and irresponsible transnational corporations catering for
the world market," he says, "we must instead create a network of loosely connected local ecologies, largely in the hands of small and medium
companies that are integral parts of local communities and societies, and
for whom they feel deeply responsible."

In an age when the pronouncements of free-market economists,
high-tech zealots, and giddy globalists are accepted as absolute truths,
akin to the ten commandments or laws of physics, Goldsmith's defiant
and wise admonition that there is another way for our civilization to
develop—a way that has guided human cultures for most of our history—stands as a radical and refreshing challenge to conventional
wisdom. This man, who doesn't care if anyone thinks his ideas are out-
rageous, actually offers a thoughtful message about restoring sanity to
our relationship with the natural world.

SELECTED RESOURCES

The Ecologist
  Unit 18, Chelsea Wharf, 15 Lots Road, London SW10 0QJ,
  United Kingdom
  www.theecologist.org

The Way: An Ecological World-View (Univ. of Georgia Press, 1998)

The Case Against the Global Economy and for a Turn Toward the Local,
  ed. with Jerry Mander (Sierra Club, 1996)

Blueprint for Survival,
  with the editors of *The Ecologist* (Houghton Mifflin, 1972)

PAUL HAWKEN

"Commerce can be one of the most creative endeavors available to us, but it is not worthy of business to be the convenient and complicit bedfellow to a culture divorced from nature. While commerce at its worst . . . appears to be a shambles of defilement compared to the beauty and complexity of the natural world, the ideas and much of the technology required for the redesign of our businesses and the restoration of the world are already in hand. What is wanting is collective will."

A T THE CENTER of Paul Hawken's vision for Western capitalism is a simple idea: "The ultimate purpose of business is not . . . simply to make money," he writes in *The Ecology of Commerce,* "nor is it merely a system of making and selling things. The promise of business is to increase the general well-being of humankind through service, a creative invention, and ethical philosophy." To achieve those principles, Hawken advocates retooling government and business so that, simply put, sustaining our environment comes first.

Like many business success stories, Hawken's is a rags-to-riches fairy tale. Born in San Mateo, California, in 1946, he grew up in poverty. "My parents divorced, and the three kids were split off to different relatives," he says. "I ended up practically on welfare, and remember a Christmas dinner of cornflakes and warm powdered milk." At twelve, young Hawken moved in with his alcoholic father. Two years later, he ran away from home, dropped out of school, and lived on the streets, bouncing from one basement crash pad to the next.

"I was rebellious," he says, "a hell-raiser. But I don't think that part of my life should be romanticized. There is nothing romantic about it." Nevertheless, his hardscrabble youth gave him a drive for success. At the age of twenty-one, he joined up with a group of advocates for macrobiotics—a whole foods diet that places a special emphasis on fruits, vegetables, and grains grown in the region where you live. It was an exotic idea at the time, but working with macrobiotics pioneers Aveline and Michio Kushi, Hawken turned a small Boston co-op into the natural-foods giant Erewhon Trading Company.

After starting or salvaging a number of other businesses, Hawken eventually hit the jackpot with Smith & Hawken mail-order import company, selling British-made gardening tools. The prominence and profitability of the company gave Hawken a very credible platform from which he could offer his outspoken views on the ecological and ethical dimensions of business.

His ascendance hasn't been without controversy. Hawken earned a reputation as a difficult boss, leaving a trail of disgruntled detractors in his wake. The "Smith" of the Smith & Hawken empire is one of them; the partnership disintegrated with enmity on both sides. "If someone says to you that I'm not perfect," he allows, "I say 'hear, hear, that is exactly right.' I am not special." But even the naysayers grant that Hawken's message about environmentally sound business practices is both powerful and influential.

To the rest of the world, Hawken's success proved that ecological responsibility can coexist with a healthy profit margin. Smith & Hawken pioneered responsible ecological practices, from recycling office products to supporting tree farmers who employed sustainable practices. But Hawken himself was not so sure. As his company's success grew, he became more convinced that his best efforts fell short of environmentally sound practice. "The recycled toner cartridges, the sustainably harvested woods, the replanted trees, the soy-based inks . . . were all well and good," he muses, "but basically we were in the junk-mail business. All the recycling in the world would not change the fact that doing business in the latter part of the twentieth century is an energy-intensive endeavor that gulps down resources." Something more revolutionary was in order.

In 1991 he left Smith & Hawken and has devoted the past decade to discovering what a sustainable business revolution might look like.

Gradually he came to realize that even the very best corporations, the standard-bearers for the socially responsible business movement, were on a path to global destruction. "If every company on the planet were to adopt the environmental and social practices of the best companies—of, say, The Body Shop, Patagonia, and Ben & Jerry's—the world would still be moving toward environmental degradation and collapse," he says.

In fact, the entire notion of socially responsible business is, at heart, a "have-your-cake-and-eat-it fantasy," says Hawken. In part, that's because doing business—any business—exacts an environmental cost. "A jet flying across the country," he elaborates, "a car rented at an airport, an air-conditioned hotel room . . . all cause the same amount of environmental degradation whether they're associated with The Body Shop, the Environmental Defense Fund, or R. J. Reynolds."

Socially responsible business is a band-aid approach, Hawken says. Instead, he argues for a wholesale change in business and government. His central idea is what he calls a "declaration of sustainability," which translates into a seemingly simple paradigm shift from industrial and economic procedures that ignore waste and the environment to new practices that take these factors into account. He advocates nothing short of replacing our "throw-away" culture.

Many of Hawken's reforms depend on the actions of government. The federal tax code should be rewritten, Hawken urges, because it offers few financial incentives for businesses to implement environmental programs, and in fact allows write-offs for fines and legal fees incurred by continuing pollution. The corporate charter, which gives states the power to incorporate businesses—and terminate them—provides another tool for political leaders to bring about a sustainable economy. "Incorporation is not a right," Hawken argues, "but a privilege granted by the state." And this privilege should be contingent upon good environmental practices.

Hawken has ideas for businesses, too. Chief among them is a shift to production systems that mirror the cycles of nature. "Linear industrial systems take resources, transform them into products or services, discard waste, and sell to consumers who discard more waste when they have consumed the product," he writes. Instead, businesses should adopt cyclical systems in which waste from one process is the raw material (or food) for another. Hawken calls this a "closed-loop system." In a sustainable economy, for instance, companies wouldn't sell big-ticket items like automobiles and televisions. Instead, manufacturers would license their goods to consumers, who would return them after they were used up for the company to reuse parts and recycle material—a practice already in place in some countries. "If a company knows that its products will come back some day," he says, "it creates a very different approach to design and materials."

Citizens and shoppers play a major role in the creation of a sustainable economy, according to Hawken. When people gain the power to affect a corporation, such as revoking its charter or pressing lawmakers for green taxes, companies will quickly become more responsive to the health and welfare of the citizenry. And of course there's the power of the dollar: Don't buy from bad companies, he counsels, but "write and tell them why you won't. . . . Talk, organize, meet, publish newsletters, boycott, patronize, and communicate."

All terrific ideas, you say, but how can we really hope to stop the polluting, profit-worshipping machine and turn it around? Hawken doesn't have any simple answers to this one, but he's convinced it can happen: "This [a sustainable economy] is not Arcadian; it's as plausible as the system that precedes it," he insists. Indeed, unlike our current economic model, an ecologically healthy economy is less artifical and contrived since it is created on the basis of "the natural, everyday acts of work and life accumulat[ing] into a better world as a matter of course, not a matter of altruism."

And Hawken promises that because a sustainable economy should be "fun and engaging, and strive for an aesthetic outcome," there's great potential for millions of everyday Americans to get behind the idea. Environmentalists have been quick to take the moral high ground and ally themselves against aesthetics (excepting the aesthetic of natural wilderness). As a result, the green movement is often seen as puritanical, anti-fun, and backward. But, as Hawken points out, "good design can release humankind from its neurotic relationship to absurd acts of destruction."

SELECTED RESOURCES

Natural Capitalism: Creating the Next Industrial Revolution (Little, Brown, 1999)

The Ecology of Commerce (HarperBusiness, 1993)

Growing a Business (Simon & Schuster, 1987)

The Next Economy (Holt, Reinhart, and Winston, 1983)

Seven Tomorrows: Towards a Voluntary History,
   with James Ogilvy and Peter Schwartz (Bantam, 1982)

HAZEL HENDERSON

"Don't wait for anyone to deputize you or authorize you or empower you. You have to just start out with yourself—where you are, what you know, what your impulse is—and put one foot in front of the other."

A HIGHLY INFORMED adversary to the uninspired thinking that goes on inside most corporate boardrooms and government agencies, Hazel Henderson is both tireless and formidable in pointing out what's wrong with current global trends and how things could be made better for the great majority of people on this planet. While she doesn't promise easy solutions, she offers eminently practical proposals to problems often dismissed as unsolvable. Sensing the rising power of multinational corporations thirty years ago, she was one of the first activists to articulate a vision of socially responsible business. Now she promotes an innovative plan to reduce military violence around the world through a security insurance agency, in which nations would be assured military assistance from U.N. peacekeeping forces if they were attacked.

Many of her suggestions are targeted right at the heart of the economics profession. "Economics, far from being a science, is simply politics in disguise," she declares. The numbers that economists use to justify various courses of action—whether regarding employment, environmental risk, or global trade—are simply cooked up to create desired outcomes, then served with a garnish of empirical evidence.

"Poor people don't hire economists," she notes. "It's banks, brokers, governments, and large corporations."

And Dr. Henderson has impeccable credentials to back up her outspoken views—although not the sort you'd imagine. She's never enrolled in an economics course, nor even attended college. Her doctor of science degree from Worcester Polytechnic Institute is honorary—an acknowledgment of decades of research, analysis, and activism. It's on the basis of work in the real world—where she's shown how mainstream economists routinely overlook significant factors like environmental health, community, and the needs of developing countries—that she has been selected as an adviser to the National Science Foundation and the U.S. Office of Technology Assessment, appointed to the Horace Albright Chair in Conservation at the University of California at Berkeley, and named a fellow of the World Business Academy. Futurists Alvin and Heidi Toffler, authors of *The Third Wave,* have said, "At a time when conventional economics is tottering into senility, a handful of thinkers are forging imaginative alternatives. Hazel Henderson is among the most eloquent, original—and readable—of the econoclasts."

Henderson's suggestions how government and business should conduct themselves—which she has shared in numerous books and a column syndicated to four hundred newspapers in twenty-seven languages—comes from sharp observation of how things really work. Her classrooms were the seaside English village where she grew up, the Caribbean islands where she spent five years as a "hotel bum" working at various resorts, the American Airlines ticket counter at Rockefeller Center, and the environmental movement. Growing up eating most meals out of the family garden was a basic course in ecology, she says, and the hotel work offered her the chance to observe and meet promient people in many fields. The advantage of working for an airlines was free travel all over the world. She contends that those experiences served her better than Oxford or Georgetown would have. Never schooled in the narrow methodology of academic disciplines, her mind has been free to make connections and draw conclusions that elude many of her highly degreed peers. "If I had been inducted into Economics 101," she laughs, "I would have suffered brain damage."

Henderson's education has been gloriously multidisciplinary. She read books on any topic that engaged her imagination and sought meetings with anyone who could help her uncover anything she wanted to know. So it's no surprise that her work weaves in and out of many fields. "Practicing social innovator" is the term she uses to describe what she does, adding, "I always knew I was unemployable, so I invented my own job and have been self-employed for thirty years."

Henderson started down this career path in the early 1960s as a young mother concerned about the effect air pollution was having on her daughter and other children in New York City. She helped start a group called Citizens for Clean Air, and in a short time convinced local television stations to report the air pollution index in their nightly newscasts. Then she persuaded an ad agency to create TV commercials (for free) drawing attention to pollution, and talked television stations into running them (for free). These were astounding accomplishments in an era when littering was still viewed as socially acceptable behavior. "I absolutely did not know that it couldn't be done," she says. "I thought, well, they're nice people. They'll see the merit of this, and one thing kept leading to another."

In a 1968 appearance on NBC's *Today* show, she talked about coming oil shortages and the obsolescence of internal combustion engines, both radical ideas at that time. Next, she teamed up with Ralph Nader on a campaign to make General Motors more accountable to the public. "I remember going down to Washington to testify before Congress," she says, "and here I am against this guy from General Motors. He is being paid hundreds of dollars an hour and I'm having to pay my own train fare and hire a baby sitter. I began to learn an awful lot about the system."

Meditating on how much power corporations can wield against citizens in political fights, Henderson hit the books to learn more about how business operates. Her research led her to write an article about the social responsibility of business, a rarely discussed concept back in 1968. "I decided that I should send it around to various business magazines just for the hell of it," she says. "I sent a copy to *Harvard Business Review*, to the only woman I could find on the masthead. I actually rolled on the floor in delight when they said they were going to run it."

Offers to speak at business schools came pouring in—usually from students, not faculty—and Henderson found herself a spokeswoman for ideas that within a few years emerged as a new social movement. "I could not have really imagined the speed with which the whole idea of socially responsible business and ethical investing could have taken hold," she says. In 1982 she was asked to join the advisory council of the Calvert Social Investment Fund, one of the first socially conscious investment firms. "That was a big leap for me to be actually identified with an asset management company. I had always been on the other side, a Nader Raider type of person, but I thought if I am going to stay in this capitalist country, I have to figure some market strategy of pursuing my goals to make society more ecofriendly."

Working with the Calvert Group, she created a set of economic and social measures based on her Country Futures Indicators, to gauge the quality of life in various societies around the world. The Calvert-Henderson Quality-of-Life Indicators are designed to be a more accurate alternative to the widely used gross national product, which charts economic growth with no distinction between what's good or bad for the people in a country: Economic activity that increases because of an AIDS epidemic, for instance, counts as economic growth just the same in the GNP as that created by a worthwhile new invention.

A lot of Henderson's time is now occupied with another business project, WETV, a global television network that brings programming on ecological issues, socially responsible business, and indigenous people's culture to thirty-one countries, with plans to extend that to sixty, including the United States. WETV is a partnership of humanitarian aid agencies in Canada and Europe, private investors, and citizens groups in the developing world.

She is also promoting a new idea for national security. Following the lead of Costa Rica, which abolished its military in 1948, Henderson proposes with Alan F. Kay a security insurance agency, administered under U.N. leadership, whereby nations could buy insurance policies providing peacekeeping forces and humanitarian assistance to protect them in case of attack. More of their resources could then go to meeting the needs of people rather than military spending. The temptation to invade a neighboring nation would disappear if you knew it would be protected by an international security force. The policy would require that qualifying nations pay premiums to fund the peacekeeping troops and reduce or eliminate their own armies and weapons stockpiles. As outlandish as this might sound, the U.N. Security Council has debated the idea and it has been declared feasible by the Center for Defense Information, a Washington think tank staffed by former military leaders.

Researching, speaking, teaching, and consulting on all her projects keeps Henderson on the road for almost four months out of each year, and she's always happy to get home to St. Augustine, Florida, where she moved in 1986 to be near the ocean. The laid-back town's old-fashioned amenities (it's the oldest European settlement in North America) mean that she can live inexpensively: "I sold my car as soon as I got here—you can walk everywhere in town—and I haven't bought new clothes in a decade, the town is so full of great secondhand shops. All my furniture is secondhand, too." She keeps an office in the historic heart of town, outfitted with an extensive research library, and lives on an island just a short stroll across what she calls a fairy-tale bridge. "I like to walk on the beach and do my thinking," she says. And when ringing phones, e-mail messages, and unanswered mail threaten to overwhelm her, she says, "I go to my favorite meditation place in the morning and ask the great spirit and mother Gaia, What is the best thing that I can work on today? When I come back I look at the in box and just set it aside and do something else. Otherwise you get run by the system, and the system is quite pathological."

SELECTED RESOURCES

www.hazelhenderson.com

Beyond Globalization: Reshaping the Global Economy (Kumarian, 1999)

Building a Win-Win World: Life Beyond Global Economic Warfare
  (Berrett-Koehler, 1996)

Creating Alternative Futures: The End of Economics
  (Putnam, 1978; Kumarian, 1996)

JERRY MANDER

"Technologies do act as drugs. They are what society offers to make up for what has been lost. In return for family, community, a relationship to a larger, deeper vision, society offers television, drugs, noise, high speed, and unconsciousness. These are the things that keep you from knowing that there's anything else available."

© Mikkel Aaland

THE FIRST THREE decades of Jerry Mander's life offered few outward signs of the radical thinker and activist he would become over the following three decades. You just don't expect a kid raised amidst the booming self-satisfaction of postwar suburbia—someone with an early memory of being "awestruck" at the technological wonders showcased at the 1939 New York World's Fair—to write a book entitled *Four Arguments for the Elimination of Television*. You don't expect to hear a graduate of the Wharton School of Business—and captain of the University of Pennsylvania golf team to boot—to argue passionately that the escalating power of corporations poses a menace to the world. And you don't expect a successful advertising executive—president of a company that handled prestigious accounts like Triumph sports cars, Land Rovers, and Paul Masson wine—to target consumer society as a threat not just to the environment but to human civilization as well.

But this is the path Mander has traveled, from an American Dream boyhood in a sparkling new subdivision of Yonkers, New York, to his current role as director of the International Forum on Globalization, perhaps the world's leading organization challenging the prevailing vision of a high-tech, free-market, globalized economy as the ultimate fulfillment of human progress.

"The fantasies of utopian existence promoted by proponents of the technological, industrial mode of life for the past hundred years are now demonstrably false," he says. "The system has not lived up to its advertising. Life really is better when you get off the technological-industrial wheel and conceive of some other way. It makes people happier. It may not make them more money, but getting more money hasn't worked out. Filling life with commodities doesn't turn out to be satisfying."

Mander's "some other way" began in the 1960s, when he was working as a theatrical press agent in San Francisco and teamed up with a comedy troupe to create satirical ads criticizing the war in Vietnam. These caught the eye of the legendary ad man Howard Gossage, who scooped Mander up for his agency, which Mander later headed. Mander masterminded clever campaigns to sell people on particular brands of shirts and cars and wine, but also did a lot of pro bono work on behalf of environmental groups, including a famous campaign that helped the Sierra Club save the Grand Canyon from being flooded by a proposed dam. Proponents of the dam said their plans would actually improve this natural wonder because tourists could get a closer view of the canyon walls from excursion boats. This inspired Mander to work up an ad asking, "Should we flood the Sistine Chapel so tourists can get near the ceiling?"

Working closely with and learning from David Brower, then head of the Sierra Club and later founder of Friends of the Earth and Earth Island Institute, Mander devised media campaigns that played an instrumental role in creating North Cascades and Redwoods national parks and stopping U.S. production of the environmentally damaging supersonic transport plane. In 1971, he founded Public Interest Communications, the nation's first nonprofit advertising agency, which specialized in media strategies for activist and community groups. That firm evolved into the Public Media Center, an influential player in numerous political debates, from Robert Bork's Supreme Court nomination to the abortion rights movement.

Mander is a senior fellow at Public Media Center, and he still sports the stylish, confidently creative look of a successful ad man: He dresses in dapper, well-tailored clothes and lets his hair grow into a shock of white curls that make him stand out in any crowd. Most of his energies

now go directly into political organizing: as program officer of the
Foundation for Deep Ecology, a funder of hard-hitting environmental
activism. He is also director of the International Forum on
Globalization, which brings together activists from around the world to
craft strategies for stopping environmental and human rights abuses by
multinational corporations.

Mander traces his radical critique of technological society back to
a picnic in the 1970s at Mount Tamalpais near San Francisco. "It was a
beautiful sunny day with breezes blowing, and I was watching my kids
play on a mountainside, leaping around the rocks. Then I got it that one
of them was Captain Kirk and the other one was Spock. While we were
out enjoying the sun and breezes, they were reenacting *Star Trek*. "I realized then that we were raising a generation of people who grew up
with television and are walking through the world with television as
their main mental bank of images."

The television was eventually removed from the Mander household, and he began to have serious doubts about his own role in pur-
veying these images to sell products, which influenced his decision to
leave commercial advertising. This event was also the inspiration for
Four Arguments for the Elimination of Television, a best-seller published in
1978 and subsequently translated into twelve languages. Mander notes
that in the forty years before that, not one of more than six thousand
books about television suggested that we get rid of it; critics always
advocated controlling or improving it. Expanding on the ideas of
Canadian media theorist Marshall McLuhan, Mander argued that stupid programs and silly ads are not all that is wrong with television:
Something in the very nature of the medium is altering human society and human consciousness itself. "All information was processed
through television," he says. "People's direct experience with things
wasn't as important as media versions of reality.

"I never intended at the beginning to advocate the elimination of
television, but once I started working on it I came up with hundreds of
points—personal, political, psychological, family, politics, community.
And I thought, are we better off with or without this?"

Looking around, Mander soon saw that we embrace all new technologies—cars, pesticides, computers, biotechnology, cloning—with
open arms. Manufacturers, the media, and ads tell us how miraculous
these things will be, and no one explores the downside, the unintend-
ed consequences of powerful new technologies. Only later, when the
sky is blanketed with smog, when our food is tainted, when the pace of

life has revved up to impossible levels, do we realize the full cost. An exception is nuclear power, says Mander: The bombing of Hiroshima and Nagasaki demonstrated the worst-case scenario before the PR mavens could enrapture us with visions of "electricity too cheap to meter." He envisions vigorous public debate and a democratic decision making process before any powerful new technology is unleashed.

The technology that most concerns Mander now is not machinery or an industrial process, but the economic and political system that has grown up around multinational corporations. "They can bring down nations' economies at the stroke of a key," he says. And the lightning-fast flow of information and money made possible by computers gives corporations enormous powers to defuse opponents. If workers unionize in Mexico or the Italian government enforces environmental regulations, a company can simply shift operations elsewhere.

"The net result is monoculture," he notes, "the global homogenization of culture, lifestyle, and level of technological immersion, with the corresponding dismantling of local traditions and cultures. Soon, every place will look and feel like every place else."

Equally alarming, says Mander, are international trade deals like the General Agreement on Trades and Tariffs (GATT) that dictate what laws nations can and cannot apply. The will of the people for environmental or labor or cultural protections, expressed through their democratically elected governments, can be overturned if international trade officials see a dampening effect on world trade.

You can't accuse Mander of thinking small—he's devoted his life to challenging the most powerful institutions and ideas of our time. It's hard work. To keep his spirit and energy up, he spends time, hiking and observing wildlife, most often in Point Reyes National Seashore in the Bay Area. But the outdoors has been an inspiration all along, beginning with the woods filled with deer, foxes, and owls right behind his boyhood home in Yonkers. When that special place was bulldozed in the 1950s to make way for the New York Thruway, Mander remembers, it was his first lesson that what is sold to us as progress does not always make our lives better.

SELECTED RESOURCES

The International Forum on Globalization
  1062 Fort Cronkhite, Sausalito, CA 94965
  www.ifg.org

The Case Against the Global Economy: And for a Turn Toward the Local, ed. with
   Edward Goldsmith (Sierra Club, 1996)

*In the Absence of the Sacred: The Failure of Technology and the Survival of the
   Indian Nations* (Sierra Club, 1991)

Four Arguments for the Elimination of Television (William Morrow, 1978)

WILLIAM MCDONOUGH

"Many people believe that new industrial revolutions are already taking place, with the rise of cybertechnology, biotechnology, and nanotechnology. It is true these are powerful tools for change. But they are only tools.... The model for the next industrial revolution may well have been right in front of us the whole time: a tree."

A N OFFICE complex where every worker enjoys natural sunlight and fresh air. A school building that creates more energy than it uses and purifies all of its wastes on-site. A factory that discharges water as clean as what comes in. The imaginary creations of an ecotopian science fiction writer? Not at all. They're the actual creations of Charlottesville, Virginia, architect and industrial designer William McDonough, who holds high hopes they can help direct us toward the future of modern design, high-tech engineering, and industrial production.

McDonough is no wild and woolly dreamer, but a highly practical designer whose work has been championed by the mainstream business world. *Time* magazine included him among its "Heroes for the Planet," and the White House named him the first recipient of the Presidential Award for Sustainable Development. The sunny office described above, built in San Bruno, California, is corporate headquarters for the Gap. It features huge atriums that bring natural light and air to all parts of the building, as well as a roof planted with native plants, natural air-flow cooling, low-toxic materials, sustainably harvested wood, and the second-best energy conservation of any commercial building in Northern California. Equally important, Gap's headquarters is a place where employees—from the janitor up to the CEO—like to work. It won the 1998 *Business Week/Architectural Record* Award. "This isn't a green building award," McDonough says proudly. "This is a design-for-business award."

He won this award the previous year, too, for a Herman Miller Corporation building in Zeeland, Michigan, where both office and factory-line employees work in natural sunlight. "Sixteen people who left for higher wages at another company all came back, saying, 'We couldn't work in the dark.' "

The energy-producing school building is under construction at Oberlin College in Ohio. The clean-water factory, located in Switzerland, makes McDonough-designed textiles for the SteelCase corporation. "When the Swiss inspectors got to the mill to test the water, they thought their equipment was broken," McDonough says. "It was so clean."

He's also worked for Nike, Wal-Mart, Monsanto, the Environmental Defense Fund, and the Heinz Family Foundation. He's been hired to revamp Ford's River Rouge assembly plant in Dearborn, Michigan, where Henry Ford perfected modern industrial production with the assembly line. In announcing the project, company chairman William Clay Ford Jr., Henry's great-grandson, said, "The revitalization of the Rouge complex is a terrific opportunity to demonstrate sustainability by transforming the icon of twentieth-century industrial manufacturing into the model of twenty-first-century sustainable manufacturing."

All of these projects point the way toward the next industrial revolution, in which the machine-age ideal of efficiency will be replaced by the natural world's principle of effectiveness. McDonough points to the cherry tree to explain his ideas. No one would call a cherry tree efficient—it scatters thousands of blossoms in the process of creating fruit and the hope of germinating more cherry trees. But it is effective; new cherry trees do sprout. Plus, the blossoms are beautiful to look at, delightful to smell, and do no harm to the earth. "Who would notice piles of cherry blossoms littering the ground in the spring and think, "How inefficient and wasteful'?" he asks. "The tree's abundance is useful and safe. After falling to the ground, the blossoms return to the soil and become nutrients."

This line of thinking challenges the conventional wisdom not only of the business world but also of the environmental movement. In recent years, "eco-efficiency" has become the rallying cry of many green activists. Sure, a little pollution is better than a lot, and recycling is better than throwing things away, but McDonough thinks we can do even better by looking at how natural systems operate. In a rainforest, a prairie, or a coral reef, there is no waste—one organism's waste is another's food. This is the first principle of the next industrial revolution, says McDonough.

Working with German chemist Michael Braungart, McDonough has been boldly plotting the overthrow of business as usual. They've designed yogurt cartons, running shoes, and curtains that can be used as garden mulch when you're through with them. They've created beauty aids and kids' dolls free of toxic chemicals. They advocate leasing "durable" goods like computers or cars and eventually returning them to the manufacturer so their components can be reused. Interface, the largest commercial carpet manufacturer in the world, is already adopting this idea. McDonough designed a Wal-Mart store in Lawrence, Kansas, with the right proportions and materials so that it can be easily renovated into an apartment building, and he is mapping out an Indiana housing development where suburbanites can get around without a car.

Drawing further on lessons from the natural world, McDonough outlines another principle of the next industrial revolution: Respect diversity. Plants and animals vary greatly from Borneo to Baltimore to Bavaria, and so should building materials and styles. This notion first struck him when he was working on a project in Jordan for the late King Hussein and saw the tents traditionally lived in by Bedouin families. They were brilliantly designed for a place where temperatures regularly surpass 110 degrees, using coarsely woven natural fabric that provides life-saving shade yet lets in breezes and pinpoints of light. When it rains, the fibers swell to keep the dampness out. McDonough speaks enthusiastically of what we could achieve by marrying this kind of traditional design brilliance with modern materials. "Today we can do great things with glass. Let's see how, combined, these methods can work."

The third fundamental precept of the next industrial revolution is this: Use solar power. Plants take all the energy they need from sunshine—creating no toxic air, acid rain, global warming, or nuclear waste. McDonough follows nature's lead in his Oberlin building, which will run on solar power and produce more energy than it consumes. It also will treat its wastewater with a "living machine" constructed of fish, snails, plants, and microbes by John Todd of the New Alchemy Institute.

As a student fresh out of architecture school at Dartmouth and Yale in the 1970s, McDonough designed the first solar-heated home in Ireland, though he's aiming for different results now. "People then were designing solar collectors for people to live in, instead of designing houses for people to live in," he says. "Good designers began to avoid 'green design' because it was so ugly. Now we know how to do it with grace."

McDonough traces his interest in ecological design back to a childhood in Hong Kong, where his father worked for Seagram's. "During the dry season, we'd have four hours of running water every fourth day, and we needed to save water in pots and bathtubs," he recalls. "So when we moved to Westport, Connecticut, I didn't really fit in. Other sixteen-year-olds were driving around in Porsches and I was checking faucets to make sure they weren't leaking. I never could connect with the notion of living like there is no tomorrow."

Indeed, he's been inspired by the Iroquois ethic of taking into account the next seven generations in all undertakings. That's the foundation for all the work at his architectural firm, at the industrial design firm he launched with Michael Braungart, and in his teaching at the University of Virginia. He recently stepped down as dean of the architecture school, in part to spend more time with his own next generation, an infant daughter and young son, as well as to work on an old house he bought in Charlottesville. "It's right in town, so I can ride my bike everywhere," he says. "And I'm going to make the roof absorb water. It's going to be fun." In the tradition of another Charlottesville resident, Thomas Jefferson (who designed the University of Virginia campus), he's also planning to conduct various horticultural experiments on his one-acre lot. Jefferson, too, is an influence, McDonough says, noting how the creator of Monticello understood that good design can help fulfill the promise of life, liberty, and the pursuit of happiness.

SELECTED RESOURCES

William McDonough + Partners
  410 E. Water St., Charlottesville, VA 22902
  www.mcdonough.com

McDonough Braungart Design Chemistry
  410 E. Water St., Suite 500, Charlottesville, VA 22902
  www.mbdc.com

The Hannover Principles: Design for Sustainability (Island, 1997)

BILL MCKIBBEN

"If consumer society has one Achilles' heel, it's not that it is going to destroy the earth—it is, but that's not the Achilles' heel. The Achilles' heel is that consumer society doesn't make us unbelievably happy."

© Nancie Battaglia

BILL MCKIBBEN has been taking aim at the powers that be ever since he was a teenager in suburban Lexington, Massachusetts. He spent summers dressed as a minuteman guiding tourists around the historic town green and reenacting the events of 1775, when local villagers fired upon Redcoats in the first skirmish of the War of Independence. "Maybe that accounts for my rebellious nature," he muses. "I've never had a sense there was anything un–American about standing up to power."

In outspoken best-sellers such as *The End of Nature,* a sharp warning about the consequences of environmental degradation, and *The Age of Missing Information,* a meditation on the numbing mindlessness of television, McKibben has chronicled the opening shots of another revolution no less sweeping in its challenge to the existing political and economic order—and one whose prospects for victory at the outset look every bit as slim as those of the ragtag Minute Men's chances against the military might of the British Empire.

But this battle is against the rising use of fossil fuels, the global spread of consumer culture, the titillating allure of advertising, and the unquestioned worship of economic growth. If these forces are not overcome, McKibben argues, we'll see a steady upsurge in environmental and human devastation: global warming, famine, social alienation, war, over-population, extinction of plant and animal species.

"We are in much worse shape than we were twenty years ago," he says. "You can point to all kinds of environmental successes—cleaning up the Great Lakes, cleaning up the air over Los Angeles—but it doesn't amount to a hill of beans because the system creating those problems keeps going. What we've learned in the past twenty years is that it's going to be a lot harder than we thought. The vested economic interests causing environmental impoverishment are very powerful.

"The market forces pushing convenience, individualism, and comfort are still stronger than the attraction of community, fellowship, and connection with the natural world," he adds. "This is the core of the environmental crisis and of an accompanying spiritual crisis. What we call the environmental crisis is really a crisis of desire. We're losing the battle to offer people an alternative set of things to desire. Disney and GM are creating our desires."

This revolution must be an insurgency of simplicity and elegance rather than armed resistance, says McKibben: "Our task over the next twenty years is to demonstrate that to live simply is more elegant, more satisfying, and more pleasurable than consumer society. It doesn't work to just tell people to get out of their cars to save the upper atmosphere. Instead we need to encourage them to ride a bike. It's elegant. It's fun. It makes you feel better. It's important not to say that TV will rot your brain; say instead that it's satisfying to take a walk in the moonlight."

Unlike many advocates of the simple life who think it's a fine idea for everyone else, McKibben strives to practice what he preaches. For Christmas, his family and many neighbors in upstate New York try to keep expenses to $100. But rather than letting this limit holiday festivities, he's transformed it into a celebration of a different kind of wealth. "I know what I will be doing Christmas Eve," he wrote in the book *Hundred Dollar Holiday.* "My wife, my . . . daughter, my dad, my brother, and I will snowshoe out into the woods, choose a hemlock or a balsam fir, and saw it down." And there are always presents aplenty under the tree: hand-carved walking sticks, homemade sausage, bright calendars featuring family photographs, pledges to give a back rub or stack a cord of firewood.

Discussions about curtailing consumerism and limiting growth frequently get sidetracked by prickly questions about economic justice. It's dandy for folks in Marin County or Boulder to embrace the simple life, but try selling it to slum dwellers in Latin America or peasants in Asia.

Yet McKibben believes that's exactly where this revolution is beginning. In his influential book, *Hope, Human and Wild,* he points to the
Brazilian city of Curitiba and the Indian state of Kerala as shining
examples of environmental sustainability.

Curitiba, a city of 1.5 million in southern Brazil with a per capita
income of $2,500, has much to teach Paris, Prague, and San Francisco
about urban charm and vitality. It's one of the greenest cities in the
world, with hundreds of new parks and plazas added in recent years, and
it boasts one of the best bus systems anywhere. Deciding that subways
were too expensive, the city created a network of busways—streets
reserved exclusively for buses, which means fast, convenient service for
riders. Although it has more cars per capita than other Brazilian cities,
it uses 25 percent less gasoline because people drive less. Like Rio and
São Paulo, it has sprawling shantytowns, but schools, youth programs,
community centers and daycare facilities generously funded by the city
offer a measure of hope not found in most Third World slums. And its
slums are surprisingly clean, thanks to an innovative program that offers
poor Curitibans a bag of groceries in return for each bag of garbage
they turn in to the city.

But Curitiba offers more than efficient government services.
McKibben rhapsodizes about the lively street life, cultural amenities,
and urban innovations such as a municipal skateboard ramp and
Saturday-morning art lessons where kids draw on huge sheets of paper
spread out on the city's main pedestrian street. Downtown Curitiba, he
says, "is as alive as any urban district in the world. . . . [It's] a rich and
diverse and actual place that makes the American imitations—the South
Street Seaports and Faneuil Hall marketplaces—seem like the wan and
controlled re-creations that they are." After spending a month in
Curitiba with his wife, writer Sue Halpern, and daughter, Sophie, in a
city that would be classified as impoverished by the standards of any
Western nation, McKibben wrote, "We decided, with great delight, that
Curitiba is among the world's great cities."

Kerala, a densely populated state on the southwest coast of India
with a long tradition of peasant activism, is another place that has much
to teach far wealthier societies about economics and human dignity,
McKibben says. The leftist parties that have long governed the state
emphasize fair distribution of resources over economic growth, with
impressive results. The government has boosted the prospects of poor
people through substantial land reform projects, and concentrates its
limited state budget on good schools, quality health care, and subsidies

to ensure low prices on basic food items. Despite a per capita income of $330 a year, McKibben notes, "its quality-of-life measures—infant mortality, life expectancy, female literacy rate, birth rate—are comparable to the United States'."

"In other words," McKibben writes, "Kerala mirrors the United States on about one-seventieth the cash. . . . It is a subversive fact, this little chunk of India, one that could potentially help undermine the developed world's instinctive resistance to change."

A third spot where McKibben finds hope for the future is another place that is often dismissed as poor and backward—the upper reaches of Appalachia in New England, and upstate New York. "It's the world's biggest experiment in ecorestoration," he says. "One hundred years ago it was all clear-cut; now it's a beautiful forest. Here was a place that was wasted. It was totally cleared for logs. Nature has a real ability to replenish itself."

It's where McKibben now calls home. He moved to the Adirondacks of upstate New York more than a decade ago after quitting a prestigious job at *The New Yorker*. He had been hired by the magazine's legendary editor William Shawn right off the *Harvard Crimson* student newspaper, and when new owners replaced Shawn, McKibben turned in his resignation the same day. Although raised in Toronto and suburban Boston, McKibben's passion for the wild beauty of the outdoors was instilled on family mountain climbing trips. Books, too, heightened his budding environmental consciousness. He cites Edward Abbey, Wendell Berry, and Gary Snyder as great influences, not only in understanding ecological principles, but in his own decision to become a writer.

He's become a pillar of the community around Johnsburg, New York, even if people might not endorse his views on, say, organic farming or the vacuousness of television. "My neighbors are very forgiving of my idiosyncracies. One of the best things about small town culture is that it's accepting, despite all the caricatures in the media. If you help out in the community, that's what matters."

His wife, Sue, is involved with the local library and he's part of the volunteer crew at Garnet Lake Fire Department and teaches Sunday school at Johnsburg United Methodist Church. "I'm not a particularly orthodox Christian," he admits. "We spend a lot more time on Noah than most Sunday school classes and we take a lot of hikes. I don't pretend to understand God, but I do know that one can't even begin to think about religion without spending some time outdoors."

These are the roles he plans to play in the coming sustainable revolution, in addition to writing and parenting. "Living here conspires to keep me hopeful," he says, "which is important if you're mostly writing about things like global warming."

SELECTED RESOURCES

Long Distance: A Year of Living Strenuously (Simon & Schuster, 2000)

Hundred Dollar Holiday: The Case for a More Joyful Christmas (Simon & Schuster, 1998)

Maybe One: A Case for Smaller Families (Simon & Schuster, 1998)

Hope, Human and Wild: True Stories of Living Lightly on the Earth (Hungry Mind, 1997)

The Age of Missing Information (Random House, 1992; Plume, 1992)

The End of Nature (Random House, 1989; Anchor, 1990)

DONELLA MEADOWS
(1941 – 2001)

"I am convinced that the next twenty years are it: the last chance to get a sustainable world. Shortly thereafter, at least according to the computer models, things just collapse. Industrial society goes almost into an environmental free fall. But I can be hopeful for what I have seen over the last twenty years. In 1972, for instance, when I wrote *The Limits to Growth*, I had never seen a big working organic farm. Now I've seen hundreds, and I know that we could get rid of all those agricultural chemicals and not starve, whereas twenty years ago I wasn't sure of that."

"TWENTY YEARS is roughly the doubling time of the world economy," said Dartmouth University environmental studies professor and syndicated columnist Donella Meadows, before her death of meningitis in February 2001. "That means twice the number of cars and twice the tons of coal burned. So twenty years from now, if we don't do anything, there will be twice as much pollution and drawdown of resources as today. My vision for the next twenty years is this: Let's not have the next doubling because the earth almost certainly can't bear it."

If convincing industrialists and investors as well as indigent people in slums and villages around the world to settle for less—less production, less profit, less Pepsi—sounds like an intimidating goal, keep in mind that Meadows was no stranger to controversy. In 1972 she wrote, with three co-authors, *The Limits to Growth,* a slim volume that sold millions of copies in twenty-eight languages with the message that the world economy cannot continue to expand endlessly without severe environmental strains and eventual social collapse.

"From my point of view as a scientist," she recalled, "there was nothing more stupidly obvious than to say that the earth is finite and growth can't go on forever. It was like saying the sun rises in the east. I was simply astounded at the number and power and loudness of people who wouldn't accept that."

Reflecting on that experience in her later years—she was just thirty, and two years out of graduate school at the time—Meadows was still struck by the ferocity of the attacks from business, universities, and government. "They couldn't allow that book to stand. They threw everything at it they could think of. There's a deep belief that growth is always good. I actually don't think we even needed to write anything in the book. Just the title, *Limits to Growth,* was already such an assault on the idea of industrial growth that it couldn't be allowed."

Meadows and two of her co-authors—ex-husband Dennis Meadows, a systems management professor at the University of New Hampshire, and Norwegian business executive Jørgen Randers—updated their work in 1992 using advanced computer models that create future scenarios based upon continuation of current trends in 249 different ecological, economic, and demographic variables such as global birth rates, pollution levels, and total acreage of forest. They came to the conclusion in *Beyond the Limits* that the day of environmental reckoning is closer than they originally imagined. "Things moved a lot faster toward limits than we anticipated, and some new ones have appeared, like ozone layers that nobody knew about," she said. "I now think that we are over the limits, that we are beyond carrying capacity. We are going downhill.

"I think many more people understand that now. To say the earth is finite and we cannot grow forever doesn't sound so cockeyed as it did in 1972."

Still, the new edition sparked its own flurry of outraged criticism. "We got back the same arguments as before: 'Technology will solve all our problems.' 'The price system will solve all our problems.' 'We have to grow in order to end poverty.' We've had 250 years of industrial growth. Poverty is still with us. How much growth is it going to take?

"I am very disheartened to hear the political debate just talk about growth, growth, growth, growth, and nobody stands up and challenges it. Growth of what for whom for how long, and why is that so good? Nobody can do that. You are just not permitted in the United States in the public media to challenge the basic tenets of industrialism."

But having done exactly that with *The Limits to Growth* and *Beyond the Limits,* Meadows learned about the immense power of mind-sets in dictating how people see the world and how social and environmental issues are discussed. "I put forth information that didn't fit into the 'industrial growth forever' mind-set, and they exploded at me. I started thinking, What's going on with these people?

"We all have mind-sets," Meadows said, noting that when faced with an opposing set of views about the world, we often lash out in defensive anger, focusing on the exceptions and the anomalies in order to discredit the opposing view and expose its believers as totally wrong. "Another way is to start talking about mind-sets and admit that everybody has one. Let's just assume that all individuals are reasonable, but they resist letting in information that challenges their mind-set."

Owning up to this in her own life, Meadows made a point of looking at how deeply held beliefs narrowed her thinking. For many years, she admitted, her training as a scientist prevented her from appreciating the value of spirituality. This, in spite of the fact that it was her deep emotional attachment to the prairie fields and forest preserves near her childhood home in suburban Chicago that originally sparked her interest in science. "I wanted to know how nature worked," she recalled. Her Christian upbringing came to seem foolish in light of the empirical methods of understanding the world she learned as a chemistry major at Carleton College and in the biophysics Ph.D. program at Harvard. "Scientists go through an antireligious, antispiritual brainwashing," she said. "If you can't measure it, it doesn't exist."

Ironically, the research for *The Limits to Growth*—conducted according to disciplined scientific methodology and using the most up-to-date computer modeling of the time—led to a spiritual awakening. "I was trying to deal with the terrifying futures I saw ahead," she said, "and I wanted to help steer humanity toward a more positive future, but I began to feel like a pretty frail instrument. I realized that I needed to feel a power greater than myself. Otherwise I would have just given up. I needed help."

She never became a weekly churchgoer, and when she went it was as much to sing hymns as to learn Bible lessons. But she meditated regularly, explored the teachings of numerous faiths, and spent time each day wondering about the eternal questions of the universe in her own "pretty unorthodox, quite eclectic" way.

Meadows hoped that the new emphasis on diversity in public life represents a dawning recognition that people see things in many different ways. "My greatest wish," she said, "is that I will see in this diverse world a hugely enhanced skill in dealing with diversity. I see people understanding that they have mind-sets and that other people do too, and I hope that they can get beyond them to the level where they can talk and respect each other, even though they differ deeply in their worldviews."

Meadows remembered moderating a debate about abortion at which the photos of bloody fetuses brandished by anti-abortion activists challenged her own worldview. "I still ended up pro-choice," she said, "but I ended up finding some common ground with those people. I want there never to be an abortion in the world. I'm not willing to outlaw it, but I'm willing to do all kinds of things to make sure that a woman never has to face the choice of abortion."

Reducing the number of abortions would mean wider access to birth control, good sex education in the schools, and campaigns against irresponsible sex, she said. She supported protests against oversexualized pop culture, particularly Calvin Klein ads with half-dressed teenagers in seductive poses. That's a marked change from the "If-it-feels-good-do-it" ethos of the sexual revolution that she espoused in the 1960s.

Perspectives like these found their way into her syndicated column, "The Global Citizen"—a weekly installment of fresh thinking about environmental, economic, and social issues that appeared occasionally in daily newspapers like the *Los Angeles Times* and *Philadelphia Inquirer* and regularly in a number of alternative press publications. The column was delightfully eclectic, ranging from provocative assertions that a soaring stock market is not necessarily good news to thoughtful praise for public libraries, root cellars, ladybugs, and *Pad Thai* (as representative of eco-friendly peasant food from around the world that tastes great without a lot of meat or imported ingredients). She also traveled widely as a coordinator of the International Network of Resource Information Centers, a coalition of researchers, policy makers, and activists in fifty nations who bring a big-picture perspective to issues of sustainable development and resource management.

Remarkably for someone who captured public attention with dire warnings about the future, a message many did not and still do not want to hear, Meadows did not grow discouraged. Almost thirty years later, she was still promoting sustainable alternatives to runaway industrial development and environmental degradation. What kept her going?

"Two things keep me getting up in the morning," she said. "One is utter terror. A collapse of human society would not mean just discomfort and death, but the loss of human knowledge and tradition and society, which I hold dear. This is not a feeling I really want to share with other people. It's not a very good motivator. But I also believe that the terror scenario isn't inevitable. There are strong possibilities for a way other than keeping on the industrial growth route that leads over the cliff. It's more pleasant, more humanly satisfying. It's a sustainable society, one that lives within its ecological limits. I've done the numbers. I believe it's possible for seven billion or eight billion people to live in a way that doesn't degrade the earth, in a way that meets basic human needs better than we do today—including the nonmaterial ones."

Meadows didn't just dream about a sustainable world, she lived a version of it at Cobb Hill, a new community of twenty-two families bringing vitality back to two abandoned dairy farms near Hartland, Vermont. It is a co-housing community where people live in separate solar-powered homes but engage in common activities such as weekend dinners, gardening, yoga classes, volleyball, and childcare programs. Cobb Hill encompasses a dairy farm, a maple sugar business, orchards, and organic gardens that supply many homes and restaurants in the region. Some residents make their livelihood through these enterprises, while others work off the farm. It's also the home of Meadows' Sustainability Institute, where she wrote, researched, and taught about an alternative vision of the future. Her colleagues will carry on the work.

"I spend about half my day with intellectual work and about half in physical labor, raising organic food," she said. "We create a lot of our own power, and at the same time I'm on the Internet talking with people all over the world."

Despite the enormity of environmental problems, Meadows lived in a way that supported her basic belief that people actually can make a difference in the world. Even if you never write a best-selling book, there's much to do in your own home, with your neighbors and work colleagues, in your community. Gandhi's first principle was that you don't have to go along with a society you don't agree with, Meadows reminded us. "Turn off the lights when you're not in the room," she counseled. "Buy the most fuel-efficient car you can and then work on using it as little as possible. Move near a mass transit stop and sell the car. You can get elected to local government. You can talk to people, if that's your skill. Write if that's your thing. Picket McDonald's, if that's your thing."

SELECTED RESOURCES

The Sustainability Institute
www.sustainer.org

Beyond the Limits: Confronting Global Collapse, Envisioning a Sustainable Future, with Dennis L. Meadows and Jørgen Randers (Chelsea Green, 1992)

The Global Citizen (Island, 1991)

The Limits to Growth: A Report for the Club of Rome's Project on the Predicament of Mankind, with others (Universe, 1972)

THEODORE ROSZAK

"I think I see glimmers of the great change that is demanded of us in a new quality of personality now spreading through the urban industrial societies: a demand for authenticity that breaks all the old assigned identities. Perhaps such a transformation only emerges when all the things that darken our vision have fallen irreparably apart. When I'm feeling hopeful, I refer to this possibility as "creative disintegration." The disintegration I feel sure about. All the big systems will surely come tumbling down: First World, Second World, Third World. But how creatively will we use the opportunity? I wonder, I wonder."

MORE THAN even most visionaries, Theodore Roszak evades the pigeonholes of specialty, academic field, and shorthand description. Trained as a historian, he first came to fame with a sympathetic chronicle of the dissenters and seekers of the 1960s, *The Making of a Counter Culture.* But he's come to be strongly identified with a long-term effort to reimagine the relationship between the earth and the psyche of industrialized Western humanity through the books *Person/Planet, The Voice of the Earth,* and *Ecopsychology.* And he's had time to take on computerolatry, too, in *The Cult of Information,* and the promises of an aging society in *America the Wise,* along with a host of other topics.

With this versatility, it comes as a bit of a surprise when he declares that he considers himself first and foremost a novelist. "I'm a creative writer who turned to nonfiction, not a professor who's tried his hand at novels," he insists, and his list of published fiction spans two decades, from *Pontifex* (1974) to *The Memoirs of Elizabeth Frankenstein* (1995). Perhaps, he suggests, it's best to consider him a "man of letters" in the old-fashioned sense.

The graceful phrase does capture an important aspect of Roszak's intellectual background and general attitude. Born to a working-class family in Chicago—he was the first member of his family to go to college—Roszak took a bachelor's degree from UCLA, then a doctorate in history and philosophy from Princeton in 1955.

America in the 1950s was an unpromising environment for Roszak, who had discovered and been captivated by the writings of men of letters like the anarchist poet and educational theorist Paul Goodman and visionary urbanologist Lewis Mumford. Their discontent with the vulgarities, inequities, and injustices of American society was matched by a pragmatic approach to change. "They always began with a specific problem or an issue, not simply a field, like the typical academic," he says. And their analysis and scholarship were rooted in poetic vision, as in the wider and older tradition to which they belonged: Blake, Wordsworth, Mary and Percy Byshe Shelley. The early English Romantics, with their characteristic blend of radical social thought and passionate belief in the human imagination, would continue to inspire Roszak.

Meanwhile, however, Cold War America became too chilly for Roszak and his wife, Betty. "We moved to England, and I edited a small radical publication there in 1964 and 1965," he recalls. "But then the news from America changed. Word reached us of demonstrations in Berkeley. My first reaction was, 'That can't be!'"

But, of course, the once-staid campus was aflame with the Free Speech movement and would continue as a hive of free expression and antiwar protest for a decade. "Suddenly," Roszak remembers, "the things that had concerned us for a long time were being addressed: war, peace, power, technology, the responsibility of intellectuals to think critically. It was like the French Enlightenment; there was a wonderful sense of adventure, and it launched a lot of my writing."

As his writing evolved, one characteristic thread emerged: a powerful critique of the Promethean pretensions of Western civilization, of our culture's unbridled faith in technology and technological "rationality." Too often, the rationality behind nuclear weapons, pollution, and environmental degradation looked to Roszak like (in Lewis Mumford's phrase) "mad rationality." As he took this mad rationality to task in book after book, Roszak came to pay special attention to the relationship between our minds and the planet—a relationship of essential kinship, Roszak feels, that has been distorted again and again by technological civilization. In an essay in *Ecopsychology,* he explores the biophilia hypothesis: the idea that, in sociobiologist E. O. Wilson's words, there is an "innately emotional affiliation of human beings to other living organisms."

To heal our alienation from the natural world, Roszak prescribes ecopsychology, a confluence of insights from many fields that has major political consequences. "We are living at a time when both the earth and the human species seem to be crying out for a radical readjustment in the scale of our political thought," he writes. "Is it possible that in this sense the personal and the planetary are pointing the way toward some new basis for sustainable economic and emotional life, a society . . . that can ally the innately emotional and the vastly biospheric?"

Roszak's recent book, *The Gendered Atom*—"a journey through the strange sexual subtext of modern science," as he puts it in the first chapter—adds the insights of feminism to his ongoing concern with mad rationality and its effects on our ecopsyches. For Roszak, the "rape of nature" is more than a figure of speech; it is a primal scene of sexual-environmental violation that leaves scars on our collective and individual psyches.

"Environmentalism is the most sweeping critique of industrial civilization we've ever had," says Roszak. "It's far more powerful than the ideological critiques, like Marxism. And feminism is the other great movement; it's provided more transformative power than the movements based on race, which are essentially about getting into the system." The fusion of these two great movements' lessons in *The Gendered Atom* serves as the perfect illustration for the kind of challenging inquiry that Roszak has valued most highly since the fertile tumult of the 1960s.

The sixties, of course, are long over. "What disturbs me the most in what I see around me is the lack of intellectual adventure," Roszak says. "Students these days no longer seem to want to open doors, to find the forbidden knowledge. There's a prevalence of caution. And there's less and less appreciation of the different levels of thinking. With computers, the educational system has become more and more focused on information, which is the least important level; we're losing our sense of the higher levels: interpretation, judgment, wisdom, moral choice."

And yet, the baby boom generation that forced open the doors of perception and forbidden knowledge in the sixties has one more liberating role to play: becoming old. "The longevity revolution will be the biggest cultural force in the next century," Roszak predicts. "Smaller families and longer lives mean an aging population overall, and with that comes examined experience, wisdom, and a reduced need to consume."

Aging boomers will remain in the workforce longer than their parents and grandparents, says Roszak. Many of these elders will have passed through health crises that bring them close to death and back to life—a rite of passage that will bring wisdom and focused seriousness about the remainder of life. In addition, he predicts, the growth of the caregiving professions into the most important sector of the economy will shift the axis of the culture from high-tech acquisitiveness to organized caring. ("The caregiving revolution will be the one good thing that's emerged from the twentieth century," he says.)

Roszak bids us see the years of increased longevity as a precious resource, "a cultural and spiritual resource reclaimed from death in the same way the Dutch reclaim fertile land from the waste of the sea," as he writes in *America the Wise*. "During any one of those years somebody who no longer has to worry about raising a family, pleasing a boss, or earning more money will have the chance to join with others in building a compassionate society where people can think deep thoughts, create beauty, study nature, teach the young, worship what they hold sacred, and care for one another."

SELECTED RESOURCES

The Gendered Atom: Reflections on the Sexual Psychology of Science
(Conari Press, 1999)

America the Wise: The Longevity Revolution and the True Wealth of Nations
(Houghton Mifflin, 1998)

Ecopsychology: Restoring the Earth, Healing the Mind, ed., with others
(Sierra Club, 1995)

The Memoirs of Elizabeth Frankenstein (Random House, 1995), a novel

The Making of a Counter Culture: Reflections on the Technocratic Society and Its Youthful Opposition (Doubleday, 1969; Univ. of Calif. Press, 1995)

The Cult of Information: A Neo-Luddite Treatise on High Tech, Artificial Intelligence, and the True Art of Thinking
(Pantheon, 1986; revised edition, Univ. of California Press, 1994)

The Voice of the Earth (Simon and Schuster, 1992)

CHARLENE SPRETNAK

"In this unsettling historical moment, I suggest that much of the breakdown is actually part of a bigger dynamic that has the potential to effect a profound correction of the assumptions and conditions that have led to the crises of the modern era. Numerous events and developments in nearly all fields are challenging the problematic elements of the modern worldview ... as never before. They do so not merely with complaints about what is wrong but also with fresh perceptions and creative alternatives. Suddenly new possibilities are springing to life where previously deadlock and despair held sway."

CHARLENE SPRETNAK'S road to eminence as a philosopher of women's spirituality, holistic feminism, Green politics, and anti-modernist cultural theory began with her four-year-old daughter spotting a gas station.

"We were stopped at a red light," Spretnak recalls, "and she looked over at this Mobil Oil logo, which was Pegasus, the flying horse. 'Look, Mom,' she said, 'There's a horse with wings.' 'That's Pegasus,' I replied, 'and he's from a very old story. We'll go to the library and find a book, and I'll read to you from those old myths.'"

But when she got to the library, she was sidetracked from Pegasus. "I couldn't find any versions of the Greek myths except the patriarchal ones that were negative toward women—Pandora bringing evil into the world, and all that," she says. Spretnak knew that before the era of the Olympian gods—patriarch Zeus and company—Greek religion was focused on powerful and beloved goddesses. Where were their stories?

"I got a bee in my bonnet that someone ought to reconstruct the pre-Olympian versions of the myths," she says. And so, armed only with a bachelor's degree from St. Louis University and a master's degree in English and American Literature from Berkeley, this divorced single mom and university editor (with library privileges) set out on a quest that became a major work of feminist classical scholarship.

She assembled fragments of knowledge from scattered archaeology and classical-studies sources. "I accumulated tons of file cards," she says, "and when it came time to write on a particular goddess I would gather up all her cards and meditate on her, try to be her for a few days, try to live her story. Then I would write."

This story of the genesis of *Lost Goddesses of Early Greece: A Collection of Pre-Hellenic Myths* is vintage Spretnak in its passion, intellectual daring, and determination to serve a vision of empowerment. The book launched this Jesuit-educated native Ohioan, who "never intended to be a writer, only a reader," into a career that has probed more and more deeply into the possibilities for social transformation offered by feminism, spirituality, and deep ecology—and created a political vision that's also a critique of the ideology of modernity and a defense of modernity's victims around the world.

A proud generalist, Spretnak got a thorough preparation in philosophy and intellectual history at the Jesuit-run St. Louis University. "To get a degree from the Jesuits," she says, "everyone had to minor in philosophy. They're keeping alive the humanist tradition. Being marched through the history of Western philosophy was formative in terms of cultural history. And then I loved being an English major because you get to do everything: in reading the novels or the poetry of a period, you learn the history, the sociology, the anthropology, the cultural history. What I was doing in those years of discovery was seeing that the really rich, exciting experiences blurred the boundaries."

A commitment to Green politics is central to her vision: In 1984 she was one of the cofounders of the American Greens, a coalition of state and local parties united by their commitment to environmentalism, feminism, local autonomy, community-based economics, and other nonmainstream values. She published *Green Politics: The Global Promise* (coauthored with Fritjof Capra and Rüdiger Lutz) the same year. The book was the fruit of Spretnak's interest in the pioneering German Greens, who had attained considerable political influence with their opposition to nuclear missiles and attention to ecological concerns. It was also the result of her disappointment with the paranoid way the American media were covering the movement in Germany.

"It was sensationalized as this ragtag band of hippies," she says. "The American establishment was quite threatened by the fact that the Greens wanted to pull Germany out of NATO, and this was reflected in the media. I figured somebody ought to go over there and do interviews and bring back the real story of what the Greens were up to."

Again, her characteristic boldness and sense of mission led to a book examining an important set of ideas everyone else was overlooking. But her research trip to Germany showed some of the limits as well as the promise of Green thinking in that country. Spirituality, one of her most important touchstones, was rarely mentioned. After all, the Nazis had been the last major political movement to link spirituality and the earth—with their spurious insistence that German soil was sacred. Most progressives in Germany feared invoking that specter. And the Marxist left, who initially scorned the Greens but jumped aboard their bandwagon after they did well in Germany's 1979 elections, were openly scornful of any talk of spirituality. "So I came home realizing that we could learn many things from the German Green Party, but not how to incorporate the sense that the natural world is sacred," she says. Spretnak met this challenge when invited to give the annual lecture at the E. F. Schumacher Society of America, which became her next book, *The Spiritual Dimension of Green Politics.*

The spiritual dimension is key to Spretnak because, first of all, it counters what she has called "the sterility and emptiness of life in a modern, industrialized culture," while at the same time providing a firm basis for loving and honoring the earth (Native American and other earth-based spiritualities provide examples and leadership here). "Spiritual practice also teaches us how to clear the mind of hatred, greed, and delusion," she writes, "as well as to make decisions and act in a way that's grounded. . . . A truly revolutionary Green movement must find ways to connect to the earth wisdom."

In her later work, Spretnak moved beyond feminist scholarship and Green political programs to a magisterial synthesis that amounts to nothing less than a top-to-bottom critique of modern Western culture. In *States of Grace: The Recovery of Meaning in the Postmodern Age,* she explored how the great religious wisdom traditions of the world—the "Abrahamic," or Judaeo-Christian-Islamic tradition, Buddhism, Goddess spirituality, and Native American earth wisdom— can illuminate and transform our contemporary dilemmas by reasserting connectedness—with nature, the cosmos, one another. *The Resurgence of the Real: Body, Nature, and Place in a Hypermodern World,* which she considers a companion volume to *States of Grace,* even more boldly outlined a new worldview that Spretnak dubs "ecological postmodernism."

This is not to be confused with the deconstructive postmodernism of 1980s academics, with its linguistic bias and antimaterialist assumptions. Spretnak's ecological postmodernism is a ringing alternative to the West's long-term addiction to economism, the mechanistic worldview, and the dualistic belief that there is a radical discontinuity between body and mind, humans and nature, and the self and the world. And, as the title *The Resurgence of the Real* suggests, she focuses on "the dynamic processes of the Earth community," not as a rigorously defined program, but as a web of uplifting developments that are actually unfolding today.

"There's a new, post-mechanistic sense of the body as an energy system instead of a machine," she says, and she cites the explosion of interest in alternative medicine in the 1990s, an interest that was spurred on in a big way by the medical insurance industry's realization that it could contain costs—and fend off government regulation—by getting behind low-cost alternative therapies.

"Regarding nature," she says, "the new science of complexity and other tools are showing us that nature is creative and dynamic, not at all like the mechanistic model we studied in school. It operates holistically, so the toxins and other degradations we are inflicting upon nature have rippling effects that just can't be predicted. It's so complex a balance that we should be thinking about it constantly, but it's just astounding how ecological issues are being kept off the table in every governmental capital in the world."

The third element of Spretnak's ecological-postmodern trinity is a shifting sense of place—not only the growth of community-based resistance to globalization in the developed countries, but also the more visible, headline-grabbing struggles for self-determination on the part of what Spretnak calls "the ancient nations"—from tribal groups in the United States and Canada to the turbulent emerging nations of the former Soviet empire.

All of these challenges, she asserts, add up to a significant counter-force to the crushing weight of globalized modernity, with *homo economicus*—"economic man"—at its center.

Spretnak has never let theorizing fuzz her commitment to political action. She served as press secretary for a California Green Party state-level campaign in the 1994 election. Her husband, Daniel Moses, headed the party's slate as candidate for the lieutenant governorship of California. It was not exactly fat-cat politics. "We had to borrow a single-feed fax machine," she recalls. "And I would wait until after 11 P.M., when the rates were lower, to fax all the radio and TV and print media in California." She spent the days pitching stories to reporters, who gave her about twenty seconds to hook them.

"I decided not to focus on ecology since they already knew that about us from our name," she says. So I emphasized community-based economics. 'Do you really think it's a good idea for California to bet its whole future on the export market? Wouldn't it be smarter to at least have a two-track economic development program, building up community-based economics and regional trade for California?' They'd get interested, they'd interview Daniel—and then the interview would never appear. I'd call the editor and he'd say, 'Look, lady, 98 percent of the voters vote for Democrats or Republicans, so that's who we cover.' That's how the censorship works."

Undeterred, Spretnak continues political and intellectual activism from her home in bucolic Half Moon Bay California, south of San Francisco. She writes, speaks, and acts globally. She was a member of the committee that drafted a statement of purpose for the Parliament of the World's Religions, a gigantic coming together of the world's religious bodies that had its third meeting in Cape Town in 1999. She continues to build the intellectual base of Green politics, and to watch the world for more signs of spontaneous and unstoppable transformation.

SELECTED RESOURCES

The Resurgence of the Real: Body, Nature, and Place in a Hypermodern World
  (Addison-Wesley, 1997; Routledge, 1999)

The Politics of Women's Spirituality: Essays on the Rise of Spiritual Power Within the Feminist Movement (Anchor/Doubleday, 1982; 1994)

States of Grace: The Recovery of Meaning in the Postmodern Age
  (HarperSanFrancisco, 1991)

Lost Goddesses of Early Greece: A Collection of Pre-Hellenic Myths
(Moon Books,1978; Beacon, 1992)

The Spiritual Dimension of Green Politics (Bear, 1986)

Green Politics: The Global Promise, with Fritjof Capra and Rüdiger Lütz
(Dutton, 1984; Bear, 1986)

CREATIVITY AND CULTURE

IS CULTURE the friend or enemy of creativity? What happens to Mozart's fervent, youthful creativity when it becomes a cornerstone of the classical-music establishment? For that matter, what happens to Allen Ginsberg's hairy homoerotic iconoclasm when the late poet appears in a Gap ad wearing khaki trousers? Is the so-called culture industry, from megabookstores to television to the Web, a terrific delivery system for the products of the creative spirit, or a straitjacket—or something in between?

These are questions, with many complicated, postmodern-style answers. Products of the mega-mass-culture such as on-line bookselling behemoths can put the work of an obscure poet into your hands with breathtaking speed. Cable television and the Web offer ever more rapidly specializing cultural experiences, from Korean soap operas in the rural Midwest to chat groups on French-Jewish novelists to downloadable music not sold in any store. Our technology-heavy mass culture congratulates itself on its democratizing tendencies, and there can be no question that it challenges the rigidities that we associate with high culture—racism, economic and educational elitism, stuffiness—and puts cultural riches in many hands and many hearts. Yet what price do we pay for "access"?

The creators, thinkers, and writers profiled here have different relationships to "the culture," ranging from bitter critique to savvy involvement. But all of them, explicitly or implicitly, agree that while global capitalism enjoys its victorious salad days, vital dimensions are missing from "the culture" it has created—human scale, human-heartedness, respect for irreducible difference, that X factor we may as well call the human. And in their various ways, they labor heartfully to express it. If this chapter contains no big-voiced boosters of the mass-cultural status quo—no show biz heavies or Internet millionaires—it is also free of the apocalyptic hypernegativity of the radical postmodernists. For these visionaries, "the human" is a living ideal, not a mere social construct. Living in a world of gargantuan hypermedia, they struggle, often brilliantly, to free spaces within it for those moments of human truth, brilliance, and compassion that constitute true creativity, and truly touch the heart and mind amid the roar of manufactured sensation.

For some, the main way to break the media's spell is passionate, reasoned critique. Hungarian-born George Gerbner and Estonian-born Kalle Lasn draw on experiences of cultural repression and state control in their homelands to shape a mordantly skeptical view of mass culture in the "free" world. Gerbner's decades-long critique of television began with research on the effect of video violence on children and continues as an ongoing critique of corporate control of the airwaves, which are, in law at least, a public resource. For Gerbner, the reclaiming of a truly public voice within the media is the most urgent issue in the creation of a viable modern culture. Ex-marketer Lasn's brilliant anti-advertising campaigns—commercials that question the values of commercial culture by shattering the smooth surface of half-truth crafted by admen—are just the iceberg-tip of a critique that extends deep into the modern economy.

Technoskeptic and NYU communications professor Neil Postman sees galloping technology as the most compelling product and symbol of modern society's infinite, heedless social radicalism. Its insistence on "submitting all of its institutions to the sovereignty of technology," as he puts it, leaves little room for the human and the truly creative. This conscienceless technological radicalism has turned Postman, a man of the left, into a self-described conservative. Only true conservatives (congressional Republicans and other corporate boosters need not apply) are, in his reading, still asking "retrograde" cultural questions like "What improves the human spirit?"

While Gerbner, Lasn, and Postman go after the contemporary troubles that our media-saturated and technology-worshiping culture has plunged us into, Canadian historian and critic John Ralston Saul searches across a broad historical panorama to identify the intellectual roots of the problem. Technology's cold hand is only one aspect of our general enslavement to Enlightenment rationalism and its keepers: bureaucratic, corporate, and academic elites. Efficiency, systematization, and large-scale production, the concrete products of rationalistic thinking, now hold human ingenuity prisoner, and dogmas like "market forces" turn millions into passive observers of changes that, we are told, we have no choice but to accept.

Nowhere have these dogmas, and this sense of impotence before mighty forces, been more pronounced than in the Third World, where the World Bank and its sister institutions play God over entire populations. By virtue of his nationality and his loyalty to a Latin America that he fears is rapidly turning into a mirror image of El Norte, Uruguayan prose poet Eduardo Galeano is a natural critic of the new world economic order and its effect not only on culture, but also on our consciences: "Twenty years ago, poverty was the result of injustice," he has written. "Today it is the punishment inefficiency deserves." Delving into history and myth as well as hard economics and politics, Galeano tells many stories: Latin America's victimization, the poetic richness of its culture, its many betrayals (including self-betrayals).

Galeano's fragmented, highly poetic historical texts, with their atmosphere of Latin American magical realism, are acts of resistance to the homogenizing culture of Yankee-led globalism. So, in their way, are the texts of California Chicana lesbian poet and critic Gloria Anzaldua. In the name of her own irreducible humanity and the humanity of her gay sisters of color, Anzaldua has even taken on white lesbian feminists, challenging their right to define female queerness. At the same time, this resourceful writer has portrayed her own cultural contradictions with candor, wit, and beauty.

Galeano and Anzaldua occupy a dual cultural position: the critic/artist. Concerned about some current cultural and political trends, they are also producers of art—creators who appeal to the senses and the emotions as they create artistic wholes that in many ways defy analysis, yet carry a powerful message. Visionaries of this kind are both wary and hopeful, ringing the alarm bell even as they make art that is the color of hope. Indeed, their artistic experience of embodying visions, transforming materials, and moving audiences keeps them remarkably hopeful about their ability to bring about change. Los Angeles performance artist Rachel Rosenthal hears the environmental alarm bell ringing. Reading, talking, and writing don't engage enough of the human sensorium to satisfy Rosenthal, so she uses a regal mastery of theater technique to present strange, spectacular parables of planetary danger and the disembodied intellect run wild.

Science fiction master Octavia Butler suffuses her powerful novels with a female African American sensibility and fascination with the human being in extremis. Linked in symbiotic relationships with alien monsters or trapped in apocalyptic near-future ghetto landscapes, her resilient human characters do what downtrodden people have done for centuries: create the conditions for dignified survival, or find a visionary way out to a higher plane. With Butler, critique and storytelling fuse seamlessly and the reader is not so much persuaded as transported into the very minds and hearts of people in trouble.

There is a third group of visionaries here: optimistic culture-builders who, for the most part, concentrate on the positive values they know how to advance through mastery of a medium. One of the most magisterial is Bill Moyers, the television enquirer whose probing interviews with people of spirit and substance such as mythographer Joseph Campbell and poet Robert Bly have brought to television the sort of depth and resonance that critics have long called for. A Baptist minister and former presidential press secretary, Moyers is comfortable in the realms of power as well as the realms of spirit; as he explores healing, faith, poetry, addiction, and many other subjects not amenable to sound bites, he manages a rare fusion of mass appeal and intellectual nuance.

The same could be said for pop musician and classical conductor Bobby McFerrin, who, in his quiet way, has carved out an equally unconventional niche. The jazz-trained pop vocalist, who has risen high on the charts while never losing his love for jazz and the classical repertoire, brings a winning informality to the podium. McFerrin's concert hall is a town meeting of the spirit. His goal is both a splendid performance and a meeting of souls in a spontaneous joy that melts human differences and resolves human antagonisms in ways that no argument can.

William Strickland is just as determined as McFerrin to focus his energies at the positive pole. Pittsburgh born and bred, this African American ceramicist and educator works, as we used to say, "within the system"—giving the poorest citizens of the neighborhood where he grew up the twin gifts of beauty and hope. His combination art school and vocational education center not only prepares the poor for work in the big world, but also honors them as full human beings, as creative and worthy to be touched by the spirit of art as anyone.

For Strickland, the goal of a healthy relationship between creativity and culture, self and society, is human hope, joy, and fulfillment. Futurist Barbara Marx Hubbard believes that these are the values that are going to win out—and alter human evolution in the process. According to Hubbard, the myriad unprecedented crises and challenges of our era, from potential ecocide to widespread genocide, from digital electronics to biotech, have placed the human species at a critical crossroads: oblivion or an evolutionary leap toward a new and unprecedented level of wisdom and peace. No mere dreamer, Hubbard is an activist who works hard to amass and implement practical solutions to our modern dilemmas. But her distinctive note is a cautious faith that we will make the leap into light rather than annihilation. The wisdom, energy, and passion represented in this chapter, and elsewhere in this book, offers hopeful evidence that she may be on to something.

—Jon Spayde

GLORIA ANZALDUA

Annie F. Valva

"To live in the Borderlands means to put chili in the borscht, eat whole wheat tortillas, speak Tex-Mex with a Brooklyn accent, be stopped by *la migra* at the border checkpoints."

GLORIA ANZALDUA, who describes herself as a "Chicana *tejana patlache* dyke poet and queer feminist writer," brings a poetic style steeped in Chicana history and Aztec myth to bear upon issues that are too often treated in dry theoretical terms: gender, race relations, the cultural politics of the American mosaic.

While many white feminists and theorists of multiculturalism pay lip service to "difference" and "otherness," Anzaldua lives her life on several of the most compelling fault lines of American culture: male-female, queer-straight, white-indigenous—not to mention less visible arenas of difference and struggle like the battle between macho Hispanic male culture and queer feminism, and the complex politics that separate mainstream white feminists from their sisters of color.

The borderland where Anzaldua grew up was the heavily Hispanic ranch land of south Texas, territory that is neither Mexican nor fully Anglo, though it lies inside the U.S. border. The ambiguities and uncertainties of this region inform her identity and her work. "I am a border woman. I grew up between two cultures, the Mexican . . . and the Anglo," she writes in her 1987 book, *Borderlands/La Frontera: The New Mestiza*. "I have been straddling that tejas-Mexican border, and others, all my life. It's not a comfortable territory to live in, this place of contradictions."

Many of the contradictions she faced as a child have become the subjects for her adult literary and theoretical work. Despite her fierce loyalty to her fellow Chicanas, for example, she experienced painful rejection from a traditional and conservative culture as a child. "I was 'lazy,'" she recalls. "Instead of ironing my younger brothers' shirts or cleaning the cupboards, I would pass many hours studying, reading, painting, writing. Every bit of self-faith I'd painstakingly gathered took a beating daily. Nothing in my culture approved of me."

Like many budding writers, Anzaldua turned to books and stories at a young age. "I would read in bed with a flashlight under the covers," she writes. "I preferred the world of the imagination to the death of sleep." She first made up stories to bribe her sister not to expose her nocturnal bibliophilism. Her adult writing impulse springs from a more complex source: "Living in a state of psychic unrest—in a Borderland," she writes, "is what makes poets write and artists create. It is like a cactus needle embedded in the flesh. . . . When it begins to fester I have to do something to put an end to the aggravation. . . . I get deep down to the place where it's rooted in my skin and pluck away at it . . . making the pain worse before it can get better. Then out it comes."

Anzaldua saw just three directions women in her culture could turn: "to the Church as a nun, to the streets as a prostitute, or to the home as a mother." None of the three fit. For one thing, she's a lesbian. This in itself represents a dual rebellion: against the twin concepts of women as mothers and as heterosexual servants. For another, Anzaldua was determined to satisfy her cravings for intellectual stimulation. To that end, she applied and was accepted to the Pan American University and after that to the University of Texas and the University of California at Santa Cruz for graduate work.

Along with her partner and colleague, Cherrie Moraga, Anzaldua shook up American feminism in 1981 with *This Bridge Called My Back: Writings by Radical Women of Color.* This anthology was the first substantial and widely available collection of writing by nonwhite feminists, and it subverted the white, middle-class perspective of much mainstream feminism with analysis, testimony, story, and song. It is now a staple of women's studies programs across the country.

Borderlands/La Frontera interpreted the new America of rich, unstable identities from the standpoint of Anzaldua's culturally complex but deeply rooted Chicana sensibility. A second anthology, *Making Face,*

Making Soul/Haciendo Caras: Creative and Critical Perspectives by Feminists of Color, continued to enrich and critique feminism while testifying to the brutal cost of sexism and racism in America's Hispanic lands.

What makes Anzaldua unique is the way she infuses social and political struggle with joy, energy, and compassion. "If you aren't willing to listen to the Other, the one who is different from you—because you fear that person or what she or he represents," she says, "you'll pay for it. The monster that you're projecting on to the other person will get bigger and more terrifying, because your fear will feed it. The monster you've created isn't going to go away—it's going to go on tripping you up until you deal with it."

These convictions, applied to her own life, make for a remarkable absence of dogmatism and inform her delight in playing with difference as well as analyzing and "theorizing" it. While she was teaching Chicano studies, feminist studies, and creative writing at several colleges, she also wrote a complex and poignant memoir, poetry, short stories, and unclassifiable works that combine all of the above. Anzaldua has developed a powerful theory of personal and social creativity rooted in the Aztec myth of Coyolxauhqui, the moon goddess whose brother, Huitzilopochtli, dismembered her and turned her into a sacrifice.

"In taking the risk to make a work, to write that poem or story or theoretical piece," she explains, "you may feel like the moon goddess— like you are jumping off the temple steps or off a cliff. You land at the bottom and you're broken in pieces. At this stage your work is shit, it doesn't say anything. But the next step in the creative process is picking up the pieces and moving them around—restructuring that broken body of Coyolxauhqui. You don't put her together in the same way; you end up with something new, and something has changed in you because of going through this struggle. You end up not quite the same person that you were. And the viewer or reader of your piece also undergoes a change of consciousness, moving from a before to an after."

Borrowing an Aztec term, she calls that traversal the *nepantla* stage—"between the worlds." Anzaldua sees what's happening in our country, and even the world, in the same way: passage through a stage of being pulled apart. "We're trying to recompose the nation—recreate it," she says. "A person who is undergoing therapy for a trauma like incest or assault is doing the same thing, and so is a mathematician or a scientist trying to figure out new theories."

She arrives at a self-identity by a similar route. In addition to the literal cultural incongruities she faces in her daily life, Anzaldua is interested in the symbolic aspects of the borderland. In that symbolic arena she is able to find strength and wholeness that emerge from the fractured pieces of her identity: "The new mestiza copes by developing a tolerance for contradictions, a tolerance for ambiguity. . . . She learns to juggle cultures. She has a plural personality, she operates in a pluralistic mode. . . . She turns ambivalence into something else."

This "something else" is what Anzaldua calls the mestiza consciousness. It is not merely a culture built out of varied pieces, nor a "balancing of opposing powers," but a state of "continual creative motion," in which the contradictions themselves—the constant, surprising juxtapositions of cultural fragments—produce creative energy.

A "massive uprooting of dualistic thinking" (white-colored, male-female, gay-straight) is, Anzaldua says, "the beginning of a long struggle . . . one that could, in our best hopes, bring us to the end of rape, of violence, of war."

RESOURCES

Interviews/Entrevistas, ed. AnaLouise Keating (Routledge, 2000)

Borderlands/La Frontera: The New Mestiza (Spinsters/Aunt Lute, 1987; 1999)

La Prieta (Aunt Lute, 1995)

"Theorizing Lesbian Experience," *SIGNS: Journal of Women in Culture and Society,* special edition, coeditor (18:4, 1993)

Friends from the Other Side/Amigos del otro lado (Children's Book Press, 1993)

Making Face, Making Soul/Haciendo Caras: Creative and Critical Perspectives by Feminists of Color, ed. (Aunt Lute, 1990)

This Bridge Called My Back: Writings by Radical Women of Color, ed., with Cherrie Moraga (Persephone, 1981)

OCTAVIA E. BUTLER

When I began to do a little public speaking, one of the questions I heard most often was "What good is science fiction to black people?" . . . What good is any form of literature to black people? What good is science fiction's thinking about the present, the future, and the past? What good is its tendency to warn or to consider alternative ways of thinking and doing? What good is its examination of the possible effects of science and technology, or social organization and political direction? At its best, science fiction stimulates imagination and creativity. It gets reader and writer off the beaten track, off the narrow footpath of what "everyone" is saying, doing, thinking—whoever everyone happens to be this year. And what good is all this to black people?

Lauren Olamina, the teenage heroine of Octavia Butler's 1993 novel, *Parable of the Sower,* is a visionary, a prophetess, and a twenty-first-century Moses. Born into a hellish Los Angeles where feral dogs roam the streets, homeless people wander in rags, and every house that hasn't been burned or pillaged is surrounded by high defensive walls, Lauren is protected by her Baptist minister father and his flock, an ad hoc (and well-armed) community that sticks together for mutual protection.

Convinced that she's an empath, that she can feel the pain of others, Lauren struggles with the horrors that surround her, sustained mainly by a personal faith she comes to call Earthseed. Earthseed's central doctrine is a paradoxical conception of God as both all-powerful and curiously malleable, or as Lauren puts it in a poem: "God is Power— / Infinite, / Irresistible, / Inexorable, / Indifferent. / And yet, God is Pliable— / Trickster, / Teacher, / Chaos, / Clay. / God exists to be shaped. / God is Change."

When horrible violence invades her enclave, Lauren sets out into the scary wider world with a small band of followers, preaching the gospel of Earthseed, which combines despair and hope, and includes the promise of salvation and new life in space—on other worlds.

The fifty-four-year-old Butler shares some characteristics with Lauren Olamina: She's female, African American, and a lifelong Southern Californian. She's also the only established African American female science fiction writer. These attributes are important to Butler because they speak for her uniqueness of vision and approach, but they shouldn't be allowed to suggest that her main significance is ethnic, historical, or limited to a genre: She is simply one of the strongest writers in the United States today.

Unlike Lauren, Octavia Butler is not in the market with a new faith or worldview; she's a quiet and acerbic witness to the modern world who uses the resources of science fiction to explore issues that resonate with her: family and its pains and blessings, relationships between the powerful and the powerless, and what it means to feel alien.

Her most famous short story, the Hugo and Nebula Award–winning "Bloodchild," is an unforgettable tale of the intimate, edgy relationship between a group of earthling colonists on an alien planet and the caterpillarlike beings—the Tlic—who rule the planet. Over years of wary interaction, a symbiosis has been established: the Tlic choose earthling children and use their bodies to incubate Tlic eggs. In a master stroke, Butler depicts the relationship between an aristocratic female Tlic and the human family of her chosen (male) egg-host not as violent and horrible, but as intimate, even warm—the wary affection between a reasonably kind mistress and her servants.

This is Butler's way of incorporating ideas into her work—smart, sidelong, bold without being obvious. And always, there's the down-to-earth-sense of social reality that underlies the otherworldly details. "One of the things that no one ever says about 'Bloodchild,' " she says, "is that it has to do with paying the rent."

Paying the rent wasn't always easy for Butler's mother, who raised her on the sparse takings from minimum-wage jobs in Pasadena during the 1940s and 1950s. "I badgered my mother for a typewriter when I was ten," Butler recalls, "and she bought me one. It was a big expense in those days, and she got criticized for it." But Butler's mother had long been nurturing the literary passion in her shy only child. Having brought home books discarded by her employers, she would read part of a story to little Octavia—just enough to pique her interest—then hand the book to her: "Here's the book. Now you read."

"She gave me the idea that reading was something fun instead of something teachers force you to do when you would rather be doing something else," Butler says. "One of the worst things that happens to kids now is that they are told reading is for their own good, like really bad-tasting medicine."

Butler's favorite girlhood reading was fairly typical—fairy tales and myths, then horse stories, then romances. But when she was twelve, the science fiction bug bit her (Butler told an interviewer that her first exposure to science fiction was by way of a movie called *Devil Girls from Mars*). "Science fiction let me go anyplace I wanted," she recalls. "And it gave me an excuse to learn all kinds of things: space, other planets, how plants work—you name it. It's the same now. When I'm reading a book, any book, I'm not goofing off, I'm working."

Butler attended Pasadena City College and Cal State–Los Angeles, with some not-for-credit night-school writing courses at UCLA. But what really propelled her into the writing life was Clarion, a six-week Los Angeles writing course that Butler calls "SF writers' boot camp—a different SF writer or editor teaching every week, plus drop-ins, like agents. I sold two stories to writer-editors at Clarion."

A parade of eleven novels and a short-story collection followed. The much-lauded "Xenogenesis" trilogy (*Dawn, Adulthood Rites, Imago*) bristles with Butler hallmarks: an apocalyptic scenario (Earth after nuclear devastation), a resourceful African American heroine, and the paradoxes of relationship across seemingly unbridgeable divides. The Oankali, an advanced extraterrestrial race, rescue as many earthlings (Terrans) as they can and hold them in suspended animation in their vast spaceship. They restore earth to minimal livability and are ready to revive the Terrans and return them to their planet. The repellent, tentacled aliens revive earthwoman Lilith Iyapo and choose her to serve as intermediary between them and their human beneficiaries.

Perhaps the most important Butler hallmark in the Xenogenesis books, as elsewhere, is the balanced, nuanced complexity of the issues in a genre that often limits itself to adolescent simplicities. The brilliant

Oankali are hideous to look at; their rescue of earthlings comes with a price tag (they mean to interbreed), and Lilith Iyapo eventually finds herself locked in a struggle with them as well as with her fellow earthlings, who see her as a traitor.

Butler doesn't offer grand solutions to earth's complex problems, but she does have some suggestions. "If I were God for a day," says this accomplished creator of apocalyptic scenarios, "I would make sure everyone had a conscience. Whatever other mental or emotional difficulties they had, they'd have a conscience and be a little more far-sighted. That would mean that we would advance technologically a bit more slowly. . . . We would look before we leapt.

"Right now, for instance, we look at the erratic weather and say, Gee, the weather is funny. We look at the sea-level rise and say, Isn't that interesting. We look at the fact that the ice sheets north and south are smaller than they used to be and say, Isn't that fascinating. Some of us know that all of these things, and quite a few more besides, are related. But nothing is being done."

For now, what Butler is doing is crafting fiction. She writes so early in the morning that her workday is done by 8:00 A.M. Then she takes phone calls, runs errands, and prepares for the next morning's encounters with friendly/frightening aliens, strong but struggling heroines, and a planet that doesn't seem to know how to save itself.

SELECTED RESOURCES

Wild Seed (Doubleday, 1980; Warner, 2001)

Lilith's Brood (Warner, 2000); contains *Dawn, Adulthood Rites,* and *Imago* (orig. pub. 1987–1989)

Parable of the Talents (Seven Stories, 1998; Warner, 2000)

Parable of the Sower (Warner, 1993, 2000)

Bloodchild and Other Stories (Seven Stories, 1996)

Kindred (Doubleday, 1979; Beacon, 1988)

Survivor (Doubleday, 1978)

Patternmaster (Doubleday, 1976)

EDUARDO GALEANO

Amilear Persichetti

"In politics, as in everything else, I am always seeking a perhaps impossible but desirable communion between what I think and what I feel . . . to discover a language able to express at once emotions and ideas, what Colombians in the small towns on the Caribbean coast call the "feel-thinking language." It's a language which is able to reunite what has been divorced by dominant culture, which is always breaking in pieces everything it touches. You have a language for ideas and another language for emotions. The heart and the mind divorced. The public speech and the private life. History and present, also divorced."

A T THIRTEEN, Uruguayan writer Eduardo Galeano was publishing cartoons in a socialist newspaper. At twenty-one—after unsatisfactory stints as a sign painter, factory worker, bill collector, and bank teller—he became editor-in-chief of a political journal. Soon he published a novel and became director of a Montevideo daily newspaper before writing *Open Veins of Latin America,* which has sold more than a million copies around the world.

The book emerged from three months of furious effort and nonstop coffee, always between seven in the evening and six in the morning because he was working two jobs during the day at two publishing houses. Writing it was an act of revenge, he claims: "When I was a boy,

I swore I'd get back at . . . the history courses that condemned me to remember dates and names my mind refused to store."

Open Veins was a new kind of history: lyrical, accessible to the general reader, and passionate in its denouncement of the tyrants—both domestic and foreign—that stunted the growth of democratic societies in Latin America. "You cannot confuse a dwarf with a child," he told interviewer David Barsamian of *The Progressive.* "They have the same size but they are quite different. So when you have all the technocrats speaking about developing countries, they are implying that we are living in a sort of infancy of capitalism, which is not true at all. Latin America is not a stage on the way toward development. It is the result of five centuries of history."

The book's frank demands for justice—and its overwhelming success—eventually led to Galeano's jailing in what he realized was a preview of Uruguay's 1973 right-wing coup. Upon being released, he fled to Argentina, where he founded the cultural journal *Crisis,* which, he recalls, "lasted forty lovely months until a coup d'état swept Argentina too. My name turned up on a list of those condemned by the death squads. I don't like being in jail, but I like being dead even less. I had no choice but to go to Spain, and there I lived in exile for eight years."

Being ousted from his native continent, he says, left him feeling "broken in pieces. . . . I tried to create a structure from all the broken pieces of myself, like putting together a puzzle. *Days and Nights of Love and War* resulted from this open, free conversation with my own memory, as I tried to understand what had really happened and to guess who I really was."

Explaining what motivates him in this memoir, which weaves his own story into a magical yet terrifying narrative of Latin American politics, Galeano writes, "One writes out of a need to communicate and commune with others to denounce that which gives pain, and to share that which gives happiness. One writes against one's solitude and against the solitude of others. . . . To awaken consciousness, to reveal identity—can literature claim a better function in these times?"

While he has been forced to to flee national boundaries because of his strong political views, he crosses traditional literary frontiers by choice. "I don't believe in the borders that separate literary genres," he declares, "and I enjoy violating them. I also love to make fun of the customs officers who keep imagination and reality apart and raise a wall between literature called intimate and what they call socially concerned."

In the trilogy *Memory of Fire,* he offers a sweeping account of life in the Americas, from the stories of native peoples to the economic and political mythology of modern times. Packed with emotion, these books blend the magical mood of Latin American literature with Galeano's meticulous historical research, creating a year-by-year poetic pageant of the events, large and small, that shaped our hemisphere: 1492, Columbus; 1795, a slave uprising in Havana; 1950, Rita Hayworth in Hollywood. All three volumes—*Genesis, Faces and Masks, Century of the Wind*—are written in the first person, underscoring Galeano's belief in "memory not as an arrival place but a point of departure, a catapult throwing you to present times, allowing you to imagine the future instead of accepting it."

Literature, for Galeano, is not simply a matter of ideas and artistry. He wants to record the essence of human experience, etched with blood and tears into our souls. His deep commitment to the people of Latin America, expressed in decades' worth of work, earned him in 1999 the prestigious Lannan Prize for Cultural Freedom, which carries a $250,000 award plus substantial contributions to three cultural institutions of his choosing in Montevideo, Uruguay, where he still lives and where he finds inspiration in long walks along the La Plata River. "Walking, I am, and walking, I write," he states. "The words move, they walk inside me, while I walk at the edge of the city where I was born, where I live."

Galeano's commitment to justice arose in his teens, replacing the deep, mystical Catholic faith that guided him through childhood but no longer made sense in his mind. It was at this time when he first began writing. Art had been his first passion but recognizing his technical limits at drawing he began to experiment with expressing the images in his mind through words rather picture. In many cases, he designs his own books—incorporating the visual elements of type, illustration, and white spaces as an integral part of his work. He even cites Mexican artist José Guadalupe Posada as an aesthetic influence along with Uruguayan novelist Juan Carlos Onetti and Nicaraguan poet José Coronel Urtecho. But the greatest influence on his thinking, he says, have been, "people who live without believing the line that things are more important than people; the people who don't confuse being with having, the people who can still see, with the eyes of a child, the marvel of a mutilated, maltreated world that deserves, as we do, a better fate."

In looking at the world today, Galeano says: "In the nations of the South, the deification of the market and the demonization of the forces of change have resulted in the concentration of wealth, the multiplication of poverty, and the devastation of nature. The triumphal religion of the market acts not only on economic, social, and political realities, but also on our consciences. Twenty years ago, poverty was the result of injustice. Today it is the punishment inefficiency deserves.

"More than ever," he continues, "the countries of the Southern Hemisphere are submitted to the dictatorship of an international market that lends with one hand what it steals with the other. More than ever, we are submitted to the dictatorship of media conglomerates that break real communication by teaching us to confuse quality of life with quantity of things."

The American-style consumer society now taking hold throughout the hemisphere is a tragic step—a new form of tyranny replacing the blood-soaked juntas that Latin Americans have finally thrown off in recent decades, he argues. "It is the dictatorship of the single word, the single image, the single tune, and perhaps it's more dangerous than other dictatorships because it acts on a world scale. It's an international structure of power which is imposing universal values that center on consumption and violence. It means that you are what you have. . . . Now we are being more and more obliged to accept a single way. And this single way is being mainly produced in [the] United States."

Hopeful that the developing world will find its own way forward, Galeano notes that the benefits would be many—for those in rich nations as well as poor ones. "This is the challenge faced by the South: Either we convert ourselves into a sad caricature of the North, or we find the energy to generate an essentially different path. It is necessary to be clear about the reigning power structure, which converts people and countries into commodities, condemns the majority of humankind to the hunger for bread, but also condemns all of humanity, the many poor and the few rich as well, to the hunger for embraces. This world of inequality is also a world of solitude."

SELECTED RESOURCES

Upside Down: A Primer for the Looking-Glass World (Metropolitan, 2000)

Days and Nights of Love and War (Monthly Review, 1983; 2000)

Soccer in Sun and Shadow (Verso, 1998)

Open Veins of Latin America: Five Centuries of the Pillage of a Continent (Monthly Review, 1973; 1997, twenty-fifth anniversary edition, with a foreword by Isabel Allende)

We Say No: Chronicles 1963–1991 (Norton, 1992)

The Book of Embraces, images and text by Galeano (Norton, 1991)

Memory of Fire: Genesis; Faces and Masks; Century of the Wind
  (Pantheon, 1985–1988)

GEORGE GERBNER

"For the first time in human history, stories are not told by the parent or by the church or by the community or even by the native country, but by a handful of media conglomerates that have nothing to tell but a lot to sell."

VIOLENCE ON TELEVISION has become so much a part of national debate that it's hard to remember a time when it wasn't. A lot of the credit for drawing public attention to the issue goes to media crusader George Gerbner. In the 1950s, when the country was still watching *Leave It to Beaver* and *Dragnet,* Gerbner helped pioneer the academic field of Communications Studies and argued that the mass media—radio, television, film, and print—constituted a strong socializing force worthy of analysis. He also took the debate out of academia and into the chambers of Congress and households across the country. For thirty years, he has been fighting what he calls "a media monopoly entirely tied to the corporate establishment."

Gerbner's Cultural Indicators Project caught the public's attention in 1968 with a startling statistic: The average American sees an average of five violent scenes per hour during prime-time network dramas, and twenty-five violent scenes an hour during Saturday-morning cartoons. "Violence is a cheap commodity," says Gerbner, his accent still strong fifty years after leaving his native Hungary. "It needs no translation, and it can be put into globally syndicated dramatic programs, thereby making it more profitable than anything that is conceived for domestic distribution."

Television models violent behavior for young viewers, he says, but it also has a more insidious effect: eroding the very fabric of our communities, a phenomenon he calls the Mean World Syndrome. "The more people watch television," he says, "the more they express insecurity, as reflected in [their answers to] questions like these: 'What do you think your chances are of encountering violence if you go out on the street on a given night?' and 'Do you think people are to be trusted, or [that] you can't be too careful?'

"Growing up in a violence-laden culture breeds aggressiveness in some and desensitization, insecurity, mistrust, and anger in most," he continues. "Punitive and vindictive action against dark forces in a mean world is made to look more appealing, especially when it is presented as quick, decisive, and enhancing our sense of control and security."

Global media monopolies like Time Warner, Viacom, and Disney exercise great control over the content of the shows we watch, and the result is bland fare designed to create an appealing atmosphere for advertisers, Gerbner says: "In American television you see no poor people. Advertisers don't like it. You see the drug dealers, the violent element. Poor people are virtually invisible—only 1.3 percent of characters in prime-time network dramatic TV are poor—and when they're visible, they're menacing." Minorities and older women are also among the missing, he says.

You don't criticize the media Goliaths without taking a few shots yourself, and Gerbner has been mocked by network executives who say that humorous cartoon violence is simply not comparable to the violence in TV cop shows and shoot-'em-up movies like *Die Hard*. Gerbner insists that cartoons are dangerous precisely because they portray violence as funny and free of serious consequences.

In 1989, no longer satisfied with gathering data, Gerbner formed the Cultural Environment Movement, a national coalition of groups and individuals dedicated to reclaiming control of world media. "A more diverse media would look like a more diverse society," he says. "We'd have a strong socialist press, a strong communist press, a strong religious fundamentalist press, a strong regional press. [Many] of our media are local, but essentially all of the dramatic fare comes from national syndicated sources. People often forget that broadcasting is conceived in the United States as a local activity." We need to remind ourselves that the airwaves belong to us and that licenses are given in the public interest, he says. Under the current system, "the cultural arm of fascism is a monopoly media that is entirely tied to the corporate establishment."

Gerbner has reason to be vigilant against fascism. He was raised Jewish in Hungary, where a rogue army was bent on a nationalistic agenda of recapturing lost territory from the days of the Austro-Hungarian Empire. In the 1930s, when Hungarian prime minister Béla Imrédy expressed Nazi leanings, Gerbner decided it was time to leave the country, first to Italy, then to Spain and Mexico, before making it to the United States in 1939. (His family stayed behind, and all but his mother perished in the war and Holocaust.) He studied journalism at UCLA and Berkeley, and was working at the *San Francisco Chronicle* when he decided to join the U.S. Army in order to fight the Nazis. Recruited into its intelligence arm, the OSS, he served during World War II behind enemy lines with Tito's partisans in Yugoslavia. After the war, he returned to the United States and started teaching. Eventually he created and became the first dean of the Annenberg School for Communication at the University of Pennsylvania—a post he held for twenty-five years.

Now in his eighties, Gerbner shows no signs of slowing down: "Retirement is not in my vocabulary," he declares. He now holds the Bell Atlantic endowed chair in Telecommunications at Temple University and still writes and speaks about the media. He lives in Ardmore, a Philadelphia suburb, with his wife of fifty-five years, Ilona, an actress he met in Budapest after the war. They have season tickets to the orchestra, opera, and theater—and as you might expect, he rarely watches television. As chair of the Cultural Environment Movement, he is still fighting the good fight.

"There's been progress in terms of awareness," he says. "There's been little or no progress in terms of performance. Most people, including people in the media, are aware of what they're doing . . . [but] they feel trapped in a situation in which their career depends on it." Grassroots citizen action might "loosen the global marketing noose around the necks of producers, writers, directors, actors, and journalists." Wary of censorship and its fascist overtones, he advocates antitrust legislation to break up media monopolies and diversify ownership, employment, and representation. "We have to restore the ability of broadcasters, especially public broadcasters, to put on quality drama to compete. In every other democratic country—in France, Germany, Italy, Japan, and South Korea, for example—there is sufficient financing for public television to put on attractive, high-quality dramatic programs."

On the home front, Gerbner encourages parents to provide a model of watching TV selectively to avoid raising junior couch potatoes, and to rediscover the lost art of storytelling rather than let the networks shape their children's view of the world.

SELECTED RESOURCES

Cultural Environment Movement
  Box 31847, Philadelphia, PA 19104
  www.cemnet.org

The Future of Media: Digital Democracy or More Corporate Control?
  (Seven Stories, 1999)

Invisible Crises: What Conglomerate Control of Media Means for America and the World, with Hamid Mowlana and Herbert I. Schiller (Westview, 1996)

Triumph of the Image: The Media's War in the Persian Gulf: A Global Perspective, with Hamid Mowlana and Herbert I. Schiller (Westview, 1992)

BARBARA MARX HUBBARD

"For millions of years, life has evolved unconsciously through a process of natural selection. We happen to be the generation born when a new event in the history of this planet is occurring. It is only in the past fifty years that we have penetrated so deeply into the technologies of nature—the atom, the gene, the brain—such that we can now enter the process of evolution more directly through human intent. We are changing the way nature evolves, from natural selection toward ever more conscious choice. We are living through the evolution of evolution."

EVOLUTION NOT ONLY explains how the world has gotten to where it is today, says futurist Barbara Marx Hubbard, it's the key to understanding where we are headed. She believes we are entering a transformative moment in the evolutionary cycle every bit as dramatic as the emergence eons ago of human beings from animal species.

The signs are all around us, Hubbard explains: Nuclear weapons capable of pulverizing all humanity, space travel, genetic engineering, a new wave of spiritual and psychological inquiry, widespread environmental destruction, an emerging global awareness, spiraling population growth, increasing affluence in developed countries, rising inequality between haves and have-nots, breakthroughs in information technology—new facts of the universe are triggering changes that would have been unimaginable a century ago. "The human species is either at the stage of making a quantum jump or going extinct," she says. "We're becoming responsible for life on earth. No species has ever been asked to do that before."

The trend driving us most strongly in the direction of what Hubbard calls "conscious evolution" is the changing status of women. "We know that wherever women have sufficient economic development, education, and freedom, they choose to have fewer children. That maternal energy is being liberated, and experienced as the expanded desire to create, to self-express, to find meaningful work and life purpose."

Until the present generation, men largely shaped the events of the world while women devoted themselves to the domestic sphere, but that's changing now as women live longer and bear fewer children. More of women's natural capacity to conceive and nurture life could be directed at giving birth to a new and better world. "The results of hundreds of millions of women expanding their creativity to the whole planet will be the formation of a more loving and compassionate culture."

Hubbard calls this phenomenon co-creation, and she sees it as a natural response to the myriad of problems now facing humanity. It's no coincidence, she notes, that concerns about overpopulation, the women's movement, and environmental consciousness appeared at almost the same stroke during the 1960s. "Just as nature urges us to reproduce the species, now she is arising within us to empower us to evolve the species."

Hubbard offers her own life as an example. The daughter of toymaker Louis Marx, whom a *Time* magazine cover story hailed as "The Toy King of the World," she grew up in New York City with every advantage a child could imagine—including a limitless supply of new toys. "I knew even then that most of the world was struggling to be materially secure," she says. "But I knew when they got to where I already was, they would have to face the next question: What's the meaning of your life?"

When she was fifteen, this question became all the more pressing when atomic bombs blasted Hiroshima and Nagasaki. Desperate for answers about the survival of humanity, she pored over books of classical philosophy all through prep school, Bryn Mawr, the Sorbonne, and raised questions about the meaning of life with everyone she came across. Her quest ended when she met painter Earl Hubbard in a Paris café, married him, moved to Connecticut, and had a baby.

"I loved giving birth," she recalls. "I loved my children dearly and gave them all my time. But after each child was weaned, the same longing—for something more I was born to do—came forth. Not knowing what it was, I had another child, and another and another, until I had five."

Hubbard struggled with depression, thinking she must be neurotic, until she read Betty Friedan's *The Feminine Mystique* and discovered that millions of American housewives felt the same way. She also read Abraham Maslow's *Toward a Psychology of Being,* in which he identified happy, joyous people—his term was "self-actualized"—as those who had found a vocation, a calling that they loved. "This was my wake-up call," she says. "I was not neurotic— I was underdeveloped! I put a plus sign on my frustration and reinterpreted it as a positive growth signal, guiding me onward."

Soon she was seeking out celebrated thinkers like Jonas Salk, Lewis Mumford, Thomas Merton, and Maslow, interviewing them about the evolution of humanity. Salk particularly became a mentor; he encouraged her to continue the search and introduced her to people that could help answer her questions. She calls this awakening her *vocational arousal,* which is now a central concept in her ideas on conscious evolution.

"It can strike at any age, from eighteen to eighty," she notes, "and it often happens through a peak experience or finding another person to emulate. It's the awakening of our passion to create. It's the third great human drive: from self-preservation to self-reproduction to self-evolution."

Vocational arousal is a key element of individual fulfillment at a time when people are living much longer, and therefore spending many years outside the traditional roles of career and parent. Hubbard stresses the importance of a calling for men as well as women, and for mothers as well as nonmothers. Indeed, her own children have told her that she became a better mother after she found a personal sense of purpose; her example, they said, inspired them to find their own places in the world. In fact, one of her daughters now works with her at the Foundation for Conscious Evolution, a think tank based in Santa Barbara that Hubbard founded.

Over the past thirty years, Hubbard has spread the message of conscious evolution in many venues, including workshops, conferences, books, and the Theatre for the Future, a multimedia vision of a positive future. At the 1984 Democratic National Convention, more than two hundred delegates signed a petition that put her name into nomination for vice president. She used this as an opportunity to advocate creation of a peace room in the vice president's office, to scout for innovations and inspirations for a better world. While Geraldine Ferraro won the vice presidential nomination, a peace room is now being set up as part of the Foundation for Conscious Evolution.

Practical projects have always been part of Hubbard's work, alongside theoretical long-range visions. She convened several summits of Soviet and American citizens in the 1980s to find bottom-up ways to defuse the nuclear terror of the Cold War. Now the foundation is engaged in grassroots initiatives in Santa Barbara and Sarasota, Florida, to discuss the impact that conscious evolution can have when applied in a local community.

"Western culture is right at the threshold of millions of people having enough affluence, enough security to be shifting from the level of basic needs to the next level, which is self-expression, chosen work, and a meaningful life," she explains. "I think this means the future will not just be incremental changes; the future will include quantum transformation, radical newness, a jump in consciousness, a jump in the species actually transforming itself rather than just seeking more and more things or better and better material well-being."

SELECTED RESOURCES

The Foundation for Conscious Evolution
  Box 4698, Santa Barbara, CA 93140-4698
  www.peaceroom.org

Emergence: The Shift From Ego to Essence (Hampton Roads, 2001)

Conscious Evolution: Awakening the Power of Our Social Potential
  (New World Library, 1998)

The Revelation: A Message of Hope for the New Millenium (Nataraj, 1995)

KALLE LASN

"The big issue of our time isn't racism or gender issues or feminism, or even environmentalism; the real problem is our culture. We need to pioneer increasingly potent tools for re-engineering our culture and taking it back from being something that is spoon-fed to us by corporations through their ownership of the TV airwaves."

O N CNN, a talking pig reminds viewers that a North American consumes five times more than a Mexican, ten times more than a Chinese person, thirty times more than a person in India. The ad ends with, "Give it a rest. November 26th is Buy Nothing Day."

In Seattle in November 1999, just blocks from where leaders of the world's most powerful industrial nations were meeting behind closed doors, a billboard enigmatically read, "This year, let's ask our leaders the big question."

In a magazine ad announcing "Absolut End," readers see the ubiquitous Absolut vodka bottle outlined as a murder-scene chalk sketch. The tagline explains, "Nearly 50 percent of automobile fatalities are linked to alcohol and 10 percent of North Americans are alcoholics. A teenager sees 100,000 alcohol ads before reaching the legal drinking age."

"Mind bombs," are what Kalle Lasn calls these anti-ads, which he and his colleagues at the Media Foundation design to interrupt the commercial drone that anesthetizes American and Canadian consumers. Lasn, a former marketing whiz and filmmaker, founded this guerrilla ad agency in 1989 to critique conspicuous consumption. The Vancouver-based foundation also publishes *Adbusters*, a devilishly fun monthly magazine that uses the high style of fashion magazines and advertising to deliver a subversive anticonsumerist, anticorporate message. In Lasn's view, this message translates into support of the environment, democracy, community, diversity, and human dignity. Despite a hefty $5.75 cover price, it has won nearly 50,000 readers with provocative images like Camel cigarette's cartoon trademark pictured as "Joe Chemo" and pointed articles like "Media Carta: The Human Rights Battle of the Information Age." Buy Nothing Day, Lasn's vision of the Friday after Thanksgiving as a holiday from shopping, has also generated reams of news coverage.

But Lasn's witty style is not welcome everywhere. He has had to sue U.S. and Canadian television networks for the right to air his anticommercials. Canadian stations blanched at airing an ad that answered a timber industry campaign suggesting the nation's forests would last forever. American networks and affiliates refused to air ads in which a zombified TV watcher with the glow of cathode rays washing over him is told, "The product being manufactured is you." The latter ad, created for Buy Nothing Day, was rejected by CBS executive Robert L. Lowary, who explained that it "is in opposition to the current economic policy of the United States."

"I get a creepy sense of deja vu listening to remarks like that," Lasn says. "I was born in Estonia, where for fifty years during the Soviet era people were not allowed to speak up against the government. Soviet dissidents used to talk about a 'public sphere of discourse' that was missing from their country. In North America today, there's a similar, if less draconian, public void. It's the lack of media space in which to challenge consumption, advertising, and corporate agendas. In the old Soviet Union, you weren't allowed to speak up against the government. In North America today, you cannot speak up against the sponsor.

"How come, in the land of the free and the home of the brave, you can't walk into a local TV station and buy thirty seconds of air time under the same rules and conditions as corporations?" he asks. "People no longer feel they own the public airwaves; they think the airwaves are owned by the broadcasters."

Lasn's family fled Estonia ahead of the advancing Russians in 1944, when he was two. He spent the next ten years in refugee camps in Germany and Australia. Despite his poverty, Lasn was identified as a brilliant student, and earned a scholarship to an Australian university.

After earning math and computer degrees, he took a job constructing war games for the Australian defense department.

Lasn soon grew disenchanted with military work, and decided to travel the world. On his way to Europe in 1965, he docked in Yokohama, and fell in love with Japan. As it happened, Lasn fell into lucrative work using his computer savvy to help marketers exploit the booming postwar Japanese economic miracle—an experience that helped fuel his anticonsumerist views. "I found that advertisers didn't really care about what they were advertising or the larger picture of how they fit into society in the culture," he says. "They just seemed to revel in their power to increase sales. The ethical neutrality started gnawing at me."

Abandoning his successful career as a marketer, he continued his around-the-world tour and noticed how the gap between wealthy and poor was growing everywhere. Setting his sights on a new career as filmmaker, in part to address global issues of justice, he moved to Vancouver in 1970 and joined a commune of documentary filmmakers who showed each other short films that questioned mainstream culture—the first mind bombs. He crafted a thirty-second spot revealing the percentage of the cost of certain products that could be attributed to advertising, but no station would air it. Although Lasn says he was "profoundly" affected by the refusal, he let the idea drop and became an acclaimed documentary filmmaker, earning up to $300,000 for a one-hour documentary. Many of his films explored Asian culture, which remains an interest.

Then, years later in a supermarket, he snapped. He was putting a quarter in a slot to rent a shopping cart—a common practice in Canadian grocery stores. "It suddenly occurred to me what a dope I was," he says. "Here I was, putting in my quarter for the privilege of spending money in a store I come to every week but hate, a sterile chain store that rarely carries any locally grown produce and always makes me stand in line to pay. I'd have to take this cart back to the exact place their efficiency experts have decreed. A little internal fuse blew." Before hiking off to the locally owned fruit and vegetable stand down the block, Lasn rammed a bent coin into the slot, jamming it. "I didn't stop to analyze whether this was ethical or not—I just let my anger flow," he says.

He was further inspired by the French Situationists, a radical intellectual movement of the 1950s that profoundly influenced the young radicals of Paris in 1968. The Situationists argued that all relationships had become transactional, work had become drudgery, and life was a series of empty "spectacles" constructed by modern capitalists to keep consumers consuming. To shock people out of their stupor, the Situationists created, well, "situations"—disruptive events that would knock people back into an "authentic life" of their own making. They advocated wildcat strikes and sabotage against capitalist and bureaucratic institutions in order to shock workers into reexamining and refusing to cooperate with their economic masters, but also focused on cultural messages: defacing billboards with preprinted placards, jamming commercial radio broadcasts with amateur signals. Picking up on their ideas of cultural sabotage, Lasn created his own situations: "mind bombs" and "culture jams." (The Situationist credo "Live Without Dead Time" is one of the *Adbusters'* Web site gateways.)

Culture jamming, he explains, "gets our consumer culture to bite its own tail." We can start creating a culture again by producing it "from the bottom up." The strategy, Lasn says, is a "pincer movement": *Adbusters'* mass media, television, billboard, and radio campaigns squeeze the culture at the top while pent-up grassroots pressures are unleashed from below. The Canadian timber ad he created illustrates how the strategy works: Although it was quashed, so was the timber industry's Forests Forever campaign when the Canadian Broadcasting Corporation began rejecting their ads too. "With our zero budget, we went against the whole might of the multi-billion-dollar forest industry and beat them at their own game," he says.

For grassroots action, *Adbusters'* Web site encourages individuals to attempt to buy time on local stations for anti-ads as well as the usual protests. Lasn sees the traditional left as "terribly dead." He insists that humans at the turn of the millennium are so absorbed by images that the battle must be fought with those weapons. "You look at lefty journals, and they're just about all text. Images can speak in the most wonderful way. Two thousand written words won't make even a little fart in the ocean. A five-hundred-word story saying the same thing with a couple of well-thought-out graphics or images, or a TV spot, is infinitely more effective."

Replacing economics with "bionomics"—a true-cost method of accounting in which environmental degradation, as well as profit, is factored in business decisions—is another of his visionary goals.

Lasn is pessimistic about the Internet as he watches its "wild spaces"—sites constructed by individuals— rapidly give way to those serving concentrated corporate interests, though he acknowledges that

Adbusters' Web site has been a powerful tool. "I look forward to a world where . . . if I believe in something strongly enough, I can say my piece," he says. "Someday, the American Constitution will say that every citizen has the right to receive information in and impart information to any medium whatsoever and nobody can stop you."

Through the sixteen-person Media Foundation, *Adbusters,* and a recent book, *Culture Jam: The Uncooling of America,* Lasn will keep pressing the big question alluded to in those Seattle billboards: How do you measure economic progress? Political leaders and economists, Lasn says, use only incomplete calculations, carefully calculating financial transactions without accounting for long-term costs to the planet's sustainability. Until they do, he notes wryly, leaders can't even answer what he sees as the basic question: "Are we going forward or backward?"

SELECTED RESOURCES

Culture Jam: The Uncooling of America (Eagle Brook, 1999)

Adbusters Media Foundation
   1243 W. Seventh Ave., Vancouver, British Columbia, V6H 1B7 Canada
   www.adbusters.org

BOBBY MCFERRIN

"We are all entertained so much these days, and I know that audiences want to be entertainers too. I want to leave them with the sense that the performance couldn't have happened without them."

SINGER BOBBY MCFERRIN should have been feeling at the peak of his game in 1988. A decade's worth of brilliant exploration of his nearly four-octave voice, from jazz improvisation to the ubiquitous top-of-the charts hit, "Don't Worry, Be Happy," had culminated in a sweep of the year's Grammy awards: best pop vocal performance, male; best jazz vocal performance, male; record of the year, song of the year. But the thrill was gone.

Hoping to get the spark back, McFerrin took a break from solo concerts and followed his varied interests into a whole new range of musical exploration: He celebrated his fortieth birthday with the San Francisco Symphony, making a noteworthy conducting debut by eschewing a baton. He pursued his interest in orchestration by arranging all the music for his innovative ten-person vocal ensemble, Voicestra, which appeared on television with the Boston Pops with McFerrin conducting. He teamed up with cello master Yo-Yo Ma to record a classical album that stayed on the charts for more than two years, and he scored his tenth Grammy for collaboration with jazz legend Chick Corea.

Musical excellence is a family legacy: Both his parents were professional singers. His mother, Sara, a soprano, taught voice. His father, the baritone Robert McFerrin, sang with New York City Opera, the

National Negro Opera Company, and the New England Opera Company. In the 1950s, the elder McFerrin became the first African American to be a permanent member of the Metropolitan Opera.

Like many children of musicians, Bobby McFerrin was a talented musician in his own right at an early age. He "wanted to distinguish myself from everyone else in my family," he says, and thus decided as a youngster to study piano instead of voice as his principal instrument. When he was just six, his parents enrolled him in Juilliard's gifted program, where he studied piano and music theory.

But McFerrin didn't follow the typical prodigy's path into performance and virtuosity—a life that demands a single-minded, narrow vision that he has never had. Even as a youngster, he had an eclectic and roving intellect. He was as fascinated by religion, playwriting, and jazz as he was by his traditional classical training, and he explored each of his interests fully: He sang in the church choir, wrote plays, and started a jazz band.

At California State University, he majored in music and studied music theory, composition, and arrangement, in addition to perfecting his keyboard skills. Still unsure of his future path, he was considering a career as a minister. Eventually, though, he dropped out of school and threw himself into the touring scene as a keyboard player, performing with top-forty bands and lounge acts, and with the Ice Follies.

After years on the circuit, touring the small-time music world all across the country, he and his wife settled in Utah in the mid-1970s. There, while he was accompanying an improvisational dance class and the students were moving to his music, McFerrin began to scat, letting his voice match their impromptu gestures. It was "a moment of clarity," he recalls. "I was feeling pretty burned out and wondering what my direction in life was going to be, when an inner voice told me I should sing."

"I hadn't realized I was a singer for a long time." he recalls. "I went through all kinds of ideas about myself and what I wanted to do. I played clarinet, piano, flute, studied cello, wrote and arranged for big band. . . . Then I discovered that I loved singing 'cause I could incorporate everything. . . . The voice is the most fluid instrument; you can slide from one end to the other. You can laugh, cry, squeal, grunt."

And how! To call McFerrin's vocal sweep unusual is a gross understatement. He performs straight-up jazz and pop, of course. But he's also famous for an abbreviated *Wizard of Oz* set in which he performs all the voices, the music, and the sound effects. He can handily imitate an entire bebop band, singing any instrument from trumpet to high hat with uncanny precision. And his mellow vocal rendition of Bach's "Air on a G String" is a riveting and emotional crowd-pleaser. "I see myself as a performance artist," he says. "Although my work includes jazz and pop singing, it also involves mime, dance, storytelling, and creative work with the audience."

McFerrin moved in 1979 to San Francisco, where he joined up with jazz great Jon Hendricks' band. It was his big break. He was singing with the vocal group when his talents caught the attention of Bill Cosby, who got him a slot at the 1980 Playboy Jazz Festival at the Hollywood Bowl. His star ascended the next year at New York's Kool Jazz Festival, which set the stage for his first album, *Bobby McFerrin*. After performing with jazz masters like Wynton Marsalis and Herbie Hancock, he decided in 1983 to go solo and unorthodox, mixing pop, jazz, comedy, and classical into a unique one-man show—"standing butt-naked on the stage," as he puts it, laughing. "I'll do an entire evening of nothing but improvisation," he says.

During these solo sessions McFerrin developed the philosophy he brought to bear in his seven years as creative chair of the Saint Paul Chamber Orchestra (SPCO). In his solo act, he blurs the lines between entertainer and entertained, asking his audiences to relinquish their passivity: "I'll have the audience give me ideas for improvisations. I'll riff off the squeak of a chair," he explains. In other words, McFerrin advocates democratization of the musical experience, a position that has served him well both as an entertainer and more recently as an orchestra conductor.

This sense of what he calls a "community in a concert hall" is in part what drew him to the SPCO, where he was named creative chair in 1994, a position he left at the beginning of 2001. His duties extended beyond conducting performances of the standard Bach-baroque-Beethoven repertoire to community outreach and education efforts: He bends genres, mixing jazz, classical, and pop, roping in new audiences and expanding the range of orchestral possibilities. He has often performed with local choirs on tour with the orchestra and designs the program to get everyone in the concert hall joining in the chorus. McFerrin is convinced that even a single evening of mutual pleasure is significant. "We keep looking at the big social and political problems," he says. "But when you're walking down the street and someone simply smiles at you—what a tremendous difference that makes."

His own musical experiments travel the same unconventional road: The orchestra recorded an album of Mozart piano concertos interpreted through the genre-crossing talents of McFerrin and Chick Corea. He's also worked all the way back to his pop and jazz roots with the well-received 1996 album, *Bang!Zoom*. Although he plans to return to the SPCO as a guest conductor, he left the position to allow more time for other commitments, including a new work he's composing for the San Francisco Opera with Pulitzer Prize–winning playwright Tony Kushner *(Angels in America)*.

Bobby McFerrin's boundless imagination and energy make it impossible to pin down his talents in just one form. More than anything else, he stands as one of our foremost musical explorers: Fusing and enriching classical, jazz, and pop into a twenty-first-century repertoire, he tests the limits of *a cappella* artistry, demonstrating music's qualities as a social and educational force as well as an artistic endeavor.

SELECTED RESOURCES

www.bobbymcferrin.com

Circlesongs (Sony Classical, 1997)

Bang! Zoom (Blue Note, 1996))

The Best of Bobby McFerrin (Blue Note, 1996)

The Mozart Sessions, with Chick Corea and the Saint Paul Chamber Orchestra (Sony Classical, 1996)

Paper Music, with The Saint Paul Chamber Orchestra (Sony Classical, 1995)

Don't Worry, Be Happy (Capitol, 1995)

Play (Blue Note, 1992)

Hush, with Yo-Yo Ma (Sony, 1992)

BILL MOYERS

"This mass medium of television seems especially intolerant of ideas. But in fact, it could bring our tribe together around a national campfire."

Don Perdue

"A PROFESSIONAL beachcomber on the shores of other people's wisdom" is how Bill Moyers, with characteristic modesty, describes his own unique role in American life. However, *The Stars and Stripes,* official Defense Department newspaper for overseas troops, notes that many people look on him as the conscience of America and some have pleaded with him to run for president—an idea he has never taken seriously. A president, after all, is the person from whom we seek answers, and Moyers finds listening much more fufilling.

For almost thirty years, he's been interviewing people from all walks of life—from everday citizens to mind-expanding visionaries in the fields of philosophy, spirituality, politics, poetry, and medicine—and letting us listen in. Few figures throughout history have introduced so many new and dazzling ideas to so many Americans. His television work, both for the networks and PBS, have won more than thirty Emmy Awards, and he is the author of numerous best-selling books on subjects such as The Bible, poetry, politics and mythology. His television special *A Gathering of Men with Robert Bly* helped launch the men's movement. His television special and book *Healing and the Mind* has moved the medical establishment to take alternative health therapies more seriously, and continues to change the lives of people struggling with illness.

In choosing what new fields to tackle, he follows the famous advice that myth scholar Joseph Campbell offered in an interview with Moyers: "Follow your bliss." His recent TV special and book, *Fooling With Words: A Celebration of Poets and Their Craft,* was inspired by Moyers' own lifelong passion for poems, which he counts as his favorite means of winding down from work and recharging his own imagination. "I do not understand the power of poetry to transfigure, but I remembered the first time I experienced it." He writes of his high school English teacher, Inez Hughes, in the introduction to *Fooling With Words:* "Standing with her shoulders high and her back straight, and holding *The Oxford Book of English Verse* as far from her body as her arms would extend, she read. For the entire hour she read, until the bell rang and the spell was broken. She had a sonorous southern voice, as versatile as a pipe organ, which rose half an octave as she read. Between her native drawl and an exactness of diction acquired in elocution courses back East, her sentences could flow like a languid stream, or break, crisp and distinct, like twigs snapping underfoot."

Although his subjects span the full range of human experience, they share one overarching theme: the human spirit. In focusing on this theme, he has dared to break television's "awful taboo against intelligent, reflective discussions of religious subjects," as former PBS president Ervin S. Duggan put it. Indeed, one of Moyers' television series was built around hours of fascinating conversations with religious scholars Huston Smith and Elaine Pagels that plumb the story of Genesis and its influence on the modern-day American psyche and culture. This was the basis for his popular book, *Genesis: A Living Conversation.*

But Moyers' discussions reach beyond religion to pursue what he says is one of the most compelling stories of our time: "The attempt to find a new vision for America which has the authority and power of a religious vision but which is inclusive, not sectarian.

"We're bombarded everywhere by the pernicious and debilitating effects of nonsense, trivia, and violence, by a stream of mass-produced, mass-consumed carnage masquerading as amusement," he adds. "I think it makes it harder for us to cooperate in solving those problems that are threatening the globe, whether it's the ecological crises or the crises of materialism and emptiness in our own society. . . . I like and admire and honor those people in our society who are trying to counter that stream of pernicious images. . . . What lifts me and encourages me are more humanizing forces. The ancient Israelites had a word for this: *Hochma*—the science of the heart. Intelligence, feeling, and perception combine to create the moral imagination. . . . That's what gives me joy and pleasure to see—and even, in a minor way, to be part of."

Like any good journalist, Moyers keeps his finger on the pulse of the American zeitgeist. When he pitched a six-hour discussion with a little-known scholar of myth named Joseph Campbell, he had trouble getting the series funded, and some station managers refused to air it. "People would say, 'What—an eighty-three-year-old mythologist talking head for six hours? You've got to be crazy. Who's going to watch this?'" says Moyers' longtime collaborator Betty Sue Flowers. But the Campbell series, titled *The Power of Myth,* gained tremendous word-of-mouth notice and was turned into a best-selling book. Moyers has a knack for knowing what audiences will find compelling before they themselves know. As Flowers puts it, "he bridges the gap between where people are and where their spirits yearn to be."

Moyers' life story is as unlikely as his longstanding success in bringing deep subjects like spirituality and poetry to millions of television viewers. How did a young Baptist seminarian from the small East Texas town of Marshall wind up as the presidential press secretary, and then go on to become one of the most beloved and honored social commentators of our time? "Lyndon Johnson once said to me that there are three ways for a poor boy in the South to do well," answers Moyers. "One was to preach, one was to teach, and the other was to politic. And so I followed all of those until circumstance, more than choice, decided my destiny." As a student at North Texas State, he wrote to Johnson, then a senator from Texas, asking for a job. "I would like to be a political journalist and would like to learn politics at the feet of someone who has accomplished a great deal," Moyers wrote.

Johnson hired the young man to answer correspondence, and then got him a job at a Texas radio station while Moyers finished up his degree at the University of Texas. The two stayed in touch during Moyers' five years in seminary, and, as vice-president, Johnson brought him to Washington to be deputy director of the just-launched Peace Corps. Later he become Johnson's chief White House spokesman. "I remember when I was press secretary standing there answering questions, thinking to myself, 'I really belong on the other side, asking questions, not answering them.'" He subsequently worked as publisher for *Newsday* and as a correspondent for CBS and PBS before founding

Public Affairs Television, where he produces shows with his business partner and wife of forty-five years, Judith Davidson Moyers.

Politics has remained a passion for the man who helped Lyndon Johnson shape the vision of the Great Society. "The public has been left stranded by media that reduce important political ideas to a 'sound bite' of 9.8 seconds, the average length of time presidential candidates were permitted to speak uninterrupted on network news in the campaign of 1988," he told an audience of political leaders. Today, "we see more and more that the things that really need to happen—whether it's [dealing with] growing inequality, children living in poverty, a lack of universal health care, pollution—can't be seriously addressed because the politicians would have to offend their bankrollers—the people who pay to play. I think this is why we have to keep fighting this cause [campaign finance reform], and why we can't yield to cynicism and frustration."

At a time when televised political coverage has been reduced to mere examinations of candidates' campaign commercials and fundraising operations, Moyers offers in-depth discussions of the ideas that "the candidates would be talking about if in fact they were free to express their minds."

Country life and a Baptist upbringing are not the kind of influences often cited in an age when sophisticated cynicism reigns. But Moyers nonetheless points to the experience of his Texas childhood as the inspiration for his vision of bringing a broad roster of interesting people talking passionately about a wide range of subjects to television.

"Growing up in a small Southern town, you are early exposed to voices. The voices of your parents in the next bedroom, the voices of the passersby on the sidewalk, the voices of the people sitting on the porch in twilight. The voice of the hairdresser. The voices of the farmers who come to the town square on Saturdays. The black voices on the west side of town. The white voices on the east side of town. The voices of the Lebanese merchants in the little stores around the square. So you get interested in the human voices and in the messages they carry."

Although we think of Moyers foremost as maestro of a chorus of strong American voices, there is also his own voice, which pulls it all together—coaxing a little more clarity or encouraging elaboration out of his conversational partners. What he once wrote about Joseph Campbell just as aptly describes his own appeal: "It was impossible to listen to him—truly to hear him—without realizing in one's consciousness a stirring of fresh life, the rising of one's own imagination."

SELECTED RESOURCES

Genesis and the Millenium: An Essay on Religious Pluralism in the Twenty-first Century, including eight ecumenical responses (J.M. Dawson Inst. of Church-State Studies, Baylor Univ., 2000)

Fooling With Words: A Celebration of Poets and their Craft (Morrow, 1999)

Genesis: A Living Conversation (Doubleday, 1996)

The Language of Life: A Festival of Poets (Doubleday, 1995)

Healing and the Mind (Doubleday, 1993)

The Power of Myth, with Joseph Campbell (Doubleday, 1988; Anchor, 1991)

A World of Ideas: Conversations with Thoughtful Men and Women about American Life Today and the Ideas Shaping Our Future (Doubleday, 1989)

The Secret Government: The Constitution in Crisis (Seven Locks, 1988)

Listening to America : A Traveler Rediscovers his Country (Harper's Magazine Press, 1971)

NEIL POSTMAN

"**Almost all technologies enhance our lives but they also detract from our lives. Most Americans are so in love with technology that they only see what it give us—not what it takes.**"

© Jerry Bauer

DON'T CALL Neil Postman a progressive. He may be a consistent and cutting critic of capitalism. He may be on the editorial board of *The Nation*. He may be the coauthor of the 1960s classic, *Teaching as a Subversive Activity*. He may have once believed in the tenets of progress, American style. But not now.

Postman calls himself a conservative, and he contends that most other Americans who use that label—loyal Republicans and corporate boosters —are actually radicals. He explained why in a speech to conservative business leaders and academics in Vienna: "A capitalist cannot afford the pleasures of conservatism, and of necessity regards tradition as an obstacle to be overcome. . . . It is fairly easy to document that capitalists have been a force for radical social change since the eighteenth century, especially in the United States. . . . In today's America . . . if anyone should raise the question, What improves the human spirit? or even the more mundane question, What improves the quality of life? Americans are apt to offer a simple formulation: That which is new is better, that which is newest is best.

"The best cure for such a stupid philosophy is conservatism. My version, not President Reagan's. A true conservative also knows that technology always fosters radical social change. . . . The United States is the most radical society in the world. It is in the process of conducting a vast, uncontrolled social experiment which poses the question, Can a society preserve any of its traditional virtues by submitting all of its institutions to the sovereignty of technology?"

This speech was given in 1987, soon after the publication of Postman's landmark book on television, *Amusing Ourselves to Death,* and he meant it as an exhortation to Austrians to stop the onslaught of commercial broadcasting in their country. Postman, chair of the Department of Culture and Communication at New York University, has spent many years researching the social consequences of television, and that's what made him a skeptic of technological progress, he says.

"Along with everyone else, I was delighted with television," he recalls, speaking with the passionate inflections and staccato lyricism of a native-born New Yorker. "But I began to see that there was going to be a downside to the wonders of television. It would change our social habits, and not necessarily for the better. It would affect our perceptions of what we might do with our leisure time. It would have some serious effects on literacy, and most of all it was having a very unhealthy effect on young people."

This first struck him in the 1950s while he was teaching elementary school in western New York. "TV was just beginning to grip the imagination of Americans," he recalls. "And it was obvious that it was taking up more of kids' time and gearing to their emotions more than schools were."

Later, while in graduate school at Columbia University, he met Marshall McLuhan, a University of Toronto professor who was just beginning to publish his ideas about the medium of communication being more important than the content. Postman remembers being "bowled over" by the implications of McLuhan's theory—the experience of watching television alters how we think about the world in the same way, no matter whether we're watching pro wrestling or the Royal Shakespeare Company. There are inherent values in the medium, which we tend to overlook. Postman soon realized that this was true of all new technologies.

"The single most important lesson we should have learned in recent years," Postman offers, "is that technological progress is not the same thing as human progress. Technology always comes at a price. This is not to say that one should be, in a blanket way, against technological change. But it is time for us to be grown-ups, to understand that if technology gives us something, it will take away something. It is not an unmixed blessing. We have to go into the future with our eyes wide open."

The best way to do that, he counsels in a recent book, *Building a Bridge to the Eighteenth Century,* is to pay close attention to the past. Technological change, which can destroy long-standing traditions and institutions with breathtaking speed, ironically may prevent us from truly moving ahead. Invoking the wisdom of philosopher George Santayana, who warned that those who cannot remember the past are condemned to repeat it, Postman asks, "Is it possible to plan a future, or even think about it, without reference to the past?"

Postman finds special meaning for our era in the eighteenth century, the time of the Enlightenment and the first stirrings of the Romantic movement, when great minds were focused on the promise, the problems, and the meaning of an emerging mechanistic society. We can draw inspiration and practical insights from the work of eighteenth-century giants like Goethe, Voltaire, Rousseau, Kant, Newton, Blake, Schiller, Samuel Johnson, Adam Smith, Thomas Paine, Thomas Jefferson, and Benjamin Franklin, not to mention the music of Bach, Handel, Mozart, and Haydn. The future can be an improvement over the present, he says, only if we keep hold of the knowledge of the past.

"Learning how these smart people look at the world brings me pleasure," Postman explains, as well as offering directly applicable lessons on how to live. "I do think the slowness of the past is something preferable to the speed with which we live today."

Technological advances are always billed as a way to increase our options, when often just the opposite is true, Postman notes: "At most jobs now you have to use a word processor. And if you don't want to, you can't work there. New technology is imperialistic. It destroys older and sometimes very good ways of doing things."

Relishing his own resistance to the new technological order, Postman avoids voice mail and e-mail. "I asked myself, do I need these things, and I didn't see any real advantage for my life," he explains. He owns a car, and is an unequivocal fan of both photocopiers and air conditioning. But he still listens to records, which sound richer to him than compact discs, and he writes his books in longhand on yellow pads and then types them on his beloved Smith-Corona. "This is the way I think best," he says, although now his publisher demands he hire someone to input them onto computer disks.

"In imagining a society of the future, I hope people would be a little more sensible about this and allow older forms of human communication to coexist with newer ways," he says. "People would have more consciousness of the effects of technology and there would be room for some of us who like to do it the older way."

The mad rush to adopt every new form of technology that pops up "creates the impression that the most serious problems we have in the world are the result of inadequate technology and insufficient information.

"Look at starvation, for example," he continues. "We already have enough knowledge to feed everyone on the planet. If crime is rampant on the streets of a big city, that has nothing to do with information. As you look at our most serious problems, you'll see they have very little to do with information. They are not amenable to technological solutions. But a lot of people think technology is the only way we should go. . . . We may be distracted from addressing the real causes of these problems."

Postman sees a number of positive signs that Americans are shedding their long-standing naïveté about the effects of technology: "Parents are really wondering about television. They're asking questions about computer games and whether they should be paying money to have their kids sit in front of their computers for hours and never go out on the street and talk to anyone. People have begun to sense that there's something not quite right when all your aspirations are related to bigger and better technology."

As we now enter an era of dizzying change, with new information technologies reshaping people's lives perhaps as fundamentally as the industrial revolution did, he says we need to encourage broad public debate about how new technologies will affect our culture. Through his writing, research, and lectures he reminds us that we should have a choice about what new technologies we welcome into the heart of our lives, and which ones we don't really need.

SELECTED RESOURCES

Building a Bridge to the Eighteenth Century: How the Past Can Improve Our Future (Knopf, 1999)

Technopoly: The Surrender of Culture to Technology (Knopf, 1992; Vintage, 1993)

Conscientious Objections: Stirring up Trouble about Language, Technology, and Education (Knopf, 1988; Vintage, 1992)

Amusing Ourselves to Death: Public Discourse in the Age of Show Business (Viking, 1985; Penguin, 1986)

Teaching as a Subversive Activity, with Charles Weingartner (Delacorte, 1969)

RACHEL ROSENTHAL

"I'm interested in communication. Many artists are not; their work is opaque.... I don't like "cool" art. I'm more interested in "hot" art, something dealing with ritual, in a sense, participatory ritual. And although the audience is not actively participating, they still are empathizing in the event, and the event itself is often a kind of exorcism or a rite of passage or a magical moment."

L OS ANGELES performance artist Rachel Rosenthal once called herself "a square peg in the round hole of theater." It's a good shorthand way to get at the many things that make Rosenthal exceptional. Start with the fact that she's bald, pierced, and seventy-five years old. Born in Paris of Russian-émigré parents, she grew up in storybook luxury (Baccarat crystal goblets, a Cordon Bleu family cook, a Monet in the living room), then later spent a decade doing improvisational theater with props and costumes scavenged from trash bins. Superbly trained in the theater, she's also a studio artist who's thrown in her lot with the art-gallery-based movement—performance art—that began by disdaining the theater. Her solo and collaborative stage pieces walk a fine line: often dreamlike and always complex, they never descend into hip-for-hip's-sake obscurity.

Most important of all, Rosenthal's work manages to be personal and planetary at the same time. She is passionately concerned about the fate of the earth, the survival of its human and nonhuman inhabitants, the perils of overpopulation, and the decline of social cohesion and personal happiness in modern societies. She explores these issues with spectacle, style, and wit, too fervent to be "cool," too avant-garde to preach—and using all the resources of the stage, from up-to-the-minute audio and video and lighting technology to gorgeous costuming and poetic language. "All the arts have to communicate together, to gang up on people's psyches," she says. "The way to make people really empathize with something is not just intellectual, but also emotional and spiritual."

Rosenthal's multidisciplinary approach—call it holistic, if you like—is rooted in her biography, too. Having fled Hitler with her family—first to Brazil and then to New York—she bounced back to postwar Paris, full of dreams of being an artist. "But I didn't know which art, because I loved them all," she laughs. "I was a dilettante." Her encounter with French experimental theater, and particularly with the writings of avant-garde theorist-saint Antonin Artaud, showed her a pathway out of the dilettante's dilemma. Responding to Artaud's call for a theater of surprise, spectacle, and savage beauty, Rosenthal realized she could explore and fuse all the arts—on stage.

Returning to New York in 1949, she found her way to the heart of American avant-garde performance: the circle of musicians, poets, and unclassifiable artists gathered around the composer John Cage. Working and socializing with high-powered figures like the choreographer Merce Cunningham and the painter Jasper Johns—and continuing rigorous theater training—Rosenthal nonetheless felt blocked. The nearly all-male Cage/Cunningham world offered precious few role models for a woman artist, and Rosenthal's beloved father still opposed the idea of his daughter making a full-time commitment to the chancy world of the theater.

So when Rosenthal's father died in 1955, it was a moment of both desolation and liberation. She packed up and moved to Los Angeles, which at the time was virgin territory when it came to innovative theater. She began by giving acting workshops, but these relatively formal exercises soon turned into a wild, vivid, poetic improvisational style she dubbed Instant Theatre. Using scavenged props and costumes, "we created a dream world on stage which was really magical and astonishing," she remembers.

Rosenthal had found her voice, and in that process became a leader rather than a promising follower. But she would go through many more theatrical metamorphoses, becoming deeply involved with the

California feminist art scene in the 1970s, and crafting solo performances that explored the psychological legacy of her privileged French past, her awareness of her body, and other aspects of her identity and self-image. In one piece, called *Thanks*, she asked audience members to impersonate people from her life whom she wished to thank, including a family maid and her father.

Step by step, Rosenthal became more and more concerned with the intersections of her own life and the life of the planet. As early as 1960, in a drive through the canyonlands of the West, she was awestruck. "I fell absolutely in love with those rock formations," she recalls. "It was as if the earth was showing off, putting on an incredible show." Rosenthal was increasingly drawn toward earth-based spirituality—goddess worship and . shamanism—and increasingly concerned with sounding the environmental alarm.

"In the 1980s, it became more and more clear that I was becoming a sort of Cassandra, warning people that what we're doing, and our way of thinking about ourselves and our planet, is going to lead to catastrophe," she says. "Many of the things that I was saying then have now become quite fashionable. Unfortunately, as I keep saying, none of my performances ever become obsolete. . . . The issues are still at the forefront because none of them are being solved."

Rosenthal's ability to touch and move audiences is a compound of theatrical skill and the self-testing and self-revelation that are characteristic of performance art. When she turned sixty in 1986, for example, she shaved her head, and audiences saw a new Rachel: an androgynous crone/wise woman. "I had been growing old without feeling I was growing old," she says. "Then the big six-oh hit. The interesting thing was that as soon as I became aware that I was aging, I aged. I saw the skin sagging and the lines coming in. It's fun, and kind of marvelous—because I hate things that remain the same. The changes show the passage of life and time through a body, and that is a good thing."

Rachel's Brain, a 1987 performance that marked a watershed for Rosenthal, is a witty assault on the dominance of the head over the body and the heart in Western culture. Portraying Marie Antoinette, "the Flower of the Enlightenment, the Head of State"—complete with gaudy gown and enormous wig—Rosenthal runs through a litany of smug truisms about the superiority of the brain, conceptual thought, Newtonian theory, and technology. The monologue darkens as Marie senses bacterial invaders taking over her brain and body. Abruptly, she meets her fate: decapitation. This violence ushers in a phantasmagoria of scenes: Rosenthal dissecting a brainlike cauliflower; an image of a laboratory monkey with electrodes wired to its brain; Rosenthal as an ancient ape-man and as Koko, the famous symbol-using gorilla. They're virtuoso variations on the theme of our estrangement from our bodies, our senses, nature, and animal life.

Ur-Boor, a piece from the 1999–2000 season of the Rachel Rosenthal Company, takes on the vexed issue of civility: the power of courtesy and simple kindness to make society function. A society of the future tries to maintain civility by selecting a scapegoat called the Ur-Boor, upon whom it ritually piles all of its nasty, boorish impulses. The poor Ur-Boor, played by Rosenthal, has been exiled to a tiny, decrepit space capsule in orbit high above the earth. With the aid of spectacular visual effects, Rosenthal helps the audience reflect on social norms, the power of solitude, the role of the scapegoat in modern society . . . and many other questions that her poetic way with language and image bring to the fore.

While Rosenthal's poetic and witty way with images precludes sermonizing, there's no doubt about her intention to directly teach and promote social change. She holds a question-and-answer session with the audience after every performance. "I try to give people a sense of how important one person can be," she says. "I tell them that all the big changes that have occurred throughout the history of civilization have been initiated by one person. You drop a stone in the well, and you get concentric circles. Hopefully the circles become larger and larger. Often I meet people I don't know on the street and they say, 'That piece of yours changed my life; that workshop you gave set me on a quest.' I think that's a success story."

SELECTED RESOURCES

Rachel Rosenthal Company
   2847 S. Robertson Blvd., Los Angeles, CA 90034
   www.rachelrosenthal.org

Rachel Rosenthal,
   ed. Moira Roth (John Hopkins University Press, 1997)

JOHN RALSTON SAUL

"The question that must be asked about efficiency is whether it should be treated as a driving force in a civilization or even in a society or . . . economy. Or is it no more than one of those useful little tools which can help us all to do better if [it is] used appropriately?"

© Beverley Rockett

A NOVELIST and former oil company executive whose political thrillers probe the theme of what makes a good society, Canadian gadfly John Ralston Saul is a Renaissance man in more ways than one—he's convinced that the West needs a new Renaissance to awaken our powers of reflection, judgment, and active citizenship. These qualities, he believes, have been buried under the weight of a technocratic society in which major decisions are made at the top and the role of citizens is to comply.

His controversial 1992 book, *Voltaire's Bastards: The Dictatorship of Reason in the West,* argues that cherished concepts like rationality and reason are not noble ideals, as we have all been educated to believe. They actually are foundations of a little-recognized dogma that rules the modern world and colors most people's thinking on subjects ranging from economic policy to what makes great art. Arising out of the eighteenth-century Enlightenment's crusade to unseat the Catholic Church's central role in society, reformers like Voltaire, Descartes, and Thomas Jefferson championed reason as the path to truth and goodness. After centuries of clerical control over intellectual inquiry, this was a refreshing development. But rationality and reason have now become as rigid as the theocracy they toppled. Today, the "blind reason" of computer models and economic theories control modern civilization in much the same way that papal dictates ruled medieval culture. What rose to take the place of God, Saul says, is "a theology of pure power. The new holy trinity is organization, technology, and information."

Saul provocatively concludes that reason and rationality probably have created more misery than they have alleviated. He points to the Holocaust as the prime example of rationality: It was planned and carried out with a horrible efficiency that would have been impossible without the emphasis on order, systemization, and large-scale production that are the hallmarks of our era. The same goes for the Vietnam War, the global arms trade, and environmental degradation.

In *The Doubter's Companion: A Dictionary of Aggressive Common Sense,* Saul continued his assault on the ideological underpinnings of modern culture in a lighter vein by rewriting the dictionary definitions for many central concepts of our civilization. Ronald McDonald, for instance, is not just a clown but also "a postmodern philosopher. In somewhat the same way that Voltaire was the public intellectual face of the Enlightenment, Ronald McDonald is the face and the voice of consumer culture."

Social critic Camille Paglia described Saul's work this way in *The Washington Post:* "Rejecting the exhausted stereotype of left versus right, [Saul] opens up new lines of enquiry and creates new constellations of meaning. With his sophisticated international perspective and blunt freedom from cant, he offers a promising persona for the future: the intellectual as a man of the world."

A lifetime of study in widely diverse settings has honed Saul's unusual perspective. Raised in Alberta, Manitoba, and Ontario in a military family, he graduated from Montreal's McGill University and went on to get a Ph.D. from King's College, London. Moving to Paris, he served as correspondent for a trio of publications: Toronto's *Financial Post* newspaper, *Wine and Spirits* magazine, and England's *Arts Review* magazine. Living for long periods in North Africa and Southeast Asia as part of his duties as director of a French investment firm and as executive of a Canadian oil company, he also served as secretary of the Canada-China trade council.

His years in business and the media taught him that even at the highest levels of our civilization, the economic and political elites are fearful of straying from conventional wisdom about efficiency, hierarchy, and technology. The absolute—and in his word "naive"—faith of world leaders in their own visions of the future startled Saul. "People were always saying 'This can't happen' or 'That can't happen,' but then it did happen." Of course, this is nothing unusual, he notes: "The whole history of the human race is that we convince ourselves things are true for a short while, but then reality reasserts itself and we start over."

We can understand many things—depressing things—about the modern world from studying Homer, he says: "The Homeric idea was that people's margin for maneuver was small because the gods and destiny were in charge. Later Socrates and the Greek law giver Solon said: That's garbage! Human beings have room to organize and change themselves a lot, within the limits of reality. Now, 2500 years later, our elites tell us again: The gods rule! Only the new gods are the market, and any other force we just have to passively accept."

Waging war against the civic hopelessness that has grown out of this kind of fatalism, Saul wields a sharp pen against the corporate and political managers who foist fatalism upon us. How do they do it? By monopolizing and corrupting language.

"The elites control what they consider a higher language, a technical language inaccessible to the lower orders—and to other elites too! This language is supposedly at one end of the spectrum, and, say, *Roseanne* is at the other. But the highest language is the one that can be used and understood by citizens, and the opaque languages of the specialists are dialects, lower forms that actually suck the blood from language."

When our language has been so degraded, it's no wonder that political thinking that dares to question the status quo seems to have dried up. As a remedy, Saul suggests reclaiming the spirit of the Renaissance, "when people looked at their entire history afresh, threw all the cards up in the air."

Regaining a sense of balance in our civilization is what's key, he counsels. "Cultures need to balance reason, common sense, memory, experience, ethics, creativity, and intuition. When a culture has too much memory, it may be a monarchy obsessed with the past. When ethics dominates, you have some kind of church rule. In our day, reason—rationalism—dominates, to the point of irrationalism. All our emphasis is on deciding and then administering solutions. But any idiot can be decisive," he laughs. "We've lost the capacity to find out what's truly going on and then talk about that."

Losing this capacity can be attributed in part to our lack of a common functional language: "We need to say to the elites, particularly when they tell us that we must obey market forces, or that certain degradations of our life are inevitable: Gentlemen, we're the ones who put you where you are, and we don't want this from you anymore."

He sees signs that people from all around the world are beginning to challenge the prevailing worldview: "When things start happening, it's usually because people have stopped believing what they are supposed to believe, even if they don't know what else to believe in. I think that's happening right now."

SELECTED RESOURCES

The Unconscious Civilization (Free Press, 1997)

Reflections of a Siamese Twin: Canada at the End of the Twentieth Century (Viking, 1997)

The Doubter's Companion: A Dictionary of Aggressive Common Sense (Free Press, 1994)

Voltaire's Bastards: The Dictatorship of Reason in the West (Free Press, 1992; Vintage, 1993)

The Paradise Eater, a novel (McGraw-Hill, 1988)

The Next Best Thing, a novel (Doubleday, 1986)

Baraka, a novel (Doubleday, 1985)

The Birds of Prey, a novel (McGraw-Hill, 1977)

WILLIAM STRICKLAND

"I give my faculty and students the tools and I say, "There is no limit to what you can do." Institutions tend to limit people, to tell them they've got to fit into this box or that hole. What I'm saying is, the world is a blank canvas and it's all about making your mark."

IT WAS 1963. Bill Strickland was a high school kid with little future. His decaying inner-city Pittsburgh neighborhood didn't offer its young people much in the way of hope, and Strickland himself didn't have any plans for life after graduation.

Wandering the halls of Oliver High, he noticed a ceramics classroom. There, bent over a potter's wheel, sat art teacher Frank Ross, making a pot. Though today he's not sure exactly what fascinated him about the sight, fascinated he was. He approached Ross. "I'd like to learn whatever that is," he said.

The moment marked the beginning of a twenty-year mentorship with Ross, a lifelong devotion to pottery, and—though Strickland had no inkling of it at the time—a career applying art and imagination as well as business savvy to tap the power and change the lives of people at the bottom of America's economic ladder.

Today Strickland, fifty-five, is executive director of two complementary institutions: the Manchester Craftsmen's Guild (MCG), a ceramics school that he founded, and the Bidwell Training Center (BTS), an adult education center he took over and revolutionized. They share a handsome building on his home turf, the Manchester neighborhood on Pittsburgh's North Side. This work has made him a nationally recognized pioneer in vocational education, with a MacArthur "genius" grant and consultancies for the National Endowment for the Arts. He's also a serious jazz fan, an orchid fancier, and a certified jet pilot who flew 727s for Braniff on weekends until the airline went belly-up.

It all began with the MCG, a direct outgrowth of Strickland's love for ceramics and for education. Mentor Frank Ross did more than merely encourage Strickland to go to college: "He took me by the hand out to the University of Pittsburgh," Strickland recalls. "He saw that I had a mind, a resource he wouldn't let me waste." At the university, Strickland studied diplomatic and labor history while continuing to throw pots. In 1968, riots shook the Manchester neighborhood, and the twenty-one-year-old Strickland decided to take action. Ceramics had changed his life—why couldn't it be a way out of despair for others?

In an old row house donated by the Episcopal Diocese, he set up after-school ceramics classes for neighborhood kids. Even in those modest beginning days, his thinking had a breadth and inclusiveness that set him apart from most community activists. "I knew the community was in terrible shape," he recalls. "Anything I did would have a positive impact. I was creating visibility in the community, having an impact on education, improving the housing stock. A lot of things came out of that one decision to do ceramics."

Strickland's vision of many positive results from strong, simple ideas bore fruit. The MCG grew, and with it Strickland's reputation as a community leader. In 1972, the Presbyterian Church approached him to take over its ailing Bidwell Training Center, an adult education facility that had fallen into tax trouble. Strickland saw the BTS as a logical partner for the Craftsmen's Guild. He could work simultaneously with two of the most vulnerable groups in the ghetto: at-risk kids and hard-luck adults striving to become employable.

But Strickland's real masterstroke came in 1983, when he launched a capital campaign to build an $8 million facility to house both schools. What Strickland had in mind was an edifice that would lift the spirits of his students as well as shelter them, a stunning building that told people who had fallen through the cracks that they deserved both dignity and beauty. He engaged architect Tasso Katselas, a pupil of Frank Lloyd Wright, to design the facility. (A trip with Frank Ross to Wright's iconic Fallingwater House in Bear Run, Pennsylvania, in 1967 "made a big impact on my vision and plans for the future," says Strickland.) When it was done, with financial help from Strickland's carefully cultivated contacts in Pittsburgh's business community as well as foundations and government sources, he decorated it with first-class sculpture and paintings.

"The various things I do in my life—from making pots to flying airplanes to raising orchids," he says, "are different pieces of a single puzzle. What ties them together is my desire to live a full life. And I'm about creating environments where other people have the opportunity to do the same thing."

Both Guild and Center bristle with programs and facilities that go beyond conventional notions of training. Bidwell's free-of-charge courses are models of rigor—no one coasts to a diploma. The BTC culinary arts program provides the entire school with gourmet meals. (In 1991, it spun off a for-profit catering service that now has contracts with the Andy Warhol Museum Café, the Carnegie Mellon faculty dining club, and a number of other high-profile clients.) The MCG offers a season of top-notch jazz performances along with its art classes (last year's offerings included legendary drummer Louis Bellson and trumpeter Clark Terry), and Strickland has even turned the high-quality recordings he's made of these performances into a record label. In 1997, the label's initial release, *The Count Basie Orchestra with the New York Voices,* won a Grammy.

Strickland is also moving the MCG-BTS model into new environments. In May 1999, Strickland, San Francisco mayor Willie Brown, and jazz great Herbie Hancock jointly announced plans for the creation of the Bayview Hunters Point Center for Arts and Technology (BAYCAT), a vocational-education center with a strong arts component, including a performing arts center, in one of San Francisco's most blighted inner-city areas. As befits the Center's location near Silicon Valley, high tech will be emphasized at BAYCAT—but so will other Strickland mainstays, like culinary education, music, and art. Groundbreaking is planned for the fall of 2001.

If these activities seem to cross the line between selfless service and entrepreneurial chutzpah, Strickland sees no problem. "Good entrepreneurs are innovative by definition," he says. "The nonprofit world can benefit from the level of enthusiasm and risk-taking that entrepreneurs bring. So often nonprofits look through the wrong end of the telescope—toward the narrow end—and become one-dimensional, flat, institutionalized, and unresponsive to the environment around them."

Still, Strickland is no tycoon-in-the-making. He lives in a modest house two minutes from Manchester/Bidwell. ("My whole life is being played out within six city blocks," he quips.) Divorced, he maintains a savings account for his daughter Julie's college education, indulges himself with a closetful of impeccable suits, and still works passionately with pottery.

"Clay is very dramatic," he says. "You take an inert lump of it and five minutes later you've got a vessel. Then glaze and firing, and you have a permanent record of your work, something capable of attracting people's attention." It's a good metaphor for the "social sculpture" that Strickland is attempting with the clay of human lives, human hope, and human energy.

RESOURCES

Bidwell Training Center
  1815 Metropolitan St., Pittsburgh, PA 15233
  www.bidwell-training.org

Manchester Craftsmen's Guild
  (same address)
  www.manchesterguild.org

BODY, PSYCHE & SENSES

THERAPISTS OFTEN counsel us to maintain firm boundaries. This advice may be right for dealing with dysfunctional families and problematic associates, but not for every realm of our lives. Lack of boundaries—the feeling that you don't know where your mind and body end and the world begins—can be a sign of psychosis and codependency, but also of ecstasy and enlightenment. As an intellectual principle, the loss of boundaries is a potent reminder of our connections to one another, the natural world, history, culture, and perhaps even subtle energies in the air. The human animal exists fundamentally as a living system in communion with other living systems.

One of the many transitions our culture is passing through as we enter a new millennium is a conflict over the very nature of the human body. On one side, breakthroughs in biological understanding have modified the old mechanical model of the body spawned in the Enlightenment into an information-processing model—genetic codes, it is asserted, determine everything from whether we'll turn into criminals to which gender we prefer as lovers. On the other side of the debate you'll find these visionaries: each offers images of participation, communion, and an understanding of our bodies that suggest comparisons not to computers but to ecosystems. These images focus on the whole of ourselves, refusing to see our bodily or mental health apart from the social, economic, ecological, and spiritual health of the entire social and planetary organism.

In keeping alive the idea of the sacred, of communion, the visionaries here take risks—the risk of seeming "soft," of making connections that can't be proven, of leaps of faith as well as leaps of insight. Trained physician Larry Dossey has the greatest respect for scientific medicine—but he uses its techniques to examine things that scientific medicine has had no time for: the power of prayer in healing, for example. Dossey's holism—his attention to all of reality, not just the part that appears in medical textbooks—teaches him to respect and investigate everything that brings healing.

For New York dancer Gabrielle Roth, the relationship between the
health of the body, the health of the soul, and human communion is
both immediate and dramatic. Her classes in ecstatic dance, which fill
large rooms with happily gyrating bodies, go beyond exercising the
body to work on the mind and soul, aiming to lift the dancer into a
joyous sense of communion with all the rhythms and vibrations of life.

Psychologist James Hillman is similarly all-encompassing. He
refuses to consider the "dark" side of the psyche as something to
"fix"—rather, it's a repository of poetic power and truth. His Jungian
practice, deeply in debt to the magic and poetry of the Renaissance, is
concerned with bringing the human being into a state of vibrant aliveness that honors darkness as well as light. Increasingly, Hillman is coming to see the very model of psychotherapy as too individualistic, too
focused on the family romance and the personal problem, in an age
whose social, political, and environmental dilemmas require concerted
cooperative action.

As Hillman's practice suggests, the risks of unorthodoxy must be
taken, because healing is urgently necessary at the collective as well as
the personal level. The nearly three hundred years since the onset of
Enlightenment rationality and the birth of modern industry has been a
time of bewildering change, great physical and psychic violence, and
enormous growth in wealth, physical comfort, religious doubt, and
individual autonomy. It has made and kept many fabulous promises, and
it has also left many scars. In her books, New Mexico pyschologist
Chellis Glendinning casts a dark eye on some of the deepest personal
and social wounds of our time: the traumatic psychic effects of nuclear
war and the nuclear industry, environmental rape, and the marginaliza-
tion of indigenous people. Glendinning sees our entire culture as an
addictive system from which men and women of good will need to
recover. Poet and essayist Susan Griffin ranges even wider as she uses
historical documents and personal testimony to assess the psychic and
social costs of violence against women, against the landscape, and
against our better instincts—frequently masked, in families as in the
world's political capitals, by silence.

Jane Maxwell works on the front lines of human suffering in the
Third World, helping women harness their own ingenuity and the wisdom of their cultures in order to improve health care and their physical
well-being. The books she works on under the auspices of the Berkeley-
based Hesperian Foundation do more than just help women in the
developing world maintain good health; they promote the healing of

exploited cultures too, by expressing deep respect for the courage, resiliency, ingenuity of women living far from the centers of global power.

Some of these visionaries work on what we might call the nuts and bolts of the relationship between the self and the society, by concentrating on specific issues that link the two. Vicki Robin's healing path passes straight through one of the greatest and least discussed traumas of our modern lives: our relationship with money. Her Seattle-based New Road Map Foundation outlines a program of simplicity, clarification of values, self-fulfillment, and financial autonomy that is powerful therapy for individuals and potentially healing for our entire overworked and overspent society.

Restaurateur Alice Waters uses food as the hinge between the inner and outer worlds. Her famous Berkeley restaurant, Chez Panisse, is a sort of laboratory for awakening the senses of a nation grown used to iceberg lettuce and tomatoes that taste like wet cardboard. For her, enlightenment passes from the palate to the conscience; as we discover the earth-care, love, and mutual cooperation it takes to grow a really good strawberry, we just might want more of those values in our lives along with the shortcake.

Henry and Karen Kimsey-House start their work at the moment when we discover that we want a better life—but we aren't sure how to get there. These pioneering "personal coaches" guide clients along the path to fulfillment and psychic health—not as therapists dealing with sickness, but as exhorters and perspective-providers who bring out their clients' own ability to answer their own questions. By helping clients tap into their own powers of values clarification, motivation, and problem-solving, the Kimsey-Houses help build a society of humans who are fulfilled from within, and thus less tempted to find the "answer" in the addictive excitements of the entertainment-industrial complex or the supposed joys of material accumulation.

And then there's Tom Hodgkinson—English entrepreneur of idleness, celebrator of sloth. In a world that has dutifully learned the lesson of staying busy, but forgot why that was supposed to be so great, he dares to hold up the torch of another tradition in his magazine, *The Idler*: gentlemanly and gentlewomanly do-nothingism—which he recommends as an integral part of a truly productive, consequential life. Leaning, loafing, observing a blade of summer grass. Breathing, letting go, and just feeling boundless, boundaryless, and, for once, happy.

—Jon Spayde

Doctor, advocate for prayer in healing, mediator between alternative health movement and the medical establishment

LARRY DOSSEY

"It is difficult to retain a spiritual instinct if one travels the path of science. The method of modern education is clear: One must choose either logical, analytical, and rational approaches, or irrational, religious, superstitious, and "right-brained" ones, which include prayer. But the choice between science and spirituality appears increasingly artificial today, even from a scientific perspective."

SANTA FE PHYSICIAN and author Larry Dossey has served as a bridge between the worlds of science and spirituality for fifteen years. As a respected medical doctor, author of eight books, and editor of the peer-reviewed journal *Alternative Therapies in Health and Medicine*, Dossey has challenged the orthodoxy of mechanistic medicine with his assertions that prayer can have a powerful effect on healing. His appointment to cochair a panel on mind-body interventions at the National Institutes of Health, the most respected medical research institution in the world, shows the impact his work has had on the medical establishment.

Dossey entered the national spotlight with his 1993 best-selling book, *Healing Words*, in which he explores the question of the power of prayer in healing. He discovered more than fifty medical studies that found prayer and positive thoughts to have an effect on a patient's health—even for people who didn't know they were being prayed for.

Eliminating the possibility of a placebo effect, some of these experiments proved a positive effect even on bacterial and fungal cultures. Skepticism— drilled into him during his rigorous scientific training as an internist and successful career that began with years of private practice and then work at hospital in Dallas, where he eventually was elected chief of staff by his colleagues—led Dossey to dismiss the studies at first. But, ironically, it eventually began to seem to him "unscientific" to continue to ignore the evidence.

"Almost all physicians possess a lavish list of strange happenings unexplainable by normal science," he says. "A tally of these events would demonstrate, I am convinced, that medical science not only has not had the last word, it has hardly had the first word on how the world works, especially when the mind is involved. After scrutinizing this body of data for almost two decades, I have come to regard it as one of the best-kept secrets in medical science."

In a recent book, *Reinventing Medicine,* Dossey argues that this growing awareness of a spiritual dimension of healing should be incorporated into the daily practice of modern medicine. He argues that it is useful even if we don't yet know how it works—after all, we didn't know how penicillin worked at first, and we still don't know how general anesthesia works. He charts the progression of modern medicine through three periods: "Before Era I—roughly the decade of the 1860s—the practice of medicine was not a pretty sight. Exposure to the medical profession was actually a risk factor for health. In Era I, the era of mechanical medicine, the body was viewed as a complex mechanism that was best treated with mechanical interventions: medications, surgery, irradiation, and so on.

"Although Era I still dominates the medical landscape," Dossey explains, "in the 1950s another great historical period, Era II, dawned with the advent of psychosomatic medicine, now called mind-body medicine. In Era II one recognizes the possibility of influencing other, distant persons. This can be done through intercessory prayer and prayerfulness, imagery, visualization, love, compassion, and so on." Resolving conflicts between spirituality and medicine is a theme of Dossey's own life. The son of a sharecropper in the cotton fields near Waco, Texas, he has a background more fitting for a country singer than a New Age icon. "Prayer and Protestantism permeated those bleak prairies and, with few exceptions, everyone living on them," he writes in *Healing Words.* "The one-room country church, situated forlornly amid cotton fields at a crossroads, was the hub around which life revolved."

When he was sixteen, he was traveling around Texas with a gospel quartet and playing piano for a hellfire-and-brimstone tent evangelist. He planned to become a minister, but at the last minute he decided a college education would provide him with better career options, so on his brother's advice he entered the University of Texas in Austin. The university atmosphere proved to be his religious undoing. "Under its withering influence, and aided by my discovery of Bertrand Russell, Aldous Huxley, and other intellectual giants, my religious fervor wilted like a central Texas cotton field in September," Dossey writes. "I became an agnostic."

He went to medical school and later served as an army surgeon in Vietnam. When he returned, his discovery of Eastern mysticism and more esoteric Western mystical traditions started him on a path back to spirituality. From his medical practice and simple observation of life, he sensed there were forces in the universe that could not be explained by the cold, hard facts of science. When a herniated disc forced him to give up his full-time medical practice, he began to apply his spiritual beliefs to medicine by investigating the role of nonscientific factors like prayer and mental attitude on healing.

Today, Dossey and his wife, Barbara Dossey (a nurse who has written several noted textbooks on holistic nursing), live in a house on the edge of Santa Fe surrounded by gardens, fountains, and apple, pear, peach, and plum trees. Although writing projects, a busy speaking schedule, and editing a medical journal keep him busy, Dossey tries to practice what he preaches: The man who once worked long hours as a physician—and suffered severe migraines as a result—now meditates, plays the flute and piano, and makes prize-winning needlepoint with his wife. He takes a month off every year for a horseback trip with Barbara and friends deep into the wilderness of Wyoming.

Americans are suffering an epidemic of time sickness, he says, which involves very real medical problems: sleep disorders, migraine headaches, high blood pressure, irritiable bowels, and low-grade depression. Victims of this disease are obsessed with the notion "that time is getting away, that there isn't enough of it, and that you must pedal faster and faster to keep up. The trouble is, the body has limits that it imposes on us. And the body will not be fooled if we try to beat it into submission and ask more of it than it can deliver in a twenty-four-hour day. It will let us know."

Dossey prescribes prayer, meditation, or biofeedback for time-sick patients, which he thinks can help them slow down and disconnect from the tyranny of the clock. "Therapy for time sickness is more than just solving high blood pressure or making headaches go away," he notes. "It involves changes of behavior that lead to insight and wisdom." Dossey has been criticized by some medical authorities, who question the validity of the studies he cites in his books. And he's rankled a few alternative health devotees with his warnings against blind acceptance of a bewildering array of alternative therapies without proof of their effectiveness. He insists that prayer should be used alongside, not instead of, mechanical treatments. Although he's pleased that a large segment of the public has come to understand the role of the mind and spirit in healing, he scolds those who take this idea too far and make people feel that their illnesses are a result of emotional or spiritual weakness. "When I was practicing medicine, I spent a lot of time counseling patients with New Age guilt," he says. "Ill health is not a moral failing."

While he feels pressures from both sides, Dossey also sees the two sides gradually growing closer. The number of medical schools with courses on spirituality and health care has risen from three to sixty in just five years. "I used to be quite concerned about the chances of success of this movement," he admits. "I have no doubt about it anymore. Now it is possible to tell a new story, one that allows science and spirituality to stand side by side in a complementary way, neither trying to usurp or eliminate the other."

SELECTED RESOURCES

Reinventing Medicine: Beyond the Mind-Body to a New Era of Healing
   (HarperSanFrancisco, 1999)

Be Careful What You Pray For—You Just Might Get It: What We Can Do about the Unintentional Effects of Our Thoughts, Prayers, and Wishes
   (HarperSanFrancisco, 1997)

Healing Words: The Power of Prayer and the Practice of Medicine
   (HarperSanFrancisco, 1993)

CHELLIS GLENDINNING

Lindsay Holt II

"We are the product of an environment that is disconnected from the natural world, disconnected from the very world that we were evolved to be a part of, and we are suffering as a result from a collective post-traumatic stress. That doesn't mean my next-door neighbor has post-traumatic stress in the same way that I do—but he has grown up in a culture that does not allow him to experience connection to people, animals, stars and the tides as he was meant to."

THE OUTRAGEOUSNESS of the title of Chellis Glendinning's 1994 book, "My Name Is Chellis and I'm in Recovery from Western Civilization," says a lot about how this therapist likes to operate: on a broad social and historical canvas, in powerfully personal ways, and with plenty of ingenuity and humor.

Working from the tried-and-true premise that the personal is political, Glendinning—in nearly four decades of antiwar, antinuclear, spiritual, and ecological writing, radical cultural critique, and activism—has always flowed from a psychological perspective: how what she calls the imperialist order and its arrogant, errant technologies of power have devastated the lives and psyches of its human victims.

For Glendinning, these victims are many and varied: mainstream citizens psychically numbed by the magnitude of the threat of nuclear war and nuclear accidents; traditional peoples driven from their lands and livelihoods; rural people like her own New Mexico neighbors, battling to hang on to a land-based, human-paced way of life in the face of a Wal-Mart and Baywatch culture. She has brought the voices of these people and many others into her books, while relentlessly attacking a technologically based global culture whose violence is rooted in the separation of human life from nature.

A sense that something big was wrong in the world came tragically early. Between the ages of four and sixteen she was systematically molested by her alcoholic father, a trauma from which she has drawn political as well as personal lessons. "That experience led me to distrust reformism," she says. "It would be noticed that after I came back from Sunday outings with my father, I had migraines. So the remedy was no more Sunday outings. This set a pattern in my psyche of wanting to get to the bottom of things, to the real problems."

The Cleveland-born Glendinning was a veteran activist by the time she went off to college at Smith (her iconoclastic mother had taken her along to civil rights rallies), but it wasn't till she transferred to the University of California at Berkeley two years later that her mind and conscience took fire. When Randy Hutchinson, a Lakota Sioux friend Glendinning had met during a summer on a South Dakota reservation, was killed in Vietnam, she had what she calls her "first big political thought": "Randy and I had been blood siblings—we actually mingled our blood in a ritual. I hadn't even known that Native Americans could be drafted! After all we had done to them, they still had to die in our wars. I knew how much Americans feared communism—but I realized that the war system that had killed Randy was bigger, and worse."

At the same time, Glendinning was being swept up in the epicenter of the 1960s. "It was an unspeakably amazing time," she recalls, "an instantaneous intuitional outburst through the minds and bodies of eighteen-year-olds. I don't think we'll ever fully explain it."

She immersed herself in the full menu of new ideas, from antiwar activism to Reichian therapy and bodywork, from radical feminism to natural foods. She became a therapist, taught at the Esalen Institute, and organized the first major conference to focus on the political and spiritual aspects of women's health.

Through her therapy practice and years of determined research she took a long, hard look at the personal costs of our military-industrial-corporate system and the violence it unleashes. Her 1987 book, *Waking Up in the Nuclear Age,* recounts her work helping heal the psychic numbing and denial that accompanied the arms race and closer-to-home nuclear threats like Three Mile Island. *When Technology Wounds:*

The Human Consequences of Progress is a psychological portrait of people she calls "technology survivors"—asbestos workers with damaged lungs, Dalkon Shield victims coping with toxic shock syndrome, people who contracted cancer and other ills from toxic waste dumps and spills—and many other victims of the system's threats and disasters.

In her following book, *My Name Is Chellis,* Glendinning makes the political even more personal. Here she suggests that all of Western culture is suffering from mass post-traumatic stress disorder, a disease caused by the dissociation of our bodies from the earth that began in Neolithic times and has reached a crisis point under global technological capitalism.

The ground note here is Glendinning's own slow recovery from years of abuse—a recovery that has been helped along by her commitment to the environmental and cultural health of the small New Mexico communities where she has lived: Tesuque, where she moved from the Bay Area in 1985, and the village of Chimayo, where she's lived since 1993.

"The value of the small, land-based community was implicit in everything I've been committed to," she says. "Feminism looked back to prepatriarchal times. The back-to-the-land movement and small-is-beautiful thinking endorsed it, of course. But it didn't smack me in the face until I moved to New Mexico. There native and Hispanic people began teaching me things I never could have learned any other way."

Her neighbors' ability to enjoy the present moment, their humor and humanity, have continued to inspire and delight Glendinning. And their holistic way of seeing has challenged her, too: "Growing up, I saw two worlds: my mother's bright, clean world and the dark, painful, isolated world of my father. But here the division between dark and light isn't so clear. There's heroin in my community, for example—users and dealers. They aren't shoved away to the margins. They are part of the community in a way that they aren't elsewhere. If somebody robs a store for drug money, we tend to know who did it." In fact, she says, "here in Chimayo, my friends include former drug dealers and bank robbers, chili farmers, low riders, land-grant activists, state policemen, parolees . . . the works."

Glendinning has also changed cherished habits, like vegetarianism. "I've eaten pigs and cows whose names I knew," she laughs. "I even accept the presence of guns in this culture—they're vitally needed for hunting. I go down to Santa Fe and say these things, and people don't approve. But I acknowledge the culture in which I live in its own terms.

I'm not here to critique it. I'll defend it from Wal-Mart onslaughts, because everything we said we wanted from small communities back in the sixties—things we were right to want—I've found here."

SELECTED RESOURCES

Off the Map: An Expedition Deep into Imperialism, the Global Economy, and Other Earthly Whereabouts (Shambhala, 1999)

"My Name Is Chellis & I'm in Recovery from Western Civilization" (Shambhala, 1994)

When Technology Wounds: The Human Consequences of Progress (William Morrow, 1990)

Waking Up in the Nuclear Age: The Book of Nuclear Therapy (Beech Tree, 1987)

SUSAN GRIFFIN

"I am beginning to believe that we know everything, that all history, including the history of each family, is part of us, such that when we hear any secret revealed, a secret about a grandfather, or an uncle, or a secret about the battle of Dresden in 1945, our lives are made suddenly clearer to us, as the unnatural heaviness of unspoken truth is dispersed. For perhaps we are like stones, our own history and the history of the world embedded in us, we hold a sorrow deep within us and cannot weep until that history is sung."

THE VERY THING that drew some people to political causes in the 1960s may also explain most people's deep disinterest in politics today. Activism once seemed to represent a glamorous delivery from the humdrum dullness of ordinary life—the drama of marching on Washington, not the routine of commuting to work; a connection to big events unfolding in Paris and Latin America, not day-to-day concerns in Phoenix and Milwaukee; heated debates over the fine points of Marx, not arguments about whose turn it is to do the dishes. So, many Americans began to dismiss liberal-left politics as irrelevant to the experience of their lives. They came to feel that progressives were more concerned about fashionable issues and abstract ideals than real-world problems average people face each day.

Susan Griffin spent most of the 1960s in the middle of the radical political whirl, helping to organize the free speech movement at Berkeley and immersing herself in civil rights and antiwar protests.

Griffin spent most of the 1970s raising a daughter, which meant not only changing diapers and helping with homework, but also thinking and writing about politics in new ways. Feminism, with its message that the personal is political, attracted her, and so did the burgeoning new interest in ecology. Unlike a lot of activists, who at that time viewed these as two distinct movements, Griffin pondered the ways in which the natural world and women were targets of the same destructive impulses. Her 1978 book, *Woman and Nature,* outlined in impressive historical detail how Western culture has systematically sought to dominate both in similar ways for similar reasons. Women, who alone have the capacity to give birth, represent a vital link to the natural forces of life and death; threatened by this power, men want to subdue and control it.

She continued this probe of the psychic underpinnings of modern civilization in two later books, *Pornography and Silence,* which explores the inner darkness of interactions between men and women, and *A Chorus of Stones,* which weaves an account of the American nuclear industry, meditations on Nazism, and her own personal history into a disturbing narrative about the role of violence and the need for domination in our culture.

Griffin's thinking has also been shaped by illness, a long bout with chronic fatigue syndrome. "I'm better now after two harrowing years," she says. "But for a while I couldn't even cook for myself." The title of another book—a series of essays—neatly describes the place where years of intellectual exploration and personal experience have led her: *The Eros of Everyday Life.*

"What needs to happen today in politics is that we literally have to have our feet on the ground, we need to pay attention to actions and not just abstractions," Griffin says. "Philosophy means nothing unless it is connected to birth, death, and the continuance of life. To build a society that works, you have to begin from nature and the body."

Commitment to abstract economic and social theories rather than to living, flesh-and-blood reality is one of the chief mistakes made over and over by our culture, and not just by those on the left. "Our societies, both socialist and capitalist, are so insane because we have been severed from physical existence and the deep, deep intelligence that is a part of physical existence. It's like gardening. You try something in your garden, and it works, so you try a little more of it. Or if it doesn't work, then you do less of it.

"This relates to gender," she adds, "in that the men who still have the largest share of the power in society don't do any domestic work. The very people who are making our most important decisions should know how to cook, know how to grow a garden, diaper a baby, and raise young people. They should not only know these things but practice them."

The collapse of communism marks a perfect opportunity for the dawn of a new kind of politics, says Griffin: "Western civilization has defined itself in opposition to nature. Socialism went right along with that and adapted wholesale the industrial model.

"But the whole old system is passing," she continues. "It included the economic plans of both socialists and capitalists. The conservative corporate world is run on the same principles as the Soviet Union: centralized control. Decisions are made in an abstract way to control people. The Soviet Union toppled from the same forces that will topple capitalism.

"But we are beyond violent revolution. That's not a reason to be hopeless. It's a reason to change our thinking about society. I am very critical of state socialism. But I really do believe in 'from each according to his abilities, to each according to his needs.' We should begin to formulate other ways to meet people's needs; a huge government with welfare is not a good way to meet people's needs."

Searching for examples of cooperative societies and cultures where accumulated human wisdom prevails over a mechanistic mind-set, Griffin has become interested in traditional peasant life. "These are ancient cultures that we may have considered reactionary. Yet these people have been imbued with a collective ethos through their entire lives. To be a good person, we've been raised to be altruistic. But we have not felt that if someone else suffers, we suffer. In a traditional culture, you may go over every morning to the bakery to get bread. If the baker is sick, there won't be any bread."

How can we bring a solid sense of community and ecological balance to a complex, technological society like the United States? "We can't ignore the government," she says. "It's become—excuse my expression—a pimp for the corporations. But we can't put all our energy into changing government policies, either. We need to build positive models in our communities."

One way to do that, says Griffin, is to enlist the energies and hopes of those who feel that politics has little to do with what matters in their lives: "We need to get feminists and ecologists, but also people working with welfare rights, people fighting racism, people working with health care, people with the unions, people working on gay and lesbian issues, and bring them together. We need people who haven't been associated with progressive politics. People who care about the beauty of cities— landscape architects, for instance. Bring all these people together to think creatively about our society."

Griffin's integrative, holistic outlook arises from her rich but complex personal identity and history: She's the Gentile-born adoptive daughter of a Jewish family in Los Angeles, a self-described movie lover who embraced writing as her mode of expression, a wife and mother who gradually accepted her own sexual attraction to women in the 1970s, an artist who elegantly blends poetry, journalistic research, political analysis, and personal narrative in her work. She views herself as a "bridge figure" standing between the illusory boundaries we believe in.

Now at work on several novels, Griffin is also planning to undertake a subject that might seem strange coming from someone who made her name as a 1960s radical, environmentalist, and feminist critic of pornography: "It's going to be devoted entirely to courtesans and how that history connects to contemporary women's sexuality," she says. "The history is amazing, and we've been cut off from it, as women, particularly in America. . . . A lot of the sexual freedom we have today we owe not only to the feminist movement, but also to courtesans. They broke down sex, class, and gender barriers. They did things other women weren't supposed to do. They achieved independence so they could take lovers just like men. They could control their own money. They could go places alone. Use ribald language. Talk politics. Society women couldn't do this."

Griffin still lives in Berkeley, as she has for decades, and remains vigilant that the public world of work doesn't overshadow the substance of her everyday life. When she's asked what constitutes a meaningful life, she reels off a few of her favorite things: "Feeding your grandchild small spoonfuls of yogurt and ice cream. Trying to use another language. Walking in the woods. Dancing to reggae. Cooking vegetables just pulled from your garden. Ice skating. Smelling wood fire. Eating olives. Listening to friends tell stories of their lives. Growing old—it's better than you would think."

SELECTED RESOURCES

The book of the Courtesans: A Catalogue of Their Virtues
  (Broadway, Sept. 2001)

Woman and Nature: The Roaring Inside Her
  (Harper & Row, 1978; Sierra Club, 2000)

What Her Body Thought: A Journey into the Shadows (HarperSanFrancisco, 1999)

Bending Home: Selected and New Poems, 1967–1998 (Copper Canyon, 1998)

The Eros of Everyday Life: Essays on Ecology, Gender and Society
  (Doubleday, 1995)

A Chorus of Stones: The Private Life of War (Doubleday, 1992; Anchor, 1993)

Pornography and Silence: Culture's Revenge Against Nature (Harper & Row, 1981)

JAMES HILLMAN

"If the idea of mentoring were reawakened in the culture, we wouldn't go to therapy looking for a mother, a father, a mentor, a brother, a teacher, a lover—all that in one person. Also, we wouldn't need therapy as much if individuals had more of their own practice—whatever that practice is. It can be practice with nature, practice with art, practice with music, practice with spiritual discipline. But it must be a practice that invites dedication."

JAMES HILLMAN, one of the most influential psychologists of our time, has said, "The ideas of psychotherapy are some of the most pernicious now affecting the culture." He likens "depth psychology" to the "kudzu vine, thriving as a parasite." In case you hadn't guessed, Hillman isn't your garden-variety therapist encouraging self-actualization and positive vibrations. "I have a dark eye, a twisted perception," he laughs, and his casually spoken words carry weight. After all, the eye that Hillman casts on psychology, therapy, and the human condition is dark in more ways than one.

Born in an Atlantic City, New Jersey, hotel room in 1926, Hillman had an international education: Georgetown University, the Sorbonne in Paris, Trinity College in Dublin, the University of Zurich (where he earned a Ph.D.), and The C. G. Jung Institute in Zurich (where he earned an analyst's diploma). His Jungian training, and its fascination with inner forces of the shadow, goes a long way toward explaining his openness to the dark side of life.

There's his dark view of the medical model of mental health, under whose banner psychotherapy aims to "cure" the "sick" psyche. For Hillman, all the psyche's phases and faces, and especially its dark ones, are poetic, trustworthy, revelatory: To follow and learn from them (even if the learning is painful) is a way to grow psychologically. "There is an innate, I think, *gift* in human beings [wanting] to pull bugs' legs off them," Hillman writes. "Thomas Wolfe said, 'Pity is a learned emotion. A child will have it least of all.' Interesting thought. The Grimms' fairy tales are filled with horrors: tortures, ovens, boiled alive, heads cut off, witches, giants. The archetypal imagination is filled with that. If you read African fairy tales, they're full of unbelievable things happening to people: swallowed up, eaten alive, burned in the fire, the whole village destroyed. All of this belongs to our coming to terms with the fantasy world."

These horrors all have a vital place in the psyche. Hillman insists that we must come to trust "the heart's reactions of desire and anger . . . [and] fear. These deep emotions of the bowels, liver, genitals, and heart. . . . These responses of the animal blood keep us in tune, in touch with the world around—its beauty, its insult, its danger."

Translating *psyche* as "soul"—its Greek meaning—Hillman plumbs that great ancient word to its darkest and most radiant depths. "Other words long associated with the word *soul*," he writes in *Suicide and the Soul* (1964), "amplify it further: mind, spirit, heart, life, warmth, humanness, personality . . . purpose, emotion, quality, virtue, morality, sin, wisdom, death, God."

Hillman's expansive, passionate view of the soul, nourished by his love of the Renaissance, leads him to twist received psychological wisdom into "new" forms that often echo antiquity. Answering the therapeutic prejudice that the healthy mind is a barracks brought to order under the rule of the ego, Hillman offers "polytheistic psychology," which accepts and even celebrates inner inconsistency and "obliges consciousness to circulate among a field of powers. Each god has its due as each complex deserves its respect in its own right. . . . Polytheistic psychology can give sacred differentiation to our psychic turmoil."

Hillman is worried about what he calls "concealed fascism" in the United States, "not in the obvious parallels with Europe in the 1930s, but in things like the lowering of take-home pay and the concentration of media in a few hands. Even multiculturalism becomes fascism in a way, by making people mere representatives of the groups to which they belong."

The tendency (so often the other side of the multiculturalism coin) for individuals to cast themselves as victims is equally troubling to Hillman. He tends to see it as a kind of psychic bait-and-switch tactic, on both the personal and the political level: "If I'm a poor victim," he explains, "if I've been abused, revenge will be important in me. My rights. Getting mine back. Pushing away the aggressors. I see it as a kind of crazy way of justifying the heroic side. The radical, violent side—you see, I'm not really a brute, I'm a victim. And what I'm doing to other people is because I'm a victim. It's perverse."

But he saves some of his most serious criticism for psychotherapy. His 1996 book, *The Soul's Code,* is a critique of psychology and how it misreads and confuses the idea of the human psyche. Hillman finds particular fault with the self-centeredness that lies at the center of contemporary therapy. "Psychotherapy, or at least our psychological consciousness, has exaggerated self-searching to find out who you are, and neglected what the world wants from you as just as valid a way of finding out who you are," he says. In other words, modern psychotherapy is blind—in a typically Western manner—to the relationship between individual and society. "What do people find you useful for? What do they like to be around you because of? That's also a part of calling."

And that's neglecting an essential component of what it means to be human. "Aristotle said man is by nature a political animal. Tremendously important sentence that's been cited many, many times. But what he's saying there is that just as you're a sexual animal, or a family animal, you also are political—that's part of your *instinctual* life. Now, therapy investigates your sexual instinctual life. Or maybe your eating habits, if you have eating troubles. But does it investigate your political instinct? Could you be dysfunctional politically?" Yes, you could be, he insists, and psychotherapy should recognize this political dimension of the psyche.

By the same token, he is equally interested in psychic and personal rootedness. As a variety of millennial psychoses take hold of the world, Hillman is looking toward the next millennium as "the end of time"—not the apocalypse, but a hoped-for falling away of questions like cause and effect: "a dedication to what is, instead of to how it got this way, and where it's going. We need to pay attention to the spatial dimension: to care about what's here, and maintain it. To get out of our personal pasts, our case histories, and into where we are now." He's asking us, in other words, to "live so that you believe you'll never live anywhere else."

Lest you confuse this message with "Be here now," that easygoing maxim of the 1970s, Hillman is quick to point out the dark side of his current interest in the collapse of time. "I am a catastrophist," he says. "I have no salvation fantasies. The question I ask is: How do you live on a sinking ship? Another way to put it is this: You can't stop an avalanche, but you might be able to divert it." But Hillman's too complex a thinker to imagine that diverting the avalanche negates catastrophe. "I don't use the word *hope* at all," he says.

SELECTED RESOURCES

The Force of Character: And the Lasting Life
  (Random House, 1999; Ballantine, 2000)

Dream Animals, paintings by Margot McLean (Chronicle, 1997)

The Soul's Code: In Search of Character and Calling
  (Random House, 1996; Warner, 1997)

Kinds of Power: A Guide to Its Intelligent Uses (Doubleday, 1995)

We've Had a Hundred Years of Psychotherapy—and the World's Getting Worse,
  with Michael Ventura (HarperSanFrancisco, 1992)

A Blue Fire: Selected Writings, ed. Thomas Moore (Harper & Row, 1989)

Suicide & the Soul (Harper & Row, 1964; Spring, 1976, 1985)

Facing the Gods, ed. (Spring, 1980)

TOM HODGKINSON

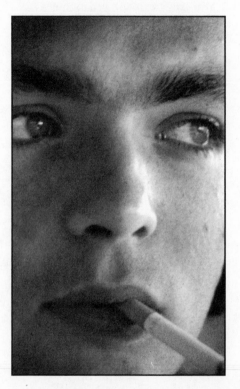

"What is an idler? The word is commonly used these days in the pejorative sense: An idler is lazy, good-for-nothing, a layabout, slacker, indolent, a slothful couch potato who contributes nothing to society. What [an idler] actually is: a rejection of worldly pressures, an individualist revolt against authority, a pleasure, a spiritual practice."

Tom Hodgkinson represents the necessary antidote to a society in which, social scientists tell us, people are working more and feeling less happy. The mischievous editor behind the British periodical, *The Idler* (the snail is its symbol), he is the Pied Piper of creative loafing, spreading a powerful message that contentment—and true productivity—rise when we have the chance to smash both external and internal time clocks.

Having graduated from Cambridge University, Hodgkinson was working at a mainstream magazine and living as just another frustrated drone—"checking the price of baked beans and things like that," he says—when he stumbled across a collection of essays by eighteenth-century author Samuel Johnson. In "The Idler," Dr. Johnson berated himself for rising late and too seldom studying scriptures—this from one of the most productive men of letters in history.

"I related to his concept of an idler as someone who was capable of working very hard, but would tend to do it after a long period of inaction," Hodgkinson says. "He has this principle of momentum: It's like a buggy that's pushed up a hill, he explained. When it starts leaving, it leaves with a violence proportionate to its own weight." This, Hodgkinson realized, was how he himself works.

Around the same time, he noticed that many of his so-called slacker friends seemed to be having more fun than he was, taking advantage of their down time to put on parties, print T-shirts, and publish fanzines. This inspired him to ditch his day job and begin cobbling together *The Idler,* which illuminates "what you might call an elbow-on-the-mantelpiece, gentlemen-of-leisure, observational way of living."

One basic principle of the idler philosophy is that work and play ought to come together. Hodgkinson speaks of the late entrepreneur Nicholas Saunders, who cofounded Britain's Institute for Social Inventions—a very loosely structured think tank that gathers and disseminates good ideas all around the world. "He came to a point in his life where he wasn't enjoying what he was doing," Hodgkinson says, "so he wrote a list of all the things he did enjoy doing—talking to friends, staring out the window in the pub—and then tried to find something that brought together as many of those things as possible. In a way, that's what we've done, too."

Granting yourself permission to contemplate is a revolutionary act, he says. "It felt to me that an idler was someone who actually thought about what was going on. You're called lazy, but you're only lazy because you don't believe in what your employer's asking you to do. We ended up questioning everything, and it led us into becoming quite anarchistic and libertarian in our political outlook."

Rejecting the political right as moralist slaves to materialism, he also disdains the left as "insufficiently self-reliant." He dismisses New Labour British Prime Minister Tony Blair's Third Way as "too publicly pious."

For example, Hodgkinson believes Blair's welfare reform appears to champion the virtue of work, but does so in a soulless, self-defeating way. "The government here is always introducing new ways of trying to get people off the dole, which on the face of it sounds reasonable enough," he notes. "But often all they're talking about is taking people off Social Security, where they're getting a very, very small amount of money, and putting them in very badly paid menial toil in which they have no interest. We should be encouraging enterprise and creativity and funding ways to let people do what they want to do, and not be beaten down and set in wage slavery."

Blairites "spend a lot of time telling people how they should run their lives." Hodgkinson believes that government intervention is often overpowering yet fruitless. "My politics has become something of a socialist-anarchist-libertarian blend," he says, noting that the one error of almost all politicians is an obsession with doing things—when sometimes not doing things is the preferable policy. "For example," he says, "where we once had roundabouts on our roads, now we have traffic lights, which are no improvement. It's as if they don't trust you to negotiate the roundabout."

Instead of the long-running skirmishes between left and right, Hodgkinson sees a different clash of ideas shaping our social system. "It seems to me there are two cultures at work," Hodgkinson says. "There's this culture where we get our self-worth from money and possessions and our work status and social status. But there are an awful lot of people who relish the opportunity not to think like that."

In *The Idler's Companion: An Anthology of Lazy Literature,* Hodgkinson cites a long tradition of idlers, from Lao Tzu and Aristotle and Pascal, on through Robert Louis Stevenson and Arthur Rimbaud and William Blake, all the way to Miles Davis and Ivan Illich and Jean Cocteau. Not to forget Oscar Wilde and D. H. Lawrence, and Nietzsche, who once criticized Americans for working with "breathless haste": "Even now one is ashamed of resting, and prolonged reflection almost gives people a bad conscience," Nietzshe wrote. "One thinks with a watch in ones hand." Says Hodgkinson, "Byron, Keats, Shelley—you didn't see them toiling away on media projects. They were sort of blowing around, writing poems, which improved millions of people's lives."

Creativity and anxiety were the twin poles of Hodgkinson's youth. Born in 1968, he was the eldest son of two journalists who "weren't particularly hip, but explored ideas." They recognized the link between mental health and stress, and wrote extensively about it in the British press. His parents often put he and his brother to bed at four or five p.m. so they could work on their own writing. "I got used to having an awful lot of sleep at a young age."

Hodgkinson has found that his vision of idleness resonates with many people. And that can present problems. He is now in great demand, consulting for the innovative British TV network, Channel Four, the liberal Guardian Newspaper, and "one or two" advertising agencies, on top of his new business of importing absinthe (the perfect idleness inducer, popular among nineteenth century free thinkers) from the Czech Republic. The profits from these businesses subsidize the money-losing *Idler*, but they also take time. Hodgkinson, who believes a perfect work week is "three by three"—three hours a day, three days a week, decided that producing five annual issues of the ten-thousand-circulation *Idler* each year contradicts its mission. In the future, he says, *The Idler* will appear only once or twice a year.

Despite these brushes with success, Hodgkinson has no intention of forsaking his idler values. Indeed, he's pondering a move to the country because the frenetic bustle of the city undercuts the possibility for true leisure. "My plan is to transfer operation half out of London to get more of a balance between country life and city life. What I really love doing now is chopping logs and making fires and sitting around a table eating and drinking wine."

This is all part of his master plan to both lead and promote the idler life, which he has put a great deal of thought into. "Can I describe my ideal day?" he asks. "It would start with waking up rather late, and then lying in bed for an hour or so. Then I would have coffee and walk around outside my cottage in the country. Then I would sit down for two or three hours of concentrated work—writing, editing, or connecting with people on the phone or whatever is the work of that day. Followed by a late lunch and a nap. And then spend the afternoon chatting with friends, going for walks. Then after that I'm magically spirited to Soho and meet up with friends and go out partying. That's my perfect day—you're working and playing in a way in which one connects up with the other."

SELECTED RESOURCES

The Idler's Companion: An Anthology of Lazy Literature,
  ed. Tom Hodgkinson and Matthew De Abaitua (Ecco Press, 1997)

HENRY AND
KAREN KIMSEY-HOUSE

"Our coaching is based on four principles: our clients are naturally creative, resourceful, and whole, not sick or in need of fixing; we follow the client's personal agenda, not some patented seven- or ten-step method; our coaches and clients design their relationship and revise it when they need to; and we work with the client's entire life, not just his or her work self or romantic self or family self."

"IMAGINE WHAT the world would be like if everyone had someone who was committed 100 percent to their welfare and growth," says Henry Kimsey-House. That's the utopian version of what he and his wife, Karen, along with business partner Laura Whitworth, are creating under the banner of "coactive coaching." From their nonprofit base, The Coaches Training Institute (CTI) in San Rafael, California, they lead a growing cadre of student coaches-in-training through the fine points of helping clients set, stick to, and achieve their goals, reach balance in their lives, and enjoy existence generally. The booming personal-coaching movement—which, unlike therapy, doesn't look backward at family traumas but forward toward clients' immediate and long-term life goals—began with the business-oriented Coach University, based in Colorado. Coach U's approach is geared to improving the productivity and job satisfaction of clients, as well as their personal lives. Other coaches are more like consultants—providers of information and advice.

The Houses' innovation, coactive coaching, differs from both of these models. First, it can include, but is by no means limited to, job performance and satisfaction. Coactive coaches let the client set the agenda, and will help with anything from grieving losses to getting organized, from changing a hopeless career path to envisioning a completely fulfilled life. Second, the coactive coach doesn't provide answers in the form of advice or information. Instead she skillfully guides the client to an awareness of her own values, her own resources, and her own answers.

In weekly half-hour telephone sessions, coactive coaches elicit the client's own powers of vision, goal-setting, and decision making through asking what the Kimsey-Houses call "powerful questions," leading clients to discover or rediscover their own values and strengths, then put them into practice. Although the powerful questions are specific to each individual coaching encounter—there's no laundry list—one of the most powerful ones, and the one that elicits the most powerful answers, is "What do you want?"

"We work in three areas," says Henry. "Fulfillment—getting what you want from life. Balance—looking at all areas of life and seeing where things are missing. And process—being conscious of where you are right now, and fully experiencing that." Sometimes process coaching is no more complex than helping a client stay with a strong emotion for a while so that it comes to feel like less of an impediment and more of an indication of energy and aliveness.

The extensive training that CTI coaches receive includes a battery of innovative skills. They learn, for example, to listen at three levels. At Level One the coach is most aware of how the client's words register in the coach's own mind and heart. At Level Two, the coach strives to understand the client in the client's own terms—there's lots of checking to be certain that the coach "gets" what the client is saying. At Level Three, the coach listens for unspoken things: underlying emotions, hidden resistances, and the overall atmosphere of the call.

The coach listens, asks powerful questions, and "furthers the action" by gently but firmly moving the client toward deeper levels of honesty, and by eliciting the client's own ideas about how to solve whatever problem is under scrutiny. If the client gets stuck in an emotion, empathetic process coaching may be called for. As the call winds up, the coach may ask the client if he or she wishes to be held accountable for an action to be taken in the next week or some other time in the near future—anything from making a difficult phone call to beginning to clean a closet to writing a list of affirmations. "Inquiries" are powerful questions that the client may be left to mull over during the time before the next call: "What would it feel like to have both enough money and enough time?" "What does aliveness mean to you?"

The results of coactive coaching are unpredictable and various, as different as the differing personalities of clients. One bookish client for whom metaphor is a powerful motivator was helped to discover that what he thought was a scattered and disorganized way of learning actually reflected a playfulness that was one of his core values. He took the sea otter as a personal totem, and came to see his forays into books as playful plunges into the ocean. The self-acceptance that resulted removed a major block to his completion of graduate school. Another client deeply valued connections with artistic people, but found it difficult to meet them. With her coach's encouragement, she thought up a weekly "take an interesting person to lunch" program: She "cold-calls" an artist or other innovator in her city and invites them to a one-hour lunch, with no strings attached—no requests for help, just the pleasure of the invitee's company. The structured format helps her overcome her shyness, and the flattering unconventionality of the plan delights her invitees. The Thursday lunches have reinvigorated her own artistic life while increasing her personal network manyfold.

In crafting their holistic vision of personal fulfillment through coaching, it didn't hurt a bit that neither of the Kimsey-Houses had any background in consulting, human resource development, or any of the other bottom-line-oriented "people" fields. Both spent many years working (and not working) in the theatre, which turned out, perhaps surprisingly, to have been first-rate preparation for coactive coaching and coach training. "My acting classes taught me that a good actor is fascinated with everything," says Henry. "They taught me curiosity about the human spirit, the power of imagination, of embodiment, and intuition. They taught me how to listen."

Still, the frantic aspiring-actor's shuffle in New York dispirited Henry. "I came to hate the business side of the theater," he recalls, "and I hated unemployment too." The answer, at least for a while, was a commitment to Actors Information Project (AIP), a New York organization that helps actors plan their careers. As vice president of program development for AIP, Henry created workshops on topics ranging from how to present yourself at an audition to long-term career strategies.

While his work with AIP was more fulfilling than cattle-call auditions, Henry still felt as if he hadn't found his vocation. He chanced to meet California-based Laura Whitworth, a onetime CPA and corporate manager who was developing a personal coaching practice. ("I thought Laura was this big-deal coach, but later I learned that I was her second client," Henry recalls.) The coaching-and-being-coached bug bit, and soon Henry was in California, where he and Whitworth joined forces, studying with Coach University founder Thomas Leonard, and eventually—in 1992—beginning to lead their own workshops.

Laura Whitworth had another friend and coaching colleague who also happened to be an ex–New York actor: Karen Kimsey. After OD-ing on the frustrations of the footlight life, Karen—who was certain she was destined to do some kind of work that helped people—took a job with The Learning Annex, a personal-growth-oriented New York adult-education center that was about to open a San Francisco branch. "I had never had any kind of regular job before," says Karen, "but I think I was able to convince them that I could act like I knew what I was doing." Karen was put in charge of the brand-new San Francisco Learning Annex, which promptly took off like a skyrocket. But being more of an administrator than a helper soon palled. "I learned I had a good head for business," she recalls. "For a while it was just great—and then it wasn't." Karen's urge to help people one-to-one had remained as strong as ever during her years as an administrator, and after considering a number of careers, she ended up at a class given by Coach U's Leonard. She hooked up with another student, Laura Whitworth, and the pair became one another's support system as both developed coaching practices.

When Whitworth and her new business partner, Henry House, gave their first coaching workshop, it was natural for them to invite Karen. "I saw this wonderful energy and friction between Laura and Henry," Karen recalls. "I knew that they were on to something huge. Henry's ideas about coaching—his sense of the client as resourceful and whole, levels of listening, and so on—were absolutely original, and Laura had such a large vision. What they were doing was giving everyone full permission to be who and what they were. I could see that this was a way that people have been dying to interact with each other: holding each other's agendas, living in a spacious, no-one-gets-to-be-wrong place. And people were also hungry for a way to look at what was most important in their lives—what had meaning."

What Henry and Laura lacked, Karen decided, was marketing savvy, the ability to make their vision big in the world. So she invited herself along as third partner, and was taken on. That was in 1992. In the next couple of years, the trio set the parameters of coactive coaching and

CTI. And then Henry and Karen fell in love and got married. "The three of us had to redesign our alliance," laughs Karen. "The principle of coactive coaching called process—being able to be with feelings, being in the moment—was born of that shift in our relationships."

Today CTI trains coaches on-site and across the country via rigorous traveling seminars and telephone courses that lead to certification by the institute. The coactive model, with its emphasis on intuition, close listening, subtle awareness at several levels, and commitment to the client as a whole person, can seem as close to a spiritual discipline as it is to a technique. And Karen Kimsey-House is unabashedly idealistic about where coaching might lead. "All three of us wanted, and still want, to change the world," she says. "But you don't do that all by yourself. You do it by impacting people. Actually, coaching itself has never been the goal for us; it's the vehicle for the interactive kind of relationship between people that we want to take out into the world more and more." Henry acknowledges that most of the people who are taking coactive coaching out into the world, as coaches and clients, are a familiar type—Baby Boomer seekers who are already used to self-examination. How will it get beyond this demographic, into the harder and more hurting corners of the country and the world?

"I think it's hundredth-monkey stuff," says Henry. "Change can come with even a small number of change agents out there. You start by preaching to the choir, then to the congregation . . . and so on. But it's also true that our model needs to look at ways of dealing with people who don't resemble us." "The world has just gotten faster and faster, bigger and bigger," says Karen. "It's become really hard for people to hang on to the things that matter to them. I see in coaching a structure to help people hold on to the things that are most important to them, and make the choices that support those values, and say no to other choices. And that's not the way we're brought up. We're brought up not to rock the boat."

SELECTED RESOURCES

The Coaches Training Institute
   1879 Second St., San Rafael, CA 94901
   www.thecoaches.com

Co-active Coaching: New Skills for Coaching People Toward Success in Work and Life, by Laura Whitworth, Henry Kimsey-House, and Phil Sandahl (Davies-Black, 1998).

JANE MAXWELL

"I'm a mother, and I try to teach my daughter that we in the developed world have a lot that we don't need, and we can give a lot away—money, but also information. Life is simply easier for white, educated, employed people with enough money, and we have a responsibility to share."

JANE MAXWELL believes in the ingenuity and resourcefulness of people who live in the countries we have the hubris to call "underdeveloped." She's seen village people conserve water with exquisite care, recycle empty baby-oil bottles as containers for gas for cooking stoves, and teach themselves to fix anything under the sun—from clocks to TVs to trucks—without the benefit of owner's manuals. During her many years as a medical anthropologist, women's health worker, and activist, Maxwell has devoted most of her abundant energy to helping rural communities in the developing world harness that resourcefulness to improve the health of their citizens—particularly their female ones.

A key member of the Berkeley-based Hesperian Foundation, which is committed to improving health care in the world's poor communities, Maxwell was the project director and guiding spirit behind *Where Women Have No Doctor,* a unique manual of female medical self-care modeled on the successful *Where There Is No Doctor,* which Maxwell also helped to research and write.

Where There Is No Doctor was the fruit of the experience of physician David Werner and medical colleagues working in villages in

Mexico in the late 1960s and early 1970s. The notebooks they kept on medical problems and treatment appropriate to a village setting soon grew into the beginnings of a book. Today *Where There Is No Doctor* is used around the world—and particularly in developing countries—for what Maxwell calls "the 90 or 95 percent of medical problems where you don't need a doctor. Calling in a doctor for most health problems is like hiring a skilled mechanic to change a tire." Nutrition, sanitation, preventive measures, self-examinations, and simple therapies are among the issues that fill this five-hundred-plus-page guide. The Hesperian Foundation constantly hears from groups and individuals for whom the book has made a difference: a junior high school in Ghana uses it in hygiene classes; radio stations in Guatemala and India broadcast excerpts from it on a regular basis; a Bolivian father who had read the book in Spanish translation is able to spot the symptoms of peritonitis in his son in time for surgery to be successful; a man in Papua New Guinea helps his wife give birth, with the book open beside him.

The Hesperian Foundation was originally formed solely to publish the volume. It has gone on to create and publish several other guides to culturally sensitive and appropriate-scale health care in poor countries—including *Helping Health Workers Learn, A Book for Midwives, Disabled Village Children,* and other titles. The foundation allows royalty-free reproduction, adaptation, and translation and gives small grants to institutions wishing to translate its materials. (*Where There Is No Doctor* has appeared in eighty languages so far.) A Creative Education Fund helps groups adapt the material for radio, street theater, and other grassroots media.

Where Women Have No Doctor grew out of the realization that, as Maxwell puts it, "men and women do not get ill the same way." Women in poor communities are, for example, more likely to get waterborne diseases because their traditional work—cooking, washing clothes— keeps them in contact with water. "And there are social factors too," says Maxwell. "In some societies, if you distribute high-energy foods like eggs and cheese to women, they may be expected to take them home and give them to men."

Out of these observations and a huge amount of medical commonsense, Maxwell and her collaborators stitched together a genuinely multicultural book, based on inquiries into the real conditions of female health in forty countries, and illustrated by no fewer than forty-nine female artists from the United States, India, Brazil, and twenty other countries.

The *No Doctor* books make their way around the world chiefly through large purchases by organizations like Oxfam, the Peace Corps, and UNICEF, who then distribute them to aid workers and local people. The Hesperian Foundation estimates that two to three million copies of the two books have been sent out into the world. Both *No Doctor* books sell in the developed world as well, says Maxwell. "Survivalists love them," she says with some irony. "And so do rich people who go on yachting vacations to remote places."

Needless to say, Jane Maxwell has not devoted her life to the needs of militia members and yachtsmen. Irish-born and London-bred, she spent her early years in a working-class environment—her father worked in a grocery store and a wine shop. "I dropped my Irish accent early," she says in a decidedly British lilt modified by almost four decades in the United States—most of that in Berkeley, where she lives with her husband, Michael Blake, and their fourteen-year-old daughter, Sacha.

She plunged into activism in her London years, leafleting for Bertrand Russell's antinuclear movement and the antiapartheid cause. "Growing up in an Irish immigrant family, I suppose it was natural for me to be on the side of the underdog," she says. "But there wasn't any voluntarism or taking up of causes in my family at all. I just started doing it on my own." Maxwell also developed an acute case of wanderlust and longed to travel abroad. A jazz fan, she decided that the East Coast of the United States would be her first destination, and when an au pair opportunity opened there in 1961, she said good-bye to England.

When the child-care gig was over, Maxwell and an English friend drifted to the Bay Area. "And I just never left," Maxwell quips. She took a job in a bank, where she led a fight to force management to allow tellers to wear buttons with political slogans, and on weekends volunteered in a center for disabled children. Evenings were devoted to civil rights work.

Aside from a short stint in nursing school in England, Maxwell had had no higher education. Eventually, at thirty-two, she entered the University of California as an anthropology major. Her junior year abroad, in Ghana, would change her life. "I saw that life could be grim in Ghana, in the capital as well as up-country," she says. I could see that people were getting sick because of things that didn't need to happen." At the same time, Maxwell was struck by Ghanaians' ability to get by with the resources they had: "They knew how to make water last. They knew how to make everything last. Their sense of reuse and recycling was just amazing. When I returned to the United States, I was much more aware of how much we have that we don't need."

Armed with her newfound understanding that, as she puts it, "intelligence has nothing to do with education," and certain that she wanted to devote herself to some combination of medicine and information-sharing in the developing world, Maxwell completed bachelor's and master's degrees in anthropology and an MS in public health. She helped out at the Berkeley Free Clinic, then as now a notable center for basic health information with an eye to empowering patients. In the late 1970s, she got wind of the Hesperian Foundation's work and came aboard.

Maxwell takes every opportunity to underline the collaborative nature of her work with Hesperian; after all, her experience and education have inoculated her against the temptation to see health work in developing countries as charity given by First World heroes to the world's poor. The *No Doctor* books collective keeps in touch with the communities they help, which are, of course, also continuing sources of information and inspiration. "I'm constantly amazed at the sisterhood among women doing this work," says Maxwell. "There's so much spunk, ingenuity, fire in the belly out there, despite the walls that they're up against everywhere. One group of women in a part of Zimbabwe that had no medical facilities used our book to learn about cancer and pregnancy, then badgered the health ministry until they sent a mobile medical unit out regularly to help with these issues." As China urbanizes at a feverish pace, the government is letting its rural health-care system wither. A consortium of women's health groups, alarmed at this trend, are translating *Where Women Have No Doctor* into Chinese. The Hesperian Foundation estimates that the first press run of the translation will be no fewer than one hundred thousand copies.

Decades of contact with developing countries, including trips back to Africa, have given Maxwell a perspective on social change that's miles away from the quick-fix mentality common in the United States. "We have short attention spans," she says. "If something hasn't changed in six months, we think we've failed. In developing countries, change comes slowly; the societies are traditional and emphasize continuity. But those very emphases can be great strengths. A few years ago, when Nigeria ordered all foreign workers out of the country, thousands of Ghanaians had to leave. Everyone anticipated a crisis, a drain on public services. Instead there was just a two-week period in which practically all of them returned quietly to their families and took up places in the traditional village economy."

So Maxwell and friends patiently watch their useful, friendly health books make their way in the world, carrying medical information and sending a message of profound respect for how life is lived out beyond the glittering centers of global power.

SELECTED RESOURCES

Hesperian Foundation
  1919 Addison St., Suite 304, Berkeley, CA 94704
  www.hesperian.org
Where There Is No Doctor (Hesperian Foundation, 1977; 1998)
Where Women Have No Doctor (Hesperian Foundation, 1997)

VICKI ROBIN

"There is a way to balance your inner and outer lives, to have your job self be on good terms with your family self and your deeper self. There is a way to go about the task of making a living so that you end up more alive. There is a way to approach life so that when you're asked 'Your money or your life?' you say, 'I'll take both, thank you.'"

THE BEST-SELLING book that Vicki Robin wrote with the late Joe Dominguez, *Your Money or Your Life,* is often shelved in the financial planning section of bookstores—right up there with books on how to make a killing in the market. But *Your Money* is financial planning with a big difference: "It's a technology for freeing people from the work-and-spend treadmill," says Robin.

The recipe for "FI"—financial intelligence, financial integrity, and financial independence—that it contains is meant to make readers conscious of just how much life energy they're trading for money. The next task is to liberate them from paid employment forever in order to further free them for service to their families, their communities, the planet, and their own wildest dreams.

This bottom-line plan for turning wannabe idealists into active, effective change-makers and fun-havers combines self-empowerment, voluntary simplicity, and careful investment into what the authors call a "new road map" for our personal and planetary future: people happily "retired" on income from government securities, free to volunteer their time for whatever jazzes them. Not least important in this plan is the net reduction in consumption of the world's resources that results when North Americans decide to scale back and live sanely on less.

And it's just part of the down-to-earth agenda of social change that Robin and friends have put forward via their Seattle-based New Road Map Foundation. The foundation, of which Robin is president, mainly helps people across the country achieve FI via books, tapes, and pamphlets. An estimated one million people have taken part in FI training since the first seminars in 1980. FI achievers like Penny Yunuba of Boston have actually made financial-independence dreams real and followed their hearts. Yunuba no longer works for a living, donating her time instead to a whole range of volunteer projects, from delivering hot meals to the elderly to volunteering with a recycling collective. She also has plenty of time to just sit and listen to friends. "I'm free therapy," she says, "because I don't have to go to a job." Dwight Wilson parlayed an inheritance into lifetime support via FI principles, then devoted himself full-time to the creation of a Peace Park in the Russian sister city of his home town. He also organized an association of Peace Corps returnees and currently works for an organization that plants trees worldwide.

The New Road Map Foundation has also carried out medical research in support of holistic healing, including a rigorous study of Lou Gehrig's disease in 1986, which documented longer survival times for patients who received psychological and spiritual counseling. Robin is currently working on a book that explores the key concept in the foundation's financial teaching: freedom.

"In interviews around the country, I'm asking what freedom means to people, when and under what conditions they've experienced it," says Robin. "People in all different circumstances of life. I'm trying to head off objections like 'He feels free because he's rich, or because he lives in the mountains,' or whatever. One of the reasons I'm doing these interviews is that freedom is an absolutely core value for me." A philosophy professor Robin interviewed first discovered freedom when he was so poor that he had to beg a meal from a woman whose house he was passing. He watched the woman struggle with her fear, and as he watched he felt such a wave of compassion for her that soon he no longer cared whether she fed him or not. The woman shouted "No," and ran back into her house. "He didn't get a meal, " says Robin, "but through love he tasted freedom, and it tasted better than food." She talked to an India-born taxi driver in Stockholm who has spent twenty years behind the wheel, scrimping and saving to support his family back home—and calls the experience not only freedom but joy. "Americans tend to talk about personal choice," says Robin. Asians talk about spiritual law, fulfilling one's obligations."

One of the earliest intimations of real freedom Robin can recall came at summer camp. She was seven, attending a camp at Tenants Harbor, Maine, run by progressive educators Bess and Henry Haskell. "It was a remarkable place," she recalls. "It was interracial and democratically run; every morning we sat down with the counselors and decided what we were going to do that day." The Haskells owned, wonder of wonders, a Volkswagen camper. "I stood on tiptoe," says Robin, "and peeked into that thing. 'Wow,' I remember thinking, 'you could *live* in this!'"

Her VW epiphany turned out to be prophetic. At several pivotal times in Robin's life, serious travel—vagabonding on the road, with no home base—pushed her life to its next level. When she was an honor student at Brown University, she says, "I made a bargain with the devil: I decided I would take the amount of money I would need for one eight-month academic year, go to Europe, and see how long I could support myself on it."

She spent more than a year, "eating oranges, sleeping in nunneries, driving around with a load of friends in a little car. I learned how far I could extend money. And I learned that the closer to the bone you live, the more interesting life becomes."

Robin's next big journey came after a few years in New York, struggling to be an actress and director. Disillusioned with the theater scene and clueless about where her life was going, she took off in an old Econoline van, crossing the United States and Canada and ending up where many a wanderer in 1969 ended up: Berkeley, California. There she met Dominguez, who had just used the principles he would later develop in *Your Money or Your Life* to retire, at thirty-one, from a brokerage career on Wall Street.

With Dominguez and other friends, Robin formed a merry band of vagabonds who traveled the byways of the United States in a rebuilt truck-house trailer they called the Ultimate Vehicle. Their mission: to be of service to social change-makers wherever they could. "We would visit intentional communities that had lost some of their spirit and help them reconnect with their original vision," she says. "Because we were traveling, we were able to help little groups that seemed to be carrying the whole world on their shoulders by connecting them with other groups who had the same problems they had." The travelers helped the

Palo Alto–based nonprofit Choosing Our Future in a campaign to improve the quality of information on television. "We did everything from helping with research and fundraising to painting the office" Robin recalls. They camped near the offices of *In Context* magazine on Bainbridge Island, Washington, and guest-edited an issue of that sustainability- and social-justice-oriented publication. Under the auspices of the University of British Columbia's Human Unity Conference (1981) they organized townwide meetings of faith-oriented nonprofit groups, helping them exchange information, share inspiration, and heal rifts.

As they traveled, more and more of the people they ran into inquired about Dominguez's ingenious financial plan for freedom, and eventually a series of tapes and seminars grew out of his and Robin's ideas. New Road Map was formally incorporated as a nonprofit corporation in 1984, and by 1990 its work had attracted the publishing industry.

Robin's life reads like a chapter from *Your Money or Your Life*—or a wheelless continuation of her days in the Ultimate Vehicle. She shares a big, rambling old house in Seattle's University district with four housemates, all New Road Map stalwarts. "We each live on from five thousand to ten thousand dollars per year, and spend about eighty-five dollars a month on groceries," she says. The housemates meet for group study sessions and "talking stick" discussions of house and personal issues—"appraisals of our inner and outer work," Robin calls them.

"New Road Map's offices are in the house, so you could say I commute by staircase. Because I don't have to work for a living, everything I do I do by choice. The result is that I don't get stressed very often—and if I do, I have the option of saying, 'I'm taking three days off!'"

It's easy to see how Vicki Robin defines freedom. "I'm not into trying to imbed frugality in public policy, or anything like that," she says. "We're simply about making people aware that they have a choice. And, in a broader sense, we're trying to find ways to communicate the power of the human spirit in the affairs of the world."

SELECTED RESOURCES

New Road Map Foundation
  Box 15981, Seattle, WA 98115
  www.newroadmap.org
Your Money or Your Life, with Joe Dominguez (Penguin, 1992; rev. ed. 1999)

GABRIELLE ROTH

"In the beginning of ecstatic dance, we are stuck in our self-consciousness—I'm dancing, aren't I cool? We come to a place of letting go of old beliefs about ourselves—I'm fat, I'm too tall to dance, I'm no good at this or that. When we move beyond these clichés, we come to the big whopper: We each have an ego, and that ego is designed to keep us separate and in fear. I work to enlarge the soul, because the bigger your soul gets, the smaller your ego gets."

IT DOESN'T look like meditation, but it is: bodies of all shapes shaking and swooping to percussion-heavy music, each clearly responding as much to an inner drummer as to the throbbing on the sound system. A slender, fiftyish woman with a mane of black hair is the mistress of the revels, moving as if possessed by the beat. Actually, Gabrielle Roth *is* possessed by the beat, and her goal is to give the beat to all of the dancers, and the rest of us, as a permanent possession.

On videotapes and in her Lower East Side Manhattan studio, Roth takes students through what is emphatically not a dance class. There are no steps to learn and no nervous following of the teacher. In Roth's world of "ecstatic dance," you follow your own emerging inner sense of how to move. Still, beneath the free-form movement is an elaborate structure of thought about the relationship between movement and many aspects of being human, from the self-image to the soul, and a compelling vision of how the soul can be reclaimed and set free. For

Roth, getting out on the floor and dancing is the quickest and surest way to shake off the many different forms of inertia that keep us fearful, passive, and predictable.

"When you move the body, the heart starts to move," she says. "All our emotional energies start to move. If we're physically stuck, movement unleashes that. If we're emotionally stuck, or mentally stuck, stuck in our beliefs about ourselves or others or the world, well, movement unleashes that. We can constantly redefine and rearrange ourselves in the context of movement."

That redefinition and rearrangement is personal, but it isn't random. In the thirty-odd years since Roth began teaching movement classes in schools and mental hospitals as part-time work to support her own formal dance study, she has developed a sequence of rhythms through which she leads her students in a "dancing path" of self-realization. After a warm-up that's part guided meditation, part shaking loose, she introduces the rhythms: flowing, staccato, chaos, lyrical, stillness. The students shift from the looping, graceful, connected motions of the flowing mode into the angular, abrupt gestures of staccato, then from the wild, anything-goes flailing of chaos into the lighter, more playful, intuitive changeability of the lyrical mode, ending with the slowed, even motionless inner attentiveness of stillness.

The sequence is many journeys at once. In Roth's two books, *Maps to Ecstasy* and *Sweat Your Prayers,* she lays out the almost inexhaustible meanings that the five rhythms have for her. Perhaps most importantly, each stands for a phase of life: flowing for the world of the womb and birth; staccato for the realm of childhood; chaos for puberty and adolescence; lyrical for maturity; and stillness for old age and death. Roth also connects each rhythm with what she calls a "sacred teacher." In earliest life, this is the mother; in childhood the father; in adolescence the self; in maturity the wider society; and in life's last act, the cosmos. These sacred teachers "are our mirrors," Roth writes. "It is from them that we learn our basic life instincts, our spontaneous ways of being, of responding to life's challenges."

In some cases, these teachers did not give us what we needed, leaving us with wounds. The healing journey, as Roth understands it, is to become conscious of what happened to us at each stage, at the same time developing an awareness that we are not our wounds, that we are bigger than our story. In her workshops, students explore these stages in journal entries, letters to absent parents, and meditative recollection, even as they move to music to re-experience the stages as pure, liberating energy. And that's only the beginning of meanings for the five rhythms—they're also associated with physical elements, emotions, life tasks (being, loving, knowing, seeing, healing), and many other things. So her students confront the elements of their lives and personal histories as they dance. Suffice it to say that in Roth's scheme, dancing is metaphorical participation in the fullness of life. "Movement is soul food," says Roth. "For me, God is the dance—the energy, the force that has kept life moving forward. When I dance, I get as close to that energy as you can get, and I want to discover myself in its embrace. I want to define myself as someone who is changing, in motion."

She has watched her students change in major ways, too, as they follow the dancing path: they lose weight, enjoy livelier sex lives, begin to move and to think more lightly and spontaneously. One woman, who began studying with Roth at sixty-five, lost forty pounds and became markedly less arthritic. She eventually became a movement teacher herself. Ecstatic dance has helped others to deal with stress, dissolve inhibiting self-images, and overall, to enjoy being physical creatures. "We have a body, a heart, and a head," says Roth. "Our ego sees them as separate, while our soul knows their unity. My dance is a path from ego to soul." When Roth set out upon her dancing path, there was much inertia to overcome. She began as many young Americans did—dancing to rock 'n' roll in her room. "I would turn on a record and just go," she recalls. "I was completely swept up in the music." Dance classes—ballet and modern—soon became a necessity for her. She was on her way to a conventional dance career.

As a college student, she found herself teaching (or trying to figure out a way to teach) movement to schizophrenics at Agnews State Hospital in Northern California, where she'd taken a job to support herself and pay for dance classes. "I looked at them and thought, 'Oh my God, that person's soul is trapped inside her body, and her body is frozen. What do I do?' My job at that moment was simply to get the heart moving." She found that the only thing she could do was enter their several worlds "and begin to choreograph their fantasies," she writes in *Maps to Ecstasy*. "We all move around the bases, swing invisible bats, do the hula, direct emergency traffic. Eventually, they all get moving, acting out each other's trips, and I just ride the waves of energy as well as I can." Dancing didn't cure the patients of schizophrenia, but it did restore vigor to bodies that were atrophying in the sedentary routine of the mental hospital. "They remained mentally absent," says Roth, "But they became physically present."

Without quite realizing it, Gabrielle Roth had found the connection between free movement and the human soul. But her own body and soul were increasingly at odds. A trip to Europe, a stint teaching high school, and more and more dance classes followed. By day, Roth sweated in dance studios mastering steps. At night, "I abandoned myself to the passion of ecstatic dance. It never dawned on me that I might be able to perform or teach this formless form of dance. The only choice I felt was available to me was to become a professional dancer. God had other plans."

Roth injured her knee while skiing. It was the familiar you'll-never-dance-again scenario, and it plunged her into a depression. In an effort to pull herself back into the world, she went to Esalen, the renowned meditation and personal growth center in Big Sur, California. There she met Fritz Perls, the founder of Gestalt therapy. The meeting blossomed into a friendship as Perls encouraged Roth to shape her own approach to movement.

"I started doing movement with Perls' therapy groups, then everybody's therapy groups," she says. "Pretty soon I was doing my own groups. This was with adults whom I considered to be nice, normal, neutral neurotics—but they were as stuck in their bodies as my schizophrenics had been, sometimes even more so."

"Our biggest problem," she says, "is how we relate to ourselves, to others, and to the wider world. In my work, I see it all so clearly, because the body can't lie. When people are disconnected from themselves on the dance floor, you can't miss it—that lost-soul look as they look all around outside themselves for clues about who and how to be." This confusion extends to how we conceive of and talk to one another; it seems to Roth that we don't have habits and language that allow us to honor the breadth and depth of each other's experiences, sufferings, intuitions, capacities—our souls, in a word.

At the same time, the pain Roth sees in so many faces and bodies inspires—of all things—hope. "The amount of despair in the world right now gives me hope because people are closer to the bone than ever before," she says. "They are closer to the real self, which can't handle the phony masks we wear and the illusions we cart around that cause so much suffering." We may be, in fact, on the verge of a new and deeper awareness of one another: "We went through God knows how many thousands of years of unbelieveable unconsciousness, sweeping everything under the rug, never saying what we meant. With the 1960s we moved into a hyper-self-conscious period of self-awareness and self-revelation. We became aware of the soap-opera nature of the human ego. Now maybe we are ready to move from self-conscious to merely conscious: conscious of what it means to be a human being—which includes shadow and light, suffering and compassion, and the fact that we are all completely unique as well as absolutely the same."

When Roth isn't dancing, teaching, writing, or pursuing a wide range of music-recording projects with her band, the Mirrors ("I'm the rock 'n' roll section of the human potential movement," she says with a laugh), she's tuned in to professional basketball. "I'm in love with the wild boys in shorts," she says. "Basketball for me is a moving meditation. There's no time to think; you are in the divine mystery, because nobody knows what's going to happen from second to second." She pauses, and coining a phrase that transcends basketball—a phrase that could stand for her whole practice—she says, "I love watching miracles arranged in bones and blood and breath."

SELECTED RESOURCES

Raven Recording, The Moving Center
  Box 271, Cooper Station, New York, NY 10276
  www.ravenrecording.com

Maps to Ecstasy: A Healing Journey for the Untamed Spirit,
  with John Loudon (1989; rev. ed., Nataraj, 1998)

Sweat Your Prayers: Movement as Spiritual Practice (Tarcher/Putnam, 1997)

Recent dance videos on Roth's Raven label:
  The Wave
  The Power Wave
  The Inner Wave

Recent sound recordings by Gabrielle Roth and the Mirrors, also on Raven:
  Tribe
  Sundari
  Refuge, with Boris Grebenshikov

ALICE WATERS

"People are transformed in the process of growing, gathering, preparing, and offering food. Everybody has to do it, three times a day, and if you can do it in a way that teaches important values, it can be transformational. It can change you and it can change the world around you."

© Stephanie Rausser

It was 1964, Alice Waters was in France for the first time, and the food was a revelation. The New Jersey–born twenty-year-old Berkeley student was entranced with French eating and the graceful ways it meshed with other aspects of French life. Her morning route from apartment to classroom passed through an open-air market full of delightful sights, smells, and tastes. She accompanied French friends as they drove from restaurant to restaurant on Sunday afternoons, determining which establishment had the freshest of whatever was in season. Only after an hour or more of serious comparison shopping would they decide where to have dinner.

Of all her French food sojourns, though, the most memorable was a trip to a tiny restaurant in Brittany. "I've remembered this dinner a thousand times," she writes in her 1982 book, *Chez Panisse Menu Cookbook*. "The old stone house, the stairs leading up to the small dining room, which seated no more than twelve at the pink-cloth-covered tables, and from which one could look through the opened windows to the stream running beside the house and the garden in back. The chef, a woman, announced the menu: cured ham and melon, trout with almonds, and raspberry tart. The trout had just come from the stream and the raspberries from the garden." Waters' sophisticated French companions, who were given to shrugging and muttering "not bad" after meals that took her breath away, lost their sangfroid, applauded the chef, and shouted "C'est fantastique!"

It's tempting to see in this beautiful little Breton scene the seed of Alice Waters' world-famous Chez Panisse, the Berkeley restaurant that, since its founding in 1971, has done more than any other to define California cuisine—and give Americans a chef's-eye view of a better way of living. Waters' devotion to freshness, seasonality, lightness, and a spirit of experiment altered fine dining forever by inspiring a generation of cooks to transform the American palate and idea of food.

Chez Panisse is, of course, much more than a trendsetter. Born of the cultural revolution of the sixties, it embodies many of the lasting values beneath the more sensational, ephemeral products of the counterculture. In establishing the small restaurant on Shattuck Avenue, Waters, with the help of a small group of friends, emphatically elevated good food over turning a profit. In insisting on absolute freshness and seasonality in all her ingredients, she took a stand against industrialized agriculture and the supermarket, that never-never land that provides twelve months of tomatoes (and 11 months of bad ones). By offering a new menu every evening, Waters and her head chefs established a balance between control and spontaneity, which is characteristic of every art, from poetry to ballet.

And in conceiving her restaurant as a tightly knit community of cooks, eaters, and environmentally careful growers, she fused food, love for the planet, and community in a compelling way. In the restaurant's early days, as Waters tells the story, it was by no means easy to find fresh and seasonal food in the Bay Area. San Francisco's many Chinese markets were her best resource, but it was still a struggle. Then an acquaintance brought Waters some radishes from his garden—the kind of radishes the French eat at breakfast—and asked if she was interested. "I said yes, grow some more," says Waters. "That was a breakthrough. It started us off on the search for people who were interested in growing things specifically for us."

Waters began to build a devoted network of growers: organic gardeners, farmers, dairymen, orchard people. "As we moved along," Waters told an interviewer in 1997, "I realized that the best-tasting food came from the people who were taking care of the land and nourishing it." Thus, conscious stewardship of the land was enshrined at Chez Panisse as both an ethical value and a flavor-maker. Today, Chez Panisse employs a full-time "forager" who seeks out growers and interviews them to determine if their practices meet Waters' culinary and ecological standards.

Where the food comes from is important for Waters, but even more important is making good food a part of daily life. Dailiness is a key to social change because it's the way new habits are formed. "Sometimes— say, in a concert—you suddenly feel like you love the world," she says. "But unless you have everyday experiences that reinforce that love, it's very hard to keep it."

Waters' food is, of course, anything but everyday. Chez Panisse is pricey (the weekend per-person fixed price is $69), and charcoal-grilled demi-glacé duck breast and filet of beef with Niçoise olives and chanterelle mushrooms aren't truck stop fare. Waters is an artist, and like any artist of progressive opinions, she hasn't always found it easy to balance uncompromisingly high standards, community building, egalitarianism, and accessibility.

"About ten years after we founded Chez Panisse," she recalls, "the restaurant almost burned down, and the whole community came to help rebuild it. At that point I realized that it wasn't my restaurant anymore—it belonged to the people who loved it. Some celebrated every birthday there, every anniversary, the birth of their children, and God knows what else. They deserved a vote in what they were going to eat." Soon after, in 1980, Waters opened the Chez Panisse Café, upstairs from her main room. The café is less expensive and offers a variety of à la carte versions of the fare served downstairs. (An even more informal Chez Panisse spin-off, Café Fanny—named for Waters' daughter— opened its doors in 1984; it's an intimate Berkeley coffee shop that serves breakfast and lunch at a stand-up bar.)

Waters' sense of community goes beyond her restaurants. At the moment, she's involved in a project to bring her love of food and its pleasures into an unlikely venue: a public school. The goal of the Edible Schoolyard Project is to help the students of Berkeley's Martin Luther King Jr. Middle School eat better and understand the relationship between good food, pride, and empowerment.

Walking past the school one day, Waters noticed that it looked dilapidated and dispirited. She began thinking that what it needed was a garden. Talks with the principal followed, and before long, Waters and a group of teachers at King not only put in a garden but also renovated the cafeteria kitchen, which hadn't been used in fifteen years—the school had become too overcrowded to maintain a lunch program.

Five years into the project, the "garden classroom" thrives as a place where kids can plant and tend the same fine (and often exotic) vegetables Waters cooks in her restaurants. In the "kitchen classroom" they prepare and savor these good things. "They don't just like pizza and ice cream," says Waters. "They really like kale and radicchio! When kids can smell and taste and touch good food, they want to eat it. When they grow it and prepare it, they want to serve it to their friends. When they understand the principle of enriching the earth with compost, they like taking out their vegetable scraps. They like working hard, and they like working together."

Waters, a one-time Montessori teacher, is unabashed about what she sees as her teaching mission. "The restaurant isn't aggressively educating people the way I would like," she says. "That's why I'm involved in the school project. Ultimately I want our garden project to be the school lunch program at King. If something like this could be institutionalized in other schools—if you could have a curriculum that taught children these essential values—it could change the world."

SELECTED RESOURCES

Chez Panisse
  1517 Shattuck Ave., Berkeley, CA 94709
  www.chezpanisse.com

Chez Panisse Café Cookbook,
  with David Tanis and Fritz Streiff (HarperCollins, 1999)

Chez Panisse Cooking, with Paul Bertolli (Random House, 1988; 1996)

Fanny at Chez Panisse,
  with Bob Carrau and Patricia Curtan (HarperCollins, 1992)
  (Seven-year-old Fanny describes her adventures with food and cooking at her mother's restaurant; includes forty-two recipes.)

INDEX

If you have enjoyed *Visionaries: People and Ideas to Change Your Life,*
you might also enjoy other

BOOKS TO BUILD A NEW SOCIETY

Our books provide positive solutions for people who
want to make a difference. We specialize in:

Sustainable Living • Ecological Design and Planning

Natural Building & Appropriate Technology • New Forestry

Environment and Justice • Conscientious Commerce

Progressive Leadership • Resistance and Community • Nonviolence

Educational and Parenting Resources

For a full list of NSP's titles, please call 1-800-567-6772 or check out our web site at:

www.newsociety.com

New Society Publishers

ENVIRONMENTAL BENEFITS STATEMENT

New Society Publishers has chosen to produce this book on New Leaf EcoBook 100,
recycled paper made with 100% post consumer waste, processed chlorine free, and
old growth free.

For every 5,000 books printed, New Society saves the following resources:[1]

35	Trees
3,125	Pounds of Solid Waste
3,439	Gallons of Water
4,485	Kilowatt Hours of Electricity
5,681	Pounds of Greenhouse Gases
24	Pounds of HAPs, VOCs, and AOX Combined
9	Cubic Yards of Landfill Space

[1]Environmental benefits are calculated based on research done by the Environmental Defense Fund and
other members of the Paper Task Force who study the environmental impacts of the paper industry.

For more information on this environmental benefits statement, or to inquire about environmentally
friendly papers, please contact New Leaf Paper – info@newleafpaper.com Tel: 888 • 989 • 5323.

NEW SOCIETY PUBLISHERS